FLORIDA STATE
UNIVERSITY LIBRARIES

JUN 22 1999

TALLAHASSEE, FLORIDA

OUT OF EQUILIBRIUM

OUT OF EQUILIBRIUM

MARIO AMENDOLA and
JEAN-LUC GAFFARD

CLARENDON PRESS · OXFORD
1998

Oxford University Press, Great Clarendon Street, Oxford OX2 6DP
Oxford New York
Athens Auckland Bangkok Bogota Bombay Buenos Aires
Calcutta Cape Town Dar es Salaam Delhi Florence Hong Kong Istanbul
Karachi Kuala Lumpur Madras Madrid Melbourne Mexico City
Nairobi Paris Singapore Taipei Tokyo Toronto Warsaw
and associated companies in
Berlin Ibadan

Oxford is a registered trade mark of Oxford University Press

Published in the United States
by Oxford University Press Inc., New York

© Mario Amendola and Jean-Luc Gaffard 1998

The moral rights of the author have been asserted

First published 1998

All rights reserved. No part of this publication may be reproduced,
stored in a retrieval system, or transmitted, in any form or by any means,
without the prior permission in writing of Oxford University Press.
Within the UK, exceptions are allowed in respect of any fair dealing for the
purpose of research or private study, or criticism or review, as permitted
under the Copyright, Designs and Patents Act, 1988, or in the case of
reprographic reproduction in accordance with the terms of the licences
issued by the Copyright Licensing Agency. Enquiries concerning
reproduction outside these terms and in other countries should be
sent to the Rights Department, Oxford University Press,
at the address above

British Library Cataloguing in Publication Data
Data available

Library of Congress Cataloging in Publication Data
Amendola, Mario.
Out of equilbrium / Mario Amendola and Jean–Luc Gaffard.
p. cm.
Includes bibliographical references.
1. Equilibrium (Economics) 2. Production (Economic theory)
3. Saving and investment. I. Gaffard, Jean–Luc. II. Title.
HB145.A47 1998
339.5–dc21   97–46966
                                                        CIP
ISBN 0–19–829380–1

1 3 5 7 9 10 8 6 4 2

Typeset by J&L Composition Ltd, Filey, North Yorkshire
Printed in Great Britain on acid-free paper by
Bookcraft (Bath) Ltd,
Midsomer Norton, Somerset

PREFACE

This book is essentially devoted to 'continue with continuation—into the future', a task to which John Hicks called others at the end of the last paper he wrote before his death. We believe that the best way to do this is to build a comprehensive analytical approach for out-of-equilibrium economics. This has required a long time, a massive effort, and much help from others. It is impossible to thank all of them but we cannot avoid mentioning William Baumol, Sergio Bruno, Richard Day, Axel Leijonhufvud, Marcello Messori, Lionello Punzo, and George Richardson for discussing with us important analytical points, and Claude Froeschlé and Elena Lega for their essential support to the simulation analysis carried out. Various institutions have provided the means for carrying out the research project underlying the book, in particular the CNR, the MURST, the CNRS and its director of the Department of Humanities and Social Sciences Alain D'Iribarne. Finally we would like to thank the editors of the *Journal of Economic Behavior and Organization*, *Structural Change and Economic Dynamics*, the *Journal of Evolutionary Economics*, and *Revue Économique* for allowing us to use material contained in papers of ours that appeared on these journals.

M.A.
J.L.G.

caminante, no hay camino
se hace camino al andar
Antonio Machado

CONTENTS

Introduction 1

Part I. Theory: The Building Blocks 9

1. Production 11
1.1 The *ex post* view of the phenomenon of production 11
1.2 Time and equilibrium 15
1.3 Complements and substitutes in the economics of production 18
1.4 Time and sequence: dissociating costs from proceeds 20
1.5 Out-of-equilibrium contexts: bringing to light the time structure of production 24
1.6 From the *ex post* to an *ex ante* viewpoint: the creation of resources 27
1.7 Out-of-equilibrium processes: the analytical implications 31

2. Money 35
2.1 When, why, and how money matters 35
2.2 The standard theory of money and its modern revisitations 38
2.3 Substitution and complementarity 41
2.4 Integrating real and monetary disequilibria in a sequential context 43
2.5 Financial constraints and production 45
2.6 Financial decisions and real choices 50
2.7 The interest rate and the time structure of economic activity 53
2.8 Monetary control 56

3. The Human Resource 61
3.1 Labour input, human capital, and the human resource 61
3.2 The wage rate in equilibrium and out of equilibrium 65
3.3 The wage fund 68
3.4 Towards a modern theory of the wage fund 70
3.5 The human constraint 73
3.6 Wages and employment 76
3.7 Learning 78

4. The Market and the Firm — 81
- 4.1 Institutions and the process of change — 81
- 4.2 Market failure and organizational co-ordination — 83
- 4.3 Optimizing strategies of firms — 85
- 4.4 The firm and the market as substitutes — 88
- 4.5 Organizational design — 90
- 4.6 The co-ordination of production — 93
- 4.7 The market and the firm as complements — 96
- 4.8 Out-of-equilibrium strategies — 99

5. Change — 106
- 5.1 Economic dynamics: methods and problems — 106
- 5.2 The equilibrium approach — 108
- 5.3 Endogenous growth — 110
- 5.4 Transitional dynamics — 114
- 5.5 Harrod's knife-edge — 116
- 5.6 The analysis of the Traverse — 119
- 5.7 Path dependence — 123
- 5.8 The sequence 'constraints–decisions–constraints' — 126
- 5.9 The decision process — 128

Part II. Analysis: Processes of Change — 135

6. Out-of-Equilibrium Modelling — 137
- 6.1 The scope and role of modelling out of equilibrium — 137
- 6.2 The guiding lines — 140
- 6.3 A sequential model — 142
- 6.4 The coherence of the model — 152
- 6.5 Complex dynamics — 159
- 6.6 Cancelling the sequence — 164

7. Processes of Change — 170
- 7.1 Changes in technology — 170
- 7.2 Changes in skills — 187
- 7.3 Credit creation — 197
- 7.4 Changes in expectations — 206
- 7.5 Limits to growth — 211

8. Rethinking the basic issues — 231
- 8.1 Consumption, investment, and saving — 231
- 8.2 Structure and cycles — 235
- 8.3 Unemployment — 239

8.4 Flexibility and viability	243
8.4 Economic policy	245
8.5 Re-reading the recent 'story' of Western economies	250
Conclusion	259
Appendix: Numerical Simulations Data	260
References	265
Index	275

Introduction

Western economies seem to have lost the philosophy of wealth creation. Growth no longer appears to be their main concern. Rates of unemployment of 10 per cent and even more are accepted as an almost natural state of the economy, while all forces are diverted to fighting inflation, cutting public deficits and re-establishing the so-called fundamental equilibria of the economy.

Governments, central banks, and international organizations hold a view of the market according to which its main function is simply the allocation of existing resources, so that price and wage flexibility will eventually take care of everything. This is, of course, a restrictive view of the market. Both in the opinion of the fathers of the economic discipline and from the historical viewpoint market economies have always been considered as the systems most conducive to the creation of wealth. It is paradoxical that the virtues of the market are invoked today in relation to a problem of the allocation of resources which is typical of intrinsically static economies and with respect to which a central planner, open or in disguise (auctioneers, complex systems of incentives, and so forth), would certainly represent a more adequate answer. As a matter of fact this is the extreme consequence of the approach to economics that characterizes equilibrium theory and which appears to be ever more dominant.

The market, together with other institutions, is instead a device organized to solve the co-ordination problems which arise in growing economies, that is, in economies which are undergoing a change. We therefore need an analytical framework suited to deal with the phenomenon of change in a comprehensive way in order to be able to go back to the heart of the problem of wealth creation.

Out-of-equilibrium economics concerns economic change. Not all types of change. For instance, it is not concerned with proportionate growth that does not affect the way the economy is working. Standard equilibrium theory deals adequately with this. But it does not deal equally well with qualitative change, i.e. change which modifies essential features of the economy and hence its functioning; in other words, change which implies structural modifications. Technical change, innovation, changes in tastes, but also the acceleration of growth, catching up, and so forth are qualitative changes: as are almost all really interesting dynamic phenomena. Qualitative change cannot be deduced from a comparison of alternative states of an economy essentially defined in its basic structure, which is what equilibrium analysis does. It implies rebuilding a different structure, which can only take place through a process in real irreversible time. This is by definition an out-of-equilibrium process, as all true processes are; the old structure, the old way of functioning of the economy no longer exists, and the new way is not yet established. We are on the way, a way that must itself be traced out step by step.

The way we look at production is as the watershed between equilibrium theory and out-of-equilibrium theory. That is why this book begins with a chapter on production. Equilibrium is an established state of affairs. As regards production, an established state of affairs implies a productive structure that is already settled and that operates in a given way. When this is the case we can focus on this regular behaviour abstracting from the underlying productive structure which brings it about. Inputs can be immediately associated with the corresponding output (and costs with the corresponding proceeds), and this renders production an essentially timeless phenomenon. Standard production theory is consistent with this analytical context. It views production as a choice of output levels: the problem of the origin of productive capacity is dispensed with by reducing it to the analytically instantaneous choice of a combination of given generic resources. Production then appears as a particular aspect of the general problem of the allocation of resources.

This is no longer possible when the attempt to carry out a qualitative change breaks the existing state of equilibrium. The first result is a 'distortion' of productive capacity, and when production is no longer synchronized we can no longer focus only on the utilization of productive capacity while abstracting from the process through which it comes about. This is what a Neo-Austrian representation of the production process essentially does: it brings back into the analysis the phase of the construction of productive capacity. Production then becomes a process 'in time', which makes it possible to show the appearance of problems of intertemporal complementarity once we are out of equilibrium.

This is only half the story, though: the part that Hicks had started explaining in his analysis of the Traverse and in the book *Capital and*

Introduction

Time, and which is the beginning of the sketching out of an out-of-equilibrium analytical context. But, alongside the distortion of productive capacity, problems of co-ordination of economic activity are likely to appear which affect the intertemporal complementarity of the decision process in the same way as the distortion of productive capacity affects the intertemporal complementarity of the production process. The main reasons for the appearance of these complementarity problems are the construction lag and a lag in the transmission of information, which are the expression of the time dimension of the production process and of the decisions process, respectively: a time dimension which becomes relevant out of equilibrium. The interaction of these lags allows us to complete the definition of an out-of-equilibrium context as a process over time sketched out by a constraints–decisions–constraints sequence.

For a clear understanding of the working of this sequence other essential elements are required. Out of equilibrium, the supply and demand of processes, of resources, and of commodities no longer match. They do not match at each given moment and they do not match over time. The construction of productive capacity is out of balance with its utilization, costs with proceeds, and decisions with the resources available to finance them. Out of equilibrium there are therefore gaps to be filled, links to be established, sunk costs to be covered. In this context money, which is just a veil in equilibrium, becomes a crucial element. It provides a bridge through time which makes it possible to re-establish the consistency of processes and activities that would otherwise no longer be viable. Money is essential in qualitative changes taking place through out-of-equilibrium processes; in this sense out-of-equilibrium theory is a monetary theory, as stressed in Chapter 2.

Together with financial resources, and dynamically interacting with them, human resources play a role in out-of-equilibrium processes which is in many aspects the mirror image of the role played by financial resources. The concept of the human resource, analysed in Chapter 3, differs both from the concept of labour input and from that of human capital. It is a richer concept, and its greater richness depends on the time perspective from which we look at it. At each given moment the human resource, looked at as a complex of skills, qualifications, and competences, appears as a state variable of the economy, one of the prevailing constraints. Over time processes take place: learning processes, which represent the construction phase of the production of the skills, qualifications, and competences that will characterize the state variable human resource in each successive period. But there is also another, more generic form of learning which constitutes the real essence of processes of qualitative change. This is learning that concerns the process of change itself: what it consists of and the way it actually takes place. Once we focus on learning processes which are not related to specific elements, given once and for all, but rather to mechanisms aimed at bringing about the change and mechanisms of adaptation to it, the organizational aspects which represent the essence of these mechanisms come into light.

Complementarity problems, co-ordination issues, and organizational aspects: what are they, how do they arise, how do they interact sequentially out of equilibrium? This is the content of Chapter 4. The aim is to sketch out the guiding lines of the strategy designed to secure the viability of the economy that is seriously threatened by the attempt to carry out a qualitative change. Out of equilibrium— where, in the absence of complete information, bounded behaviours are relevant—constraints emerge at each successive step. A sequential strategy, by establishing new and changing relations with the environment in order to deal with these constraints, appears as a tool for acquiring information and knowledge. As a matter of fact, it is only through the consideration of relations which become structured into different aggregations that we introduce irreversibility, real time, and hence true dynamic processes. This blurs the distinction between micro and macro in dynamic analysis and at the same time stresses the interaction of market and organization in structuring coherent dynamic systems, that is, their nature as complements in a process of change.

The attempt to bring about a qualitative change engenders a complex dynamic which most often represents a threat to the viability of the economy, that is, to its being able to carry out the change undertaken without collapsing along the way. Thus viability is the main problem associated with qualitative change, and interaction, complementarity, and co-ordination over time, which actually shape the process through which the economy must go to bring about this change, are the relevant issues for viability. Is the equilibrium approach, which is behind most of the so-called dynamic methods, suited to deal with qualitative change and the analytical problems that it involves? The analysis of the dominant dynamic approach in its more or less recent versions carried out in Chapter 5 shows that this is not so. It also shows how production, money, the human resource, market, and organization, appear as the building-blocks of an alternative analytical framework which allows us to deal instead with changes that are in the nature of out-of-equilibrium processes, and retraces the roots of this framework in past analytical contributions.

In Part II of the book we set out on an out-of-equilibrium analysis. The model we turn to for this analysis, moulded on the theoretical body sketched out in Part I, is expounded in Chapter 6. It is a rather complex model, aimed at illuminating the crucial analytical aspects of processes of qualitative change without emptying them of their economic content.

It is different from standard models as regards its structure, the way it works, and the use to which it can be put. In the first place it differs as to its logical architecture. Production processes over time instead of synchronized production; fix-price instead of flex-price markets; adaptive instead of optimizing behaviour; and money not merely conceived as a veil are the pillars of this architecture. As regards its working, on the other hand, the model exhibits a thoroughly sequential determination of the evolution path followed by the economy. In particular, what in the model appears as a parameter at a given moment in time is itself the result of processes which have taken place in the economy: processes during which everything—including resources and the environment, as well as technology—undergoes a transformation and hence is made endogenous to the change undergone by the economy. Everything can be considered as given at a certain moment in time, while everything becomes endogenous over time.

Finally, the model is not used to mimic or predict what the evolution of the economy will precisely be, but rather as a heuristic tool to throw light on the mechanism which sketches out the sequential path actually followed by the economy under different conditions, and on the crucial links of the sequence. In this perspective step-by-step numerical calculations appear as a more fruitful analytical method than formal solution techniques. The results thus obtained are subtle insights rather than general theorems. However, this is not a drawback, as the calculations are of illustrative value only: the simulations are laboratories for testing concepts.

Viability, we repeat, is the main issue at stake when we are dealing with an out-of-equilibrium process of change. This is the perspective under which different cases of qualitative change are analysed in

Chapter 7. The complexity of the phenomenon of economic change has led us to consider separately its different aspects, that is, changes in technology, changes in the human resource, changes in available financial resources, and changes in expectations. In each case various evolutionary paths have been investigated under different conditions, thus setting the stage for the analysis of viability. Consideration of these different aspects under a unifying light makes it possible to understand the working of the growth mechanism and its limitations, and thus also provides suggestions on how to relax the impinging constraints.

The results obtained only reveal their full potentiality when looked at through the lenses of fundamental issues and controversies in economic theory, which can thus be put in the right analytical perspective. The relation between consumption, investment, and saving; the relation between growth and the business cycle; and the relation between employment and wages; the meaning of flexibility; and the role and functions of economic policy provide the subject-matter for Chapter 8.

It has always been the concern of economists to understand how economies do not actually experience cumulative or explosive processes notwithstanding the contrasting interests and the opposite forces at work. This, it has been suggested, is the result of the behaviours of agents which, provided the obstacles to their interaction are eliminated, make the system tend spontaneously to a stable situation: to an equilibrium. Stability as evoked by the concept of equilibrium is the distinctive character of essentially static economies, whatever the dynamic attribute we want to confer on them.

Non-stationary economies, by contrast, are characterized by complementarity and co-ordination problems which probably result in self-feeding processes that take them more and more out of equilibrium. The viability of the growth process, then, and not stability, is the relevant concept. This depends mainly on the functioning of prevailing institutions (markets, governments, and so on), that is, on the ability of these institutions to provide the means and the environment that make it possible for the economy to remain viable by continuously adapting to shocks and imbalances as they arise.

The implications of this analytical framework both for interpreting economic phenomena that have the nature of qualitative changes and for choosing the policy interventions suited to deal with these phenomena are momentous.

On most issues the conclusions reached are just the opposite of those of standard theory, which, of course, depends on the change of perspective that the nature of the phenomena involved requires and that dominant theory, accustomed to believe that its usual face can stand whatever light with just a little make-up, stubbornly denies. Consideration of problems which have powerful social consequences (particularly the problem of employment) will show how the analytical approach proposed in this book cannot be confined to a pure disquisition of theory but has essential bearing on the choice of the lines of action which will shape the very future of our society.

PART I
THEORY: THE BUILDING-BLOCKS

1
Production

1.1. THE *EX POST* VIEW OF THE PHENOMENON OF PRODUCTION

The analysis of states of the economy, and of their changes, carried out with reference to equilibrium configurations relies on an *ex post* view of production, technology, and the environment.[1] This viewpoint characterizes the standard analysis of production and technology, from the neoclassical production function to linear production models, but, as we shall see, it is not confined to this approach.

By *ex post* we mean that the focus is on 'given' solutions to given productive problems—not so much in the sense that these are specific and/or exogenously determined as in that they are looked at as already analytically defined productive options; which immediately evokes the productive configurations that are the physical counterpart of these options, whichever way they are actually defined.[2]

Reference to a productive option, that is, to a certain way of dealing with a productive problem which is itself already defined (e.g. obtaining a particular commodity in a given way to satisfy a certain need), naturally draws attention to the definition or representation of the productive configuration (capacity) which is the actual expression of this option, and, then, to the utilization or functioning of such a capacity. Technology and production appear then as the two faces of the productive option in this *ex post* perspective: the 'definition' moment (technology) and the 'utilization' moment (production). The two moments are defined in strictly related terms—amounts and proportion in which given inputs are employed, amounts and composition of a given output[3]—although utilization comes logically after what must be made use of is already there. This interpretation of

---

[1] In particular, changes are analysed by means of a comparison of different equilibrium states looked at as *before* and *after* the change. The equilibrium states represent efficient solutions interpreted as (punctual or intertemporal) allocative choices.

[2] Namely, in terms of plants and equipment, skills and qualifications, forms of organization, and so on. The most common, and stylized, definition of a productive configuration is in terms of quantitative combinations of given resources or inputs.

[3] Given (specified) inputs and a given output are the obvious elements of a productive option in the above sense.

technology and production implies in turn the consideration of 'generic' inputs—that is, resources that can be employed in different production processes without loss of productive value, and hence matter only for the amount in which they are available—so that the productive options can be defined in general and abstract terms.

The basic concept, in the standard analysis reflecting this approach, is the production possibilities (technology) set listing the given productive options. This set is defined in terms of an output vector **y** and an input vector **x**:[4]

$$T = \{(\mathbf{y},\mathbf{x}): \mathbf{y} \text{ can be produced from } \mathbf{x}\}$$

and, in the single output case

$$T = \{(y,\mathbf{x}): y \leq f(\mathbf{x})\}$$

which is related to the usual production function $y = f(\mathbf{x})$.[5] **x** and **y** are vectors (and y a scalar) expressing input quantities and output levels (or flows per unit of time), and usually requiring no further specification besides this quantitative dimension.[6]

Thus production comes down to a link between input and output quantities: the mapping of a set of input vectors into the output set. We have already mentioned that this implies considering generic inputs whose most important analytical aspect is precisely availability in larger or smaller amounts, and that can therefore be combined in different proportions to shape different productive options. We have also stressed that this makes it possible to define technology and its utilization (production) in general and abstract terms, namely in terms of technical coefficients (vectors of real numbers expressing input quantities per unit of output). Production appears then as an analytically instantaneous assembling of resources: once the productive capacity with which the process of production is identified has been defined in terms of a given combination of inputs, we are already dealing with the capacity itself from the analytic viewpoint, provided the required inputs are available in the right proportions. However,

---

[4] Or in terms of a single 'netput' vector whose elements are negative if the corresponding entries serve as net inputs and positive if they serve as net outputs.

[5] Particular properties of T (non-emptiness, closedness, strict convexity etc.) are required for the existence and uniqueness of efficient solutions, which, as we shall see immediately, is what we are after with the analysis based on this kind of representation.

[6] Simply adding further dimensions to the elements of these vectors (e.g. a space or a time dimension relating availability to specific calendar times or locations) is not enough to change the *ex post* character, and the analytical implications, of this kind of representation. See Section 1.2 below.

although the process of production is defined in the same way and together with the technology, the latter is actually dissociated from production. Technology appears in fact as an exogenously determined constraint that comes down to a given solution to a particular productive problem, where both the problem (the given output) and its solution (how to obtain it) are defined independently of the particular productive process actually carried on. Dissociation of technology from production, and an essentially timeless production process,[7] are the two main aspects of this analytical treatment of the phenomenon of production.

Dealing with given (analytically defined) productive options, in terms of given resources (that is, resources existing in their own right, outside and independently of specific production processes), on the other hand, unequivocally points to the economic problem involved. A given choice set, defined with reference to given resources, is in fact implied in this vision, and this naturally calls for 'a choice', which is in the nature of an 'allocation of resources.' This interpretation of production as a particular aspect of a problem of the allocation of resources reflects the vantage point of trade and exchange from which mainstream economics keeps looking at production: a perspective that characterized the original neoclassical model, which was mainly an exchange model, and that has been essentially maintained when the model itself has been extended to assign a more important role to production. In this perspective even when the endowments of resources are allowed to change and accumulation is contemplated, this appears as a special case of intertemporal exchange: less consumption today against more consumption tomorrow.

There is thus a strict relation between the interpretation (and the representation) of production, technology, and the environment, and the economic problem that this interpretation evokes: choice coming down to allocation.[8] Of course choice implies comparison, and comparison implies ordering: hence the focus on 'best' choice, that is, on the best solution to the problem, which becomes an optimization problem. Efficiency—in the essential meaning of existence of 'no

---

[7] We shall clarify in the next section exactly what we mean by 'essentially' timeless.

[8] To use Hayek's expression, then, economics is confined to 'the pure logic of choice' (Hayek 1937) which consists in 'comparing the items in a list, known to be complete' (Shackle 1972, p. 96). And when this is the case, we shall see in what follows, behaviours are considered essentially in the absence of time. On this point see the interesting paper by Meacci (1985).

available alternative that is universally preferred in terms of the goals and preferences of the people involved' (Milgrom and Roberts 1992, p. 22)—appears then as the relevant attribute of behaviours (and of their targets); it can be defined at different levels depending on the specific choice considered each time, but it always implies an optimization process under exogenous constraints (the given environment).[9]

The traditional interpretation of the firm—the typical agent carrying out production—and the specification of its functions, faithfully reflect this approach. The definition of the firm as a production function, and of its task as the allocation of given resources in view of efficient solutions, is in fact clearly the expression of this *ex post* interpretation of the phenomenon of production and of the economic problem associated with it.

We have already underlined the two main aspects (the technological and the productive) of an *ex post* interpretation of the phenomenon of production. Choice of the combination of given resources (out of the given technology set) and choice of output levels, respectively, are the (related) problems that the firm, identified with the production function, must solve. A production plan is then defined as 'technically efficient' if there is no way to produce more output with the same inputs, or to produce the same output with less inputs, given the assumption that both inputs and output have positive value. However, the optimization process needs more than a production function defining the choice set, when the choice is among different combinations of resources to be acquired on the market at given prices. Then 'economic efficiency' becomes the relevant concept, and it means least cost choice.[10] We thus need a 'dual' cost function that—given the existing productive resources **x** and their market prices **w**—shows the minimum cost for each output level **y** when operating at the frontier of the production set, that is

$$C(\mathbf{y},\mathbf{w}) = \min_{x} \{\mathbf{w} \cdot \mathbf{x} : (\mathbf{x},\mathbf{y}) \in T\}\ [11]$$

---

[9] In particular, it can be the attribute of a punctual choice or of a choice along a path, as we shall see in Chapter 4 when dealing with R&D strategies.

[10] Of course economic efficiency implies technical efficiency, but not the other way round.

[11] Economic efficiency (least-cost input choice) embodied in the cost function does not concern in itself the choice of output levels, but it is obviously implied by profit maximization based on the same function.

1.2. TIME AND EQUILIBRIUM

The crucial aspect of the standard representation of production—and what makes it particularly suited to an 'equilibrium' analysis—is not that it does not make reference to time, but that in the perspective adopted the time dimension of production is not relevant. In this perspective in fact, although differently dated, inputs do not come before output 'in an essential way'. That is, they are analytically, and from an accounting viewpoint, contemporaneous, so that there are always proceeds against which costs can be set and a 'current' productive activity out of which they can be financed. This aspect of the timelessness of the production process is what really matters. It implies in fact a *given relation* between the basic magnitudes of the process itself (output, employment, capital) which draws attention to the functioning of the given productive capacity that brings about this regular behaviour—not to changes in this capacity (including changes in its age structure, when this is taken into account in defining it) implying a modification of the given relation.[12]

Overlooking the sequential character of production goes back to the 'circular flow' view of production of the classical economists, whose main interest was the 'reproducibility' of a system, that is, enquiring how a system becomes organized to deliver a set of commodities which secure its reproduction requirements. The stationary state is the typical example of a circular process: symmetric relations among variables prevail and this makes it possible to analytically relate current output to current inputs and not to the inputs that have actually entered their production process. Another example of a circular process is the proportionately expanding economy of von Neumann's model (1937), which, as we shall see a little later, relies on the treatment of fixed capital as a special type of joint product.

This aspect of the timelessness of production—that there is always an output against which costs can be set—has survived not only the change from the 'reproducibility' viewpoint to the 'scarcity' viewpoint associated with the rise of the neoclassical approach, but appears in general to be an essential ingredient of equilibrium analysis. Different

---

[12] This given relation is exactly what characterizes an equilibrium state. In equilibrium, then, the 'utilization' moment of the given productive option comes into the foreground, while the 'definition' moment, including its time attribute (if any), remains in the background. This remains true when the change in capacity considered is just a proportional expansion, as in steady growth.

assumptions—concerning the nature of the process of production, its organization, the characteristics of the commodities involved, and so forth—deal with it in the most important equilibrium models. Of course, the explicit hypothesis of instantaneous production is the most obvious example. But also when this is not the case, and the fact that production takes time is explicitly considered and a vertical structure of the process of production is envisaged (as in a flow-fund model à la Georgescu-Róegen), the same result can be obtained if production is organized in such a way as to make a synchronic representation of it possible. This is what we come to, for example, when production processes consisting of a temporal sequence of operations (stages) are arranged in line in the factory system to reduce the degree of idleness implied by the time structure of production, and enough of them are carried out that all stages of a given type of process take place at the same time and final output accrues in each period (Georgescu-Roegen 1965). The vertical ordering of the successive phases of production then fades away, and once again production costs in each period can be set against current output.

Another way of obtaining the same result is the enlargement of the list of commodities by the inclusion of fictitious intermediate products as the result of reducing each given process to a number of standardized processes of unit duration. This is the method followed by von Neumann (1937), who considers a production process lasting just one period, at the beginning of which all inputs (including capital goods left over from the preceding period) are acquired and at the end of which all output (including qualitatively different capital goods obtained during the current period) is sold. The device of regarding capital goods at different ages as different goods—with a regular market and a system of prices for those goods set up in each period—and that of making the period itself as short as we like by increasing the number of fictitious commodities, make the reference back to the market continuous and the matching of inputs costs and output revenues always possible.

Multiplication of commodities also characterizes the intertemporal equilibrium model of Arrow and Debreu (1954), the most rigorous, complete and successful stage-set for equilibrium analysis. This involves a succession of periods (assumed to be in equilibrium) which are different from one another and over which production and exchange take place sequentially. Although markets do open in each period of the sequence, the outcome of all periods (prices, quantities, exchange ratios) i.e. all the elements of the sequence of equilibrium states, are determined simultaneously for all periods at the initial instant of the economy by an outside observer. Past, present, and future are equilibrated all at the same time: there is no sequential adjustment of the markets. It follows that the sequence of periods envisaged is looked at, and taken into account, 'as a whole', so as to appear as one big period both from the accounting and the analytical viewpoint. In this context, the description of production as the transformation of a bundle of commodities defined by their characteristics, location, and date of delivery[13] into another seems to make it possible to consider inputs that come before output. But this is only apparently true, since the commodities considered actually all become 'current', as they are referred to a sequence that must be taken as a whole. The future markets in fact allow not only sales of current output to finance future purchases but also sales of future output to finance current costs, so that all inputs and outputs are set against each other and there are always revenues to which costs can be imputed.

The same happens in temporary equilibrium models. Temporary equilibrium, introduced by Lindahl (1930) and extensively analysed by Hicks (1939), emerged from intertemporal equilibrium, also introduced by Lindahl (1929), as the result of the breaking up of the latter when expectations are not fulfilled.[14] Temporary equilibrium determines the outcome for a single period, not for the whole sequence. The single period equilibrium is determined on the basis of expectations concerning the state of the economy in future periods and based upon past experience. Once this is determined, production and exchange take place (within the period itself); then the process is repeated for the following period and so on. There is then sequential adjustment of markets as regards expectations; however, mistakes are not transformed into stocks of commodities handed over from one period to the next.[15]

---

[13] Hicks (1939) was the first to suggest this elaborate notion of commodity. The state of the world in which commodities are deliverable is added to their definition when uncertainty is introduced (Arrow 1953; Debreu 1959).

[14] Grandmont (1977) takes the different stand of considering temporary equilibrium as the more general framework of which intertemporal equilibrium represents the specific case of self-fulfilling expectations.

[15] As a matter of fact Morishima (1992) considers stocks which are the result of mistakes by introducing, among others, a productive activity which consists exactly in the accumulation or decumulation of stocks. However this activity is strictly related to its own period, so that the transmission of stocks from one period to the other does not imply transmission of the corresponding disequilibrium.

Although markets do open in each period, the periods themselves are actually severed from the accounting viewpoint: the costs and output of each period refer to the period itself and do not pass its border. Thus, once again, they are not dissociated.

What matters in intertemporal equilibrium, from the accounting and the analytical viewpoints, is the succession of periods, but this is taken as a whole. What matters in temporary equilibrium is each given period, but this, from the accounting and the analytical viewpoint, is separated from the sequence. The same result obtains: over the whole sequence in the one case, in each period in the other, there are current proceeds against which costs can be set; inputs do not come before output in an essential way.

Hicks had already stressed the accounting aspect in explaining the difficulty of dealing with fixed capital in equilibrium analysis: namely, the difficulty of fitting fixed capital into the arbitrary period(s) over which equilibrium is defined. 'It is in fact the extension of the use of fixed capital to a duration which is longer than the accounting (say annual) period which creates the difficulty' (Hicks 1977, p. 158). Fixed capital in fact, unless the production process (by assumption or organization) is made synchronic, naturally dissociates costs from proceeds. However, the problem is more general: it arises whenever output requires a lapse of time to mature, or commodities dated over many time periods are involved. The above-mentioned models are different but similar (in their effects) ways of overcoming this difficulty; they adjust the accounting period to the time span over which commodities are dated (over which fixed capital life extends), or vice versa.

1.3. COMPLEMENTS AND SUBSTITUTES IN THE ECONOMICS OF PRODUCTION

The essence of the problem of the time dimension of production is that complementarity rather than substitution characterizes the production process. This is a point that, although in different analytical contexts and with different accents, both Georgescu-Roegen (1971, 1976) and Hicks (1973) hint at.

Georgescu-Róegen refers to the catalogue of feasible recipes that describe production processes and that 'consists of a set of points in an abstract space, as opposed to the Euclidean space.' (1971, p. 236). This set may be represented by a relation of the form

$$Q(t) = F[E_i(t), S_j(t)], \quad 0 \leq t \leq T$$

where $Q(t)$ is the coordinate for the final output, $E_i(t)$ the coordinate for the flow factors (that enter the production process but do not come out of it, or come out without having entered) and $S_j(t)$ the coordinate for the fund factors (which 'represent the material base of the process'(Georgescu-Roegen 1965, p. 86) as they 'enter and come out of the process in an economically, if not physically, identical form, and in the same amount'(ibid. p. 84), and hence can serve in any process over and over again, although needing maintenance); all defined over the time interval $(0–T)$ which corresponds to the length of the production process. Each relation corresponds to only one process. As a consequence the factors included in any of the functionals (or of the point functions when there is a complete synchronization) representing the catalogue of the recipes, cannot be substituted for. They are *complementary* factors. In the functional, S represents generically funds (equipment, labour skills, and the like) of various qualities, S_j meaning a certain amount of the fund of quality j. There may be no change corresponding to, for example, the substitution of more capital K (in the sense of machines or equipment) for less labour L. Substitution means rather that K_a and L_a are used instead of K_b and L_b.

In other words substitution concerns processes and not the coordinates (capital, labour) of one particular process. However, the substitution of a process b for a process a cannot be realized instantaneously. The reason is that the fund factors are specific to each process and that their accumulation and decumulation differ from the accumulation and decumulation of a stock of commodities in that it cannot take place at any speed. It is in fact characterized by intertemporal complementarities; these cannot be taken into account within the context of Georgescu-Roegen's representation, and are instead at the heart of the Neo-Austrian representation of the production process, as we shall see in the next section.

Dissociating commodities from processes is then as far as Georgescu-Róegen goes, but it is a step with important analytical implications. It makes it possible to stress that 'commodities are *not* produced by commodities but by processes' (Georgescu-Roegen 1976, p. 251). And that, whereas in a stationary or steady state the attention can be confined to the production of commodities (the 'utilization' moment of a production process[16]), this is no longer the case 'in any non-stationary economic system' where 'the production activity is aimed at two distinct objectives—to produce *goods* and to produce *processes*' (ibid.) and where the latter activity must come before the former.

Now the main issue about the production of processes concerns the 'construction phase' (which corresponds to a waiting period) and the costs associated with it.[17] These costs are dissociated from proceeds in the sense that, by definition, they have to be paid before the corresponding proceeds are obtained. Thus the first requirement of a proper analysis of non-stationary states of the firm (or of the economy) is a representation of production activity as the production of processes (and not only of commodities) with a focus on its time dimension. Activity analysis actually deals with processes rather than commodities in so far as it refers to complementary factors. However, with this kind of representation the substitution of the process for another is analytically instantaneous. As a matter of fact the time dimension of production vanishes when funds (as defined by Georgescu-Roegen) are reduced to flows.[18] All inputs (including capital goods) are then commodities which in any period have a complete reference back to the market and hence a price. The costs associated with a given productive capacity are immediately matched by corresponding revenues: the distinction between construction and utilization disappears and the possibility of dissociating costs from proceeds goes with it.

1.4. TIME AND SEQUENCE: DISSOCIATING COSTS FROM PROCEEDS

We have already stressed that an equilibrium (point or path) is characterized by a given relation between the relevant economic magnitudes. This reflects the established (and in some way synchronized)

---

[16] In a steady state the perfect synchronization between the utilization of productive capacity and its construction makes it possible to ignore the latter and to focus on the commodities that enter or leave the production process in each period.

[17] Which is exactly what the Neo-Austrian model takes into account.

[18] In the activity analysis the performance of the economy during a given period is adequately represented by the flows observed within the period itself. The production process is seen in fact 'as a continuous affair described only from the *ouside* by flows. What was already *inside* the process at first and at the end is of no concern to the economist' (Georgescu-Roegen 1990, p. 210).

functioning of a given, or regularly expanding, productive capacity, which also implies that costs and proceeds are somehow kept together. Whenever production, not simple exchange, is contemplated, the assumption that inputs do not come before output in an essential way is thus crucial for equilibrium analysis.

This also implies, as we shall see in what follows, that in equilibrium—whether defined at a point in time or over time—costs C and proceeds R can both be written as a function of current output

$$C = C(\mathbf{y}), \quad R = R(\mathbf{y})$$

abstracting from the underlying productive capacity (and its characteristics) and focusing on its 'utilization' moment as represented by output levels.

Explicit consideration of the time profile of the production process (e.g. by dating the variables involved) does not really change things by itself. As mentioned in Section 1.2 above, in fact, it is always possible to adjust the accounting period to the time length over which production extends, or to do just the opposite, so as to actually abstract from this time profile. Thus we need something more than simply stretching out 'in time' the process of production: we need to dissociate the accounting period from the duration of this process, in order to dissociate inputs from output and costs from proceeds. This we can do by plotting the production process over a sequence of periods, provided, however, this is a true sequence, that is, a sequence of periods that from the accounting viewpoint do not collapse into a unique period. This requires that the costs are those actually incurred and the proceeds are those actually accruing in each given period—but that, at the same time, the different periods 'belong' to the sequence in the sense that they make up the sequence itself.[19] What really makes different periods part of a sequence in the above sense is that they are linked with each other, and in such a way as to keep the time sequence right. A production process extending over more periods and characterized by intertemporal complementarity certainly provides such a link. A Neo-Austrian production process—that is, a process by which a flow of primary labour inputs is converted 'in time' into a flow of final output, and where capital goods are implied but regarded as intermediate products internal to the process and not explicitly shown—is the most obvious candidate for this role. Its full

---

[19] Two conditions that neither in intertemporal equilibrium (where the latter obtains) nor in temporal equilibrium (where the former obtains) are verified together.

vertical integration, in fact, makes it possible to focus on 'one way' intertemporal complementarity and at the same time, by cancelling the reference back to the market 'during' the process, to dissociate 'in time' costs from proceeds imputing them to different periods.

Thus, when we consider both a process of production articulated over time and a truly sequential context, inputs do come before output in an essential way. But, once again, this can be hidden under an equilibrium sequence, characterized by a given age structure of productive capacity, which makes possible a synchronic representation of production that brings costs and proceeds together again.[20] We must therefore be somehow 'out of equilibrium' for the analytical implications of a sequential context to come to light, even when the time structure of the process of production is explicitly taken into account. But what do we actually mean here by 'being out of equilibrium'? Reference to a Neo-Austrian analytical framework (Hicks 1970, 1973) will help to clarify this point.

Consider an economy where a single homogeneous commodity is produced by means of a unique primary input—labour—with an elementary process of production of a Neo-Austrian type j taking place through a sequence of periods $0, 1, 2, \ldots, n, n+1, \ldots, n+N$ which make up a phase of construction c (from period 0 to period n) and, following it, a phase of utilization u (from period $n+1$ to period $n+N$) of productive capacity. At each time t, if $\mathbf{a} = [a_0, a_1, \ldots, a_{n+N}]$ is the vector of quantities of labour required by an elementary process and $\mathbf{b} = [b_{n+1}, \ldots, b_{n+N}]$ is the vector of final output, we can write the accounting equations for total employment (L) and total final output (B) as

$$L(t) = a_0 x_0(t) + a_1 x_1(t) + \ldots + a_{n+N} x_{n+N}(t)$$
$$B(t) = b_{n+1} x_{n+1}(t) + \ldots + b_{n+N} x_{n+N}(t)$$

where $x_0, x_1, \ldots, x_{n+N}$ are the number of processes of age $0, 1, \ldots n+N$, respectively.

In a steady state x_0 will be equal to $x_1 G$, where $G = 1 + g$ and g is the steady-growth rate. Then

$$L(t) = x_0(t) (a_0 + a_1 G^{-1} + \ldots + a_{n+N} G^{-(n+N)})$$
$$B(t) = x_0(t) (b_{n+1} G^{-(n+1)} + \ldots + b_{n+N} G^{-(n+N)})$$

The bracketed expressions are independent of t, so the ratio $(B/L)(t)$

---

[20] Or, as already mentioned, suitable forms of organization of production which imply the same kind of synchronization can be considered.

is constant over time. As in steady state the real wage rate w is also constant over time, this implies the constancy of the ratio $(B/wL)(t)$. Costs (wL) and proceeds (B) are then perfectly synchronized, and both can be made to depend on the same variable: the scale of activity of productive capacity in the utilization phase, that is

$$\mathbf{x}^u(t) = [x_{n+1}(t), \ldots, x_{n+N}(t)]$$

which, in this model, reflects current final output. As a matter of fact while proceeds actually depend on $\mathbf{x}^u(t)$, costs depend not only on $\mathbf{x}^u(t)$ but also on the processes still in the phase of construction $\mathbf{x}^c(t)$ (where $\mathbf{x}^c(t) = [x_0(t), x_1(t), \ldots, x_n(t)]$. However, in equilibrium a given age structure of productive capacity, and hence constancy of the ratio between the above vectors, makes it possible to focus only on current final output (the 'utilization' moment) and to write

$$C = C[\mathbf{x}^u(t)], \qquad R = R[\mathbf{x}^u(t)]$$

A given and stable relation between the relevant economic magnitudes, we have just stressed, also implies a given relation between processes in the (different periods of the) phase of construction and processes in the phase of utilization, and a given age structure of productive capacity. The 'productive structure' thus defined has a 'horizontal' dimension, expressed at time t by the vectors of elementary processes at different stages of their life—still in the phase of construction $\mathbf{x}^c(t)$ or already in the phase of utilization $\mathbf{x}^u(t)$—being carried on; which also implies a 'vertical' dimension (the time pattern of production associated with this age structure of productive capacity). These, in equilibrium, must be consistent with each other: then, together with construction and utilization, investment and consumption and supply and demand of final output are also harmonized, at each given moment of time and over time. When this is so the time dimension of production is left somewhat in the shade; we have just seen how we can in fact abstract from the underlying productive capacity and concentrate on its utilization moment, and how costs and proceeds then become analytically, and from an accounting viewpoint, contemporaneous.

A qualitative change—as opposed to mere quantitative growth perfectly compatible with the equilibrium state just defined—implies instead a change in the way of functioning of the economic entity considered (the economy, the firm, or whatever), that is, a structural modification which, according to the above definition, is characterized in the first place by a change in the balance between processes in the phase of construction and processes in the phase of utilization, and hence a change in the age structure of productive capacity with respect to its previous equilibrium configuration. As we have just seen, not only construction and utilization, but also investment and consumption, and supply and demand, are then no longer harmonized over time. This means it is no longer possible to focus on current final output abstracting from the underlying productive capacity and, in particular, from the time structure of the production process. The ratio $(B/wL)(t)$ is no longer constant over time and, as a consequence, costs are dissociated from proceeds. When the ratio between the vectors $\mathbf{x}^c(t)$ and $\mathbf{x}^u(t)$ is no longer constant, costs and proceeds are affected in a different way, as is the case when there is a breaking of the steady state, which thus implies separating inputs from output 'in time'.

The cost function will then be

$$C = C[\mathbf{x}^c(t), \mathbf{x}^u(t)]$$

and the proceeds function will become

$$R = R[\mathbf{x}^u(t)]$$

1.5. OUT-OF-EQUILIBRIUM CONTEXTS: BRINGING TO LIGHT THE TIME STRUCTURE OF PRODUCTION

A first and general meaning of being 'out of equilibrium' is that a change in the balance of processes of production in different stages of their life is under way. When this is so, it is not possible to abstract from the underlying productive capacity, whose structure is continuously modified, and concentrate on its 'utilization' moment. The consequence, as already mentioned, is that inputs are separated in time from output and costs dissociated from proceeds.

This, we have seen, happens whenever a qualitative change is contemplated. Then the 'definition' moment (technology) of the production process—that is, its physical characteristics, including its time profile—comes back into the foreground; and this occurs in the first place, obviously, when a change in these characteristics (that is, a change in technology) is contemplated.

In the standard analysis, in which 'efficiency' is pursued, the mere appearance of a 'superior' technique encourages its adoption.[21]

---

[21] 'Superiority' and 'efficiency' are in fact defined in the same terms, whether techniques are represented by means of a production function or in different ways, e.g. in terms of wage-interest curves.

However adoption, once again, is treated within an equilibrium framework. Thus it actually becomes an analytically 'instantaneous' (total, or partial as in vintage models) process which does not allow the transition phase during which productive capacity necessarily becomes distorted to show up. Consideration of the time dimension of production in vintage models is thus confined to the 'utilization' moment (the economic life of machines, that is, the extensive dimension of capital), and hence it has no 'essential' implications, as we have defined them, in terms of the relation between inputs and output.[22]

On the other hand, we may want to stress the fact that a 'new' productive structure does not immediately come about after a modification of it is contemplated, and that the economy must actually go through the phase of construction of a different productive capacity before this happens. This is what happens in the analysis of the Traverse (Hicks 1973), which portrays the adoption of a superior technique as a process taking place sequentially over time. The explicit consideration of the time structure of the production process and of its intertemporal complementarity (with a focus on the phase of construction of a 'new' productive capacity and on its coming necessarily before the phase of utilization) allows to illuminate the fact that a change of the technique in use necessarily implies a change in the age structure of productive capacity and hence a dissociation of inputs from output and of costs from proceeds. We are in fact here clearly in an 'out-of-equilibrium' context where the different specification of the cost and the proceeds functions—as defined in the previous section—comes to be stressed, due to the fact that the modification in the age structure of productive capacity shows immediately in the one function and not in the other. The analysis of the Traverse carried out within this analytical perspective allows important insights; in particular, as we shall see in Section 5.5 below, it makes possible a demonstration of Ricardo's famous 'machinery effect', according to which the introduction of machinery has an adverse effect on employment in the short run.

A change in the balance of production processes, and a modification in the age structure of productive capacity, also obtains when, with no change in the technique in use, there is an increase in the rate

---

[22] In Joan Robinson's parlance (1974) it is 'logical time' that is considered in these and in all equilibrium models, not 'historical time'.

of growth. This means in fact an increase in the number of processes in the phase of construction not matched for a certain time (that is, as long as the higher growth rate has not yet been reached) by a corresponding increase in the number of processes in the phase of utilization. Again, the cost and the proceeds functions are affected in a different way and costs are dissociated from proceeds. However, this case poses an additional problem—which, as we shall see throughout this book, is of paramount importance for the viability of processes of economic change. While in fact the introduction of a new technique can be financed out of current productive activity by diverting to the construction of the new productive capacity the resources previously devoted to financing the production processes of the old type, this is no longer possible when an increase in the growth rate is considered. The costs incurred by bringing about such an increase—'sunk' costs that can only be recovered over time—cannot now be financed from the proceeds of current productive activity;[23] additional financial resources are in fact required as long as the age structure of productive capacity is not adjusted to the higher growth rate. The adoption of a new technique is always possible: the technical coefficients and the hypotheses as to the destination of existing proceeds will determine how (and if) the Traverse will actually be accomplished. An increase in the rate of growth,[24] on the contrary, will be possible only if additional financial resources are exogenously made available, as we shall see in particular in Chapter 2.

What makes it possible in both cases to focus on the time dimension of production (and hence on inputs coming before output in an essential way) is a change in the balance of production processes with respect to its equilibrium configuration (where production is somehow synchronized) which takes the economy out of equilibrium in the sense outlined above. Nevertheless this change can take place smoothly, with the existing production processes gradually transmuted into different ones until a new equilibrium configuration obtains. Suitable hypotheses[25] reduce the process of change to a

---

[23] Transferring resources has no meaning in this case: in fact we need 'more' resources to finance 'more' processes of the usual type.

[24] And also a higher rate of growth.

[25] Like, in the analysis of the Traverse, the existence in the economy of a single homogeneous commodity and the hypothesis of Full Performance, which imply that all output which is not consumed is invested (except for a constant 'take-out').

sequence that can be fully predetermined and where expectations play no role. In each period of the sequence leading to a configuration of productive capacity fully known beforehand, in fact, supply and demand for final output are kept in equilibrium.[26] Thus structural modifications do not necessarily stir out-of-equilibrium processes, which may imply cumulative causation or erratic fluctuations. Although evoking an out-of-equilibrium context they can still be dealt with by turning to an equilibrium approach.

However, it must be stressed, this happens only in particular cases characterized by very strong assumptions. In general, structural modifications imply a distortion of productive capacity which comes down to the abrupt disappearance of a part of the existing capacity, with the sudden appearance of imbalances between supply and demand and investment and consumption. Via expectations, and in the attempt to correct these imbalances, a 'constraints–decisions–constraints' sequence sets in that results in an out-of-equilibrium process which probably shakes the economy in such a way as to cast doubt on the viability of the change undertaken.[27] Although true for all qualitative changes (with the specific exceptions just mentioned) this can be made more evident by referring to changes which imply shifting from an *ex post* to an *ex ante* viewpoint.

1.6. FROM THE *EX POST* TO AN *EX ANTE* VIEWPOINT: THE CREATION OF RESOURCES

We have shown that, for the time dimension of production to become 'essential' in the analysis, we require both a representation of the process of production that takes the phase of construction of productive capacity explicitly into account (and hence does not focus only on the 'utilization' moment of a given productive option), and an out-of-equilibrium context. When both of these are in place the process through which a change takes place can be analysed as such, not

---

[26] The change dealt with can also imply some scrapping of production processes. However, when this scrapping reflects an intended behaviour, no true distortion of productive capacity occurs, and the equilibrium between supply and demand can still be maintained during the process of change which is thus bound to take place (see Amendola 1972).

[27] The analysis of some such processes will be carried out in particular in Part II of this book.

substituted for by a comparison between the situations prevailing before and after the change. Two examples of such changes have been considered, and the implications of considering them as processes in historical time have been stressed.

However, although bringing to light the time structure of the process of production, and stressing the implications (different in the two cases) of actually taking this time structure into account, both cases mentioned still stick to an *ex post* view of technology and production, as they both concern given productive options. The analysis of the Traverse actually concerns the adoption of a given (i.e. already defined) 'superior' technique. Even clearer is the *ex post* viewpoint in the case of an increase in the rate of growth, where the whole point is the multiplication of processes of production not only perfectly defined but already established in the economy. What about, however, the wider and certainly more interesting gamut of qualitative changes which also imply the appearance of altogether new productive options? The analysis of these changes needs more than a representation of production that takes into account explicitly the phase of construction of productive capacity and its relation with the phase of utilization. It needs interpreting 'construction' no longer as adoption or actual embodiment but as 'creation anew'. Technology and productive options, then, are no longer given or exogenously determined: they are the result of the process of change, not its precondition. This requires a shift from an *ex post* to an *ex ante* view of the phenomenon of production, which, as we shall see in the following section, not only has important implications for a great many problems (from the way in which we define the firm and its functions to the interpretation of the environment) but also has a role to play in the first place with the modelling of processes of economic change themselves.

But what does this change of perspective really mean? It must not be taken only, and primarily, in the sense of stressing different viewpoints from which to look at a 'certain' problem but rather in the sense that, by enlarging the beam of light so as to consider a wider spread of aspects, we actually come to consider an 'essentially different' problem.

When an *ex post* viewpoint prevails a lot is 'given' as regards production. In particular, technology and the environment are essentially given—which does not mean that technology is something that falls from the sky more or less fully realized—and hence has only to be adopted, as in the traditional representation of technical progress—and that the environment is just the stage on which adoption takes place and that matters only in terms of the constraints that it imposes on the adoption process. The analysis of technological trajectories defined as the actualization of the premises contained in a basic paradigm (Dosi 1982), to take an example, has in fact taught us that technology is actually developed through a sequential process that restricts the range of options left available as the technology becomes more and more specified, and that the environment plays an active part in this process. This is certainly a significant step forward with respect to the naïve interpretation of technology as something to be taken off a shelf. However, it remains the case that it is the development of a specific technology, with given potential characteristics out of which a given environment will help to single out the ones that will be translated into the actual physical expression of the technology itself, that the model of the trajectory postulates and focuses on. Although apparently less is 'given' in this model than in the traditional one, and more is left to be determined by a process, this process is still confined to the definition and the building in a certain context of the productive capacity expression of a particular technology.

The crucial hypothesis, which characterizes both the traditional approach and that focusing on technological trajectories, is that the resources that take part in the production process—whether it be the simple adoption or actual specification of a technology—are seen as existing in their own right and are hence separated from the technology that they contribute to bringing about. This also implies, in a wider sense, that these resources make up the environment in which production takes place and which is therefore given with respect to the production process itself, although it helps to shape it. Resources, in terms of which both technology and the environment are defined in the end, must logically pre-exist them.

The *ex post* viewpoint allows us to focus on (the adoption, development, and more intensive utilization of) an essentially given technology within an essentially given context. In this sense the case of technological trajectories is no different from the cases of the Traverse and of an increase in the growth rate mentioned above: the object of the analysis remains 'a given technology', whether the latter is observed as a finished object or in the process of its formation. Thus, although representing an undeniable step forward in the description of specific technological advances and in their understanding, the evolutionary approach which is behind the analysis of technological trajectories—at least in the way in which it has been developed—does not really allow us to focus on the thorough 'economic problem' at the heart of economic change, that is, the dissociation of inputs from output and of costs from proceeds that the change itself brings about while it is taking place. This is for the reason just mentioned: in the end there is no developed theory of production different from the standard theory so as to overcome the dynamic limits of the latter.

A change of perspective, from the *ex post* to an *ex ante* viewpoint, does not mean to lock less 'in the pond of ceteris paribus'—although, as we shall see in a minute, it implies going to the extreme of actually considering nothing as given. Rather, it means changing the very object of the analysis and, together with it, the economic problem involved. Qualitative change interpreted as 'creation' of altogether new productive options, not the adoption or development of something already essentially defined, comes into focus.

Innovation is the typical example of qualitative change originating within a process that takes place sequentially, a process through which a new productive option (with the corresponding specific capacity) is actually structured and, as we shall see, yet further options are envisaged. A process of construction of new forms of production which will only take on precise definition along the way, also implies the appearance of a new kind of output (to which new forms of consumption are most likely to be associated). On the other hand this kind of process can no longer be regarded as the simple assembling of given generic inputs.[28] The inputs will in fact also undergo a modification while the process is taking place and the new productive option is being structured. Thus resources and technology are no longer separate: they become one and the same thing while the change is going on. The process of change is what brings about both, and a new and different environment together with them.

In an *ex ante* perspective, therefore, we must move from the consideration of generic inputs to that of 'specific' resources, that is, resources embodying particular characteristics, and potentialities, acquired through the process of qualitative change in question, which therefore comes down to a process of 'creation' of resources. Within

---

[28] And hence can no longer be specified in terms of given combinations of the inputs themselves (whether or not regarded at different moments of time) as in the case when an *ex post* representation of technology prevails.

this perspective qualitative change is essentially a learning process, where learning is related to the abstract capacity of conceiving and implementing new productive options in general, and hence is seen as an enrichment of the potential creativity of the human resource. However, this kind of learning is the joint product of another kind of learning, related to and taking place while the production process through which a specific productive option[29] is actually being defined is carried out. Innovative production processes actually carried on and taking shape sequentially over time are then the carrier of learning resulting in a creation of resources (Amendola and Gaffard 1988).

1.7. OUT-OF-EQUILIBRIUM PROCESSES: THE ANALYTICAL IMPLICATIONS

Interpreting production no longer as allocation of resources but as creation of resources—that is, changing the economic problem involved—has momentous analytical implications. In the first place it means that what we are after is no longer choice out of a given choice set in the light of some optimality criterion (say, 'efficiency') but modification and redefinition of the set itself. Optimal allocative solutions (equilibria) are defined with reference to given[30] parameters (resources, technology, and so forth) which are instead made endogenous to a process of qualitative change. Attention cannot therefore be concentrated on the outcome of a process that cannot be specified *ex ante*, as the effective constraints that set its trend are themselves modified while the process unfolds and depending on how it unfolds. What matters, then, is the process of change itself, and hence the conditions for its 'viability', rather than the configuration that will result from it, and the characteristics of the latter. As a matter of fact the adaptive or innovative behaviours that characterize out-of-equilibrium processes as qualitative changes may bring the economy beyond limits which imply its collapse. These limits represent barriers within which the economy itself must be kept to remain viable. They may concern employment (it may not only be production processes that are seriously affected but society itself may not accept excessive

---

[29] Which, in an *ex post* perspective, will appear as a given productive capacity, with the specific physical assets, forms of organization, and skills and qualifications of the labour inputs that it implies.

[30] Or regularly moving according to exogenously determined laws.

levels of unemployment), indebtedness (which must not be so high as to threaten creditors with insolvency, in which case creditors would lose confidence and firms would go bankrupt), or other factors.[31] However, we have already stressed, this is true not only of changes that imply the creation of resources and learning but of all qualitative changes characterized by structural modifications that can only be brought about through out-of-equilibrium processes (like, e.g., a speeding up of the growth rate). To analyse a qualitative change is to explain how, and under what conditions, it takes place, to focus on how productive options are actually structured, rather than on the characteristics of particular productive solutions, and hence on comparison and choice.

This different perspective affects both the modelling of the process involved and the kind of analysis we are to carry out. In the first place commodities are no longer defined with reference to a date, a place, and a state of nature, as in general equilibrium models, but in terms of production processes with specific time profiles. Then we have a different interpretation of the terms 'exogenous' and 'endogenous'. In a model there are variables and parameters; the parameters (given magnitudes and coefficients) reflect the existing constraints. In the standard analysis the constraints which exist outside and above the economy and which determine its behaviour are taken to be exogenous. Within this context endogenization means that something that was a parameter in the above sense is now made the object of a behaviour considered explicitly in the model; the form of the behaviour function, and its coefficients, now become the exogenous constraints.

But once we recognize that the time over which change takes place is a continuing and irreversible process which shapes the change itself, as we have to do when we consider a qualitative change (and all the more so when we adopt in an *ex ante* perspective), 'it is impossible to assume the constancy of anything *over time* . . . The only truly exogenous factor is *whatever exists at a given moment of time*, as a heritage of the past . . .' (Kaldor 1985, p. 61). In the analysis of an out-of-equilibrium process (and especially in the

---

[31] As an immediate consequence, the very image of the firm, and the definition of its tasks, also need to be revised. As a matter of fact, as we shall see more clearly in Chapter 4, in this new light the firm can no longer be identified with a production function but must be regarded as an organization whose task is not to allocate given resources in terms of efficiency but to make a process of creation of resources viable.

analysis of a process involving the creation of resources), we thus, have to consider as a parameter, and hence as exogenous, not some given element chosen beforehand by reason of its nature or characteristics, but whatever, at a given moment of time, is inherited from the past. What appears as a parameter at a given moment in time is therefore itself the result of processes which have taken place within the economy: processes during which everything—including resources and the environment, as well as technology—undergoes a transformation and hence is made endogenous to the change undergone by the economy.[32] Thus, while the standard approach focuses on the right place to draw the line between what should be taken as exogenous and what should be considered instead as endogenous in economic modelling—a line that moves according to what we want to be explained by the model—out of equilibrium (and all the more in an *ex ante* perspective) the question is no longer that of drawing a line here or there but rather one of the time perspective adopted. Everything can be considered as given at a certain moment of time, while everything becomes endogenous over time.

We have considered in Section 1.5 above out-of-equilibrium contexts in which changes are brought about gradually and smoothly, so that no viability issue is involved. However, we have stressed that more generally qualitative change causes a distortion of productive capacity which stirs an out-of-equilibrium process that the economy must go through for the change undertaken to take place. When we are 'out of equilibrium' in this stronger sense the relevant problem is the 'viability' of the out-of-equilibrium process, and this problem is not one calling for general analytical solutions as in the usual perspective of formal (allocative) models.[33] A construction process (and all the more a creation process) that builds up along the way can be explored, and its viability ascertained, by working out the evolution of the economy through the sequence of periods through which the intertemporal complementarities and the interactions that characterize the functioning of the economy trace out the effects of the initial structural

---

[32] Technological trajectories, although defined as processes, do not have the full nature of processes over time as stressed by Kaldor, in that given resources and a given environment are regarded as the exogenously determined factors of the development of the technology considered.

[33] The suggestion that rational expectations would not allow cumulative processes of this kind is not relevant here, as out-of-equilibrium contexts, in particular in an *ex ante* perspective, are characterized essentially by the fact that the agents are involved in a learning process which is not consistent with rational expectations (see Hahn 1982).

modification. The use of simulations makes this possible, and this method will be amply used in Part II of this book. As a matter of fact when we are concerned with evolutionary processes whose main point of interest is the course of events that are likely to be encountered on the way and how these link up over successive periods, step-by-step numerical calculations appear as a more fruitful analytical tool than formal solution techniques. Of course the results thus obtained are subtle insights rather than general theorems. Nevertheless providing results for a large number of different disturbances makes these results general enough to provide a better understanding of the processes in question (see Baumol 1991).

Finally—but this will be the specific object of next chapter—it must be stressed that out-of-equilibrium processes have an essential monetary aspect, and hence that money plays a crucial role in determining the viability of the processes themselves.

2
Money

2.1. WHEN, WHY, AND HOW MONEY MATTERS

When, in an *ex post* perspective, production is synchronized so that inputs do not come before output in an essential way (see Section 1.2 above) the ongoing production processes can be financed out of the proceeds continuously made available by current productive activity—whether these proceeds are reckoned in real terms or as the monetary counterpart of the physical output brought about by the activity itself. This is typically so in a stationary economy but is also the case in steadily growing economies, where 'money' (meaning by this any kind of financial means used to circulate physical resources and commodities) is by assumption made to grow at the same rate as output so as to allow steady growth to take place. In both cases a given (steadily increasing) supply of goods faces the given (increasing) demand generated by corresponding (correspondingly increasing) amounts of money[1]

Money, here, comes out of the process of production;[2] its circulation is precisely suited to real activity and neither constrains nor fosters it in any way.[3] In this equilibrium context the level of activity is solely determined by the real factors in the system; the monetary aspects of the analysis recede into the background. It follows, in particular, that

with the assumption . . . that outputs are produced at the same time as inputs are made, the bad habit of ignoring the problem of how to finance production is justified . . . The problem of financing production, together with the one of

---

[1] As a matter of fact, in steady growth the essential features of a stationary economy are maintained and, in particular, no structural modification such as to dissociate inputs from output and costs from proceeds is contemplated.

[2] Or of a process of production carried out in the past, if the purchasing power that it represents is not actually used up as it comes about but is stored for use in the future.

[3] In other words, money is only required because of the existing transaction technology: it does not change the nature of the equilibrium which would be obtained in a barter economy. As already stressed by Hume (1752, p. 292), in this case money 'is nothing but the representation of labour and commodities, and serves only as a method of rating or estimating them.'

constructing production possibility sets, makes no appearance . . . Production is completely dichotomized from finance (Morishima 1992, p. 4).

This is no longer so, in the sense that money is no longer a mere double but becomes a protagonist (we shall see in which way in what follows), when we are dealing with money that comes out of credit, not out of production. The essence of the concept of credit, according to Schumpeter, is in fact 'creating a new demand for, without simultaneously creating a new supply of goods' (1934, p. 106). Credit means the creation of a new purchasing power, not a simple allocation of a given purchasing power through the redistribution of existing financial resources. Money created by credit is added to the existing money brought about by productive activity, but no additional final output corresponds to the additional demand generated by the former.[4] A tendency to take the economy out of equilibrium is thus inherent in the concept of credit.

The case of credit money is not the only case in which money is called to play a role of its own in the economic process, though. Dissociation of inputs from output and of costs from proceeds (which, as we have just seen, is at the heart of the concept of credit but is not confined to this case), not the very fact of dealing with credit money, is in fact what matters. So, even when we are dealing only with money coming out of production, structural disturbances may be taken into account which imply a distortion of productive capacity that dissociates inputs from output: which brings back to the fore the time dimension of production and the implications of considering it.

When this is so—that is, whenever a qualitative change that takes the economy 'out of equilibrium' is contemplated (see Section 1.5 above)—money comes to play an essential role. As a matter of fact, except for the few cases in which very specific assumptions allow an out-of-equilibrium context to be still amenable to equilibrium analysis (see again Section 1.5 above), a proper out-of-equilibrium analysis has an essential monetary aspect. The reason why money is called to play a crucial role is that when we are out of equilibrium production is no longer synchronized: its time structure comes back to the surface, and we cannot confine our attention to the utilization moment of the

---

[4] The steady increase in the amount of money in a steadily growing economy—although exogenously determined in the model—is clearly not a creation in this sense, as it is always matched by a corresponding increase in the amount of commodities.

production process but must take explicitly into account the phase of construction of productive capacity and its relation with the phase of utilization. A bridge through time must then be constructed to link these phases—no longer harmonized over time when we are out of equilibrium—and money does this.

Thus we might say that when production is fully synchronized money is 'neutral'. This looks quite similar to Hayek's definition of neutrality (1931, 1933). However, it does not imply that money is the only source of distortions in productive capacity, nor that this is the only role it performs. As a matter of fact structural shocks may be the result of the behaviour of firms (innovative behaviour is the most typical example) as well as of the behaviour of banks or monetary authorities (as is the case with Hayek). The breaking of the balance between costs and available financial resources may come from exogenous changes in the money supply to which the demand for liquidity adjusts or from changes in expectations which lead entrepreneurs to modify investment decisions. In any case what matters— and what Hayek had already understood—is that the structure of productive capacity becomes distorted, which is when money acquires an essential role. In this perspective the need for an active monetary policy—that is, not a mechanistic policy or a policy predefined in terms of a unique objective, such as for instance perfect price stability, but a policy aimed at rendering the economy viable by maintaining its evolution within a stability corridor (see Section 8.4 below)—comes to be stressed.

We have seen in Chapter 1 that whenever—as is the case when we consider structural changes—we shift the focus from utilization to construction and finally, in the extreme case of innovation, to creation anew, we are actually moving gradually from a problem of allocation of given generic resources to a problem of creation of new specific resources. This is the key that, following the main lines of development of monetary theory, will lead us to sketch out clearly the complementarity relation between financial and productive assets— and hence between monetary decisions and real choices—which highlights the essential monetary aspect of a process of qualitative change. In this context, as we shall see, financial resources appear both as flows and as stocks, and both flows and stocks have a role to play in the articulation of the above-mentioned complementarity relation. It will thus also be possible to put into a more adequate perspective one of the most heated and long-lived controversies of monetary theory:

the flow versus stock issue.[5] The appropriate background for a better understanding of the problems involved in the issue, however, will not be the traditional perspective of the determination of the rate of interest, but the sketching out of the sequence through which qualitative change takes place.

2.2. THE STANDARD THEORY OF MONEY AND ITS MODERN REVISITATIONS

As in the case of the standard theory of production, the allocation of resources is behind the standard theory of money. This comes down to a theory of portfolio choice that involves essentially a substitution among financial assets and which is dealt with, in the light of a criterion of a spreading of risks, within the same general equilibrium approach used to analyse all market phenomena. Money is treated as one of the financial assets which, together with the physical capital assets, appear on the capital account of the economy (or the firm).[6] For each asset there is a demand and supply and a price. Thus prices (the interest rates), and in particular the money rate of interest (the opportunity cost of holding money instead of other short-term assets), are the crucial element of the analysis. 'The key behavioural assumption of this procedure is that spending decisions and portfolio decisions are independent—specifically that decisions about the accumulation of wealth are separable from decisions about its allocation' (Tobin 1969, p. 15).

This analytical framework can be traced back to the attempt to formulate a theory of money in terms of a theory of value in Hicks's 'Suggestion for Simplifying the Theory of Money' (1935*a*), and it is at the heart of Keynes's analysis in the *General Theory* (although in a very simplified version). It is also common to modern neoclassical theories (e.g. Patinkin 1956) and to Neo-Keynesians like Tobin (1969).

All monetary theories rely on financial intermediation, explicitly or

---

[5] The debate on loanable funds versus liquidity preference is but one—although the most famous one—of the aspects of this flow versus stock controversy; see Messori (1995).

[6] Though it is an asset with specific features, and one which can even disappear when various financial assets and a big enough decrease in the risk-aversion of the agents are contemplated (see Hicks 1967, pp. 29–30).

implicitly. As just mentioned, Keynesian as well as neoclassical theories focus on substitution among different financial assets, with *speculation* as the crucial motive behind money according to Keynes—financial intermediaries are there to satisfy the agents' preferences as to the portfolio they wish to hold. What matters, then, are the financial products. Financial intermediaries hide behind financial products: banks and non-banks are the same in this respect. Tobin's analysis, the most typical expression of the standard theory, does not make a distinction between financial intermediaries. The prices of the assets—the mediators of the choice—are at the centre of the stage. In this analysis there is no room for a finance constraint: supply and demand of financial assets, including money, are always kept in balance.

The early work on financial intermediation, that rests upon the standard analysis of the role of money, fits financial intermediaries into a Walrasian framework, that is, into a framework in which all the agents appear as anonymous participants in the different markets. As just mentioned, the focus, if there are no market failures, is on financial products (or assets) rather than on financial agents (banks and other financial intermediaries).

The modern revisitations of the standard theory shift the focus from financial products to financial intermediaries, although maintaining in the analysis the character of a choice. This comes from taking into account information problems (asymmetric or incomplete information explained by its cost) and their implications for the problem of the spreading of risks (which, as we have seen, was the main criterion leading choice). Information problems imply market failures; the way in which organizations are a substitute for the market is then crucial to obtain a better allocation of resources in the presence of market failures (see Section 4.2 below).

What is the role of financial intermediaries other than the market in this context? And, strictly related to this, as we shall see in what follows, why is outside finance necessary? Within the perspective sketched out the role of intermediaries is first of all to reduce moral hazard and adverse selection, which are a consequence of asymmetric information and prevent financial relations from being optimal. Their role is also to take care of the effects of incomplete information.

One way of dealing with the first problem is by controlling the relations between asymmetric partners. Diamond (1984) stresses the role of banks which monitor the firms that they finance. This makes possible long-term financing, and commitments in long-term relationships prevent firms that are involved in projects characterized by substantial sunk costs from going bankrupt along the way.

Incomplete information, on the other hand, puts banks and firms on the same level in terms of their knowledge of future states of nature. In this case intermediation comes down to retaining the residual control rights if and when a bad state of nature arises. Whether it is better that these rights be assigned to the bank originally involved in the contract or to a third partner is a debated issue (Aghion and Bolton 1988).

The conclusion is that different financial systems corresponding to different information structures may emerge and be the expression of an equilibrium state.[7] This points again to a problem of substitution between different systems—from pure market to a whole spectrum of types of organization—in view of efficiency in the allocation of resources.

However, there are important differences with respect to the standard theory in its modern revisitations: namely (1) that prices are no longer crucial but *quantities* matter,[8] and (2) that, while dealing with the relation between banks and firms, *financing* problems are evoked and the *transaction* role of money comes to the fore (although still with reference to a choice to be rendered optimal through a spreading of risks obtained by minimizing agency costs).

However, credit still appears as financial resources exchanged on the market as a commodity, although information problems explicitly affect the exchange. In this perspective money actually disappears—in the same way as it disappears in the standard portfolio model—in the sense that it does not differ from whatever financial asset is used to register the claims of economic agents over time.

Neither the standard theory nor its modern revisitations can thus give a satisfactory explanation of the role of money. This failure, we

---

[7] Thus we do not have a general theory but an 'exemplifying' theory in the sense stressed by Fischer (1989), that is, a theory which 'can be very illuminating indeed, suggestively revealing the possibility of certain phenomena' but lacks generality, and hence 'does not tell us what *must* happen. Rather it tells us what *can* happen'(ibid. pp. 117–18).

[8] In credit rationing models (Stiglitz and Weiss 1981, 1992; Milde and Riley 1988) identical applicants receive or do not receive a loan for reasons other than the interest rate that they are ready to pay. Thus monetary policy exerts its influence, when it does, not so much through the willingness of individuals to hold cash balances (and hence through the interest rate mechanism) but through the availability of credit.

maintain, depends on the fact that, in equilibrium, money is not really essential. It becomes essential out of equilibrium, but in order to understand this we first have to sketch out a theory of money that stresses its specific role in an out-of-equilibrium context.

2.3. SUBSTITUTION AND COMPLEMENTARITY

The analysis of the properties of real and financial assets—those representing property rights in real goods, and therefore already embodied in specific forms, and the other financial claims not similarly tied down as real assets—and of the relations between them, is at the heart of the monetary theory that Hicks developed over more than fifty years beginning with his celebrated 'Simplifying' paper of 1935.

This analysis has stressed primarily substitution among financial assets, a substitution dictated by *precautionary* rather than *speculative* motives and concerning the whole spectrum of financial assets rather than only money versus bonds, as with Keynes. A sequential framework, at first only hinted at and later more and more explicitly sketched out, is in the background, and liquidity, looked at as a means of intertemporal substitution, plays a central role in it. As liquidity is more and more associated with a sequential framework, and from a property of a single choice it becomes 'a matter of a sequence of choices, a related sequence' (Hicks 1974, p. 38), speculation recedes into the background and precaution comes to the fore.

However, Hicks's analysis goes beyond that. From simple substitution (whether punctual or intertemporal) not only among financial assets but also between these and real assets,[9] it goes on to consider complementarity relations. For this purpose financial and real assets are further classified as running, reserve, or investment assets: required for the current running of a business, held for emergencies that may arise in the future, or considered for the profit that they are expected to earn, respectively. Now, what characterizes first of all running assets is exactly that they are complementary with each other. Thus

any money that is held as a transaction balance, at the moment when the balance-sheet of the business is taken, will reckon as a running asset. If

---

[9] A clear example of intertemporal substitution between real and financial assets is liquidity held because it 'gives time to think', that is, to postpone investment which 'cannot be wisely chosen if it is too much hurried' (Hicks 1974, p. 57).

production has a cycle (say a seasonal cycle) there will be a clear ebb and flow between work in progress, stocks of finished products, and this money balance; they must clearly be reckoned together as running assets of the business. Much the same will hold for the weekly cycle of the wage-earner. The amount of money that is held (on the average) in this way will be a consequence of the general pattern of production (or consumption) on which the unit is engaged; it is the money requirement for this current pattern. If sufficient money (from whatever source) is not available to satisfy this requirement, it will be necessary that the activity of the unit should in some way be contracted; but activity cannot in general be expanded just by making more money available as a running asset. Surplus money, like surplus stocks of materials, automatically becomes a reserve asset (Hicks 1967, p. 40).

Money[10] is thus strictly complementary to real running assets (not only goods in the pipeline and work in progress but also plant and machinery used to capacity) in the sense that there cannot be production of commodities unless there exist the required money balances. The *transaction* role of money is thus stressed by this complementarity relation between financial and real assets, in the same way as the precautionary motive was at the heart of the substitution relation between them.[11] But we must now take a step forward. The transaction role of money must be understood with reference to a complementarity relation which is not limited to circulating capital, as in the example just given by Hicks, but also concerns the building process through which productive capacity is actually brought about: with reference, that is, to production in a wider sense. We shall undertake this extension of the analysis in the following sections.

All this points to the importance of holding financial (and/or real) reserve assets[12] in order to dispose of the required balances (and/or physical stocks) at the right moment—so as not to be forced to make drastic adjustments in productive activity, or to be able to reconsider choices over time in view of the sequential character of investment decisions. This is not so in equilibrium, though. In equilibrium liquidity brought about by current productive activity is just that required for keeping the activity itself going on at the current pace, and the above-mentioned complementarity relation is satisfied by definition.

---

[10] And trade credit, 'the only other financial asset which can appear as a running asset' (Hicks 1967, p. 40).

[11] This has little to do with Keynes's transaction demand for money, which is a demand of money for exchanges at a given moment of time, and hence depends on money income, not for production which takes place over time.

[12] Or of having access to credit lines, which amounts to the same thing.

It is out of equilibrium, when production is no longer synchronized and the time articulation of the production process dissociates inputs from output and costs from proceeds, that a complementarity problem arises. A financial constraint then emerges which, in a truly sequential context, appears as the relevant link over time between financial and productive assets, and hence between financial decisions and real choices. This constraint on the other hand—as we shall see in what follows—is made endogenous to the sequential process whose development depends exactly on how the complementarity relation in question is actually articulated over time.

2.4. INTEGRATING REAL AND MONETARY DISEQUILIBRIA IN A SEQUENTIAL CONTEXT

What really matters then, out of equilibrium, is the time profile of the flow of financial resources made available to sustain productive activity.

Robertson (1926, 1933) is the author who first dealt explicitly with this problem, in the perspective that we must focus on 'what happens on the markets during an *interval* of time' and not on 'the position reached as the result of previous market transactions at a *moment* of time' (1940, p. 8). The idea that *quantity* rather than *price* is relevant as regards the role of money in a sequential context, and that in this context money itself appears as a constraint, is central to his 'step-by-step' analysis. This focuses on the money flow of payments which establishes a mechanical link between successive periods where the elementary period is defined as the length of time between two successive payments of money income, 'the period during which the stock of money changes hands only once in exchange for output or for the constituents of real income.' (1933, p. 65). A financial constraint then becomes effective: the income which we dispose of in each period is in fact limited by payments made in the previous period. The link is represented by the money possessed at the outset of each period, transferred from the preceding one, which sets an inter-period constraint on final demand. Investment and production are not constrained in the same way, though, and only circulating capital is actually considered.

On the other hand, there is no intra-period sequence in Robertson's analysis. There is no sequence of exchanges since, by assumption, money can only change hands once in each given period, and no sequence of production, as the above assumption also implies that the process through which production takes place cannot be taken into account explicitly.[13]

Reference to an essentially sequential context, focus on the transaction role of money, and confinement to circulating capital also characterize Hicks's monetary analysis, as we have seen. There is something more, and different, in Robertson's analysis, though. The basic assumption of his model, in fact, is that we cannot 'identify the income received in any small slice of time with the income whose expenditure (plus or minus certain other items) generates the income received in this small slice of time', as this would avert our eyes from the essence of the matter, 'namely the power possessed by the public and by the monetary authority to alter the rates of income flow—the former by putting money into and out of store, the latter by putting it into and out of existence.' (1933, p. 80).

The explicit consideration of this 'taking from' or 'adding to' the money flow as it results from the sequence of periods—together with the explicit analysis of the relation between money 'to produce and to circulate goods', which highlights its transaction role, and money 'to hold' (defined as 'hoarding') behind which we perceive a precautionary motive—is a distinctive aspect of Robertson's model. But there is a further point that must be stressed in this context. Idle money balances are not only the result of hoarding, a voluntary choice that reflects a precautionary motive as they are for Hicks; they can also be the involuntary outcome of something else. Robertson mentions in particular automatic 'lacking', a sort of crowding out due to 'an increase in the stream of money directed on to the market' (Robertson 1926, p. 49). Whatever its cause, however,[14] this is a crucial element that is added to the analysis.

---

[13] Purchase by households of the output (of the last period) with the money income (transferred from the last period) and payment back of the money proceeds thus obtained from the corresponding sales by producers to households as wages (which, in turn, will be transferred so as to make up next period's money income) are in fact simultaneous and instantaneous in Robertson's model. The inter period constraint, thus, is on final demand (which depends on the previous period payments) and not on production, as the wages paid in each given period are financed from the proceeds obtained in the same period.

[14] We shall see that there can be other reasons besides the one explicitly mentioned by Robertson for involuntary idle balances to be held. In any case, as we shall also see, this will always be the outcome of the development of the sequence in an out-of-equilibrium context.

As a matter of fact, it makes it possible to illuminate the problem of harmonization over time implied by the existence of a complementarity relation between financial and productive assets in a sequential context: a relation explicitly taken out of balance by a phenomenon like lacking. In particular, by focusing on the interaction between credit creation, capital formation, and lacking,[15] Robertson comes to stress that, whenever a complementarity problem arises—as is necessarily the case when a growth of productive capacity is to take place—this implies the existence of appropriate and hence in a certain way desirable fluctuations of prices and output which are the normal expression of changes both on the supply and on the demand side (technical changes that affect unit costs, changes in preference systems, and so on). However, the actual fluctuations usually tend to exceed what is appropriate, so that the aim of monetary policy is to bring the fluctuations back within boundaries that make it possible the creation of the new capital required to bring about the intended change.

This analytical framework is clearly the beginning of a theory of how to integrate real and monetary disequilibria; in this sense it represents an essential step towards the construction of a fully fledged out-of-equilibrium theory.

2.5. FINANCIAL CONSTRAINTS AND PRODUCTION

The two essential analytical moments of the integration of money into an out-of-equilibrium theory are the consideration of money itself as a constraint to productive activity and the consideration of production as a process articulated sequentially over time. Robertson, we have just seen, is quite clear in pointing to money as a financial constraint in a period-by-period context; and he is also aware of the need to consider explicitly the time element of production. His analysis, however, only develops one of these two strands. Confinement to circulating capital, in fact, prevents him from actually taking into

---

[15] Namely, by focusing on the analysis of the way in which different kinds of liquidity affect the relation of the length of the period of circulation of money to that of the period of production, defined as the period during which circulating capital, to which Robertson's analysis is confined, is being increased but during which output is still not affected.

account the intertemporal complementarity of production and hence from developing a thorough sequential analysis.

This is also the case with the analysis developed along Robertsonian lines by Kohn (1981), who still overlooks production as a link between successive periods and relies on expectations to build an inter-period sequence. As a matter of fact Kohn first examines the conditions for a single-period equilibrium and then goes on to consider the impact effect of an exogenous change. But, rather than working through the period-by-period adjustment of the model as expectations adjust, he solves directly for the new equilibrium position (a stationary or a steady state) whose characteristics depend on the kind of expectations postulated. We are thus back to the comparative analysis of states of the economy typical of the equilibrium approach. The development of the sequence through which change takes place—which is in the nature of an out-of-equilibrium process—remains in the dark.

A Neo-Austrian model like that considered in Chapter 1—where production interpreted as a fully vertically integrated process articulated over a succession of periods that make up a phase of construction and, following it, a phase of utilization of productive capacity—provides the required analytical backbone to the sequence through which an out-of-equilibrium process (as all qualitative changes are) takes place, and in which money looked at as a financial constraint plays an essential role. This is because consideration of the time dimension of production processes makes it possible to add to the analysis (1) the inter-period link traced out by the intertemporal complementarity of production, and (2) an intra-period sequence.

For this purpose consider an economy with two classes of economic agents: firms and households. All exchanges between them are intermediated by a financial asset, which we call 'money'; the resources required to carry out production, and to sustain consumption, are therefore financial resources, not physical output. These resources, for both producers and consumers, come from their participation in current productive activity. External financial resources are required (and a corresponding source must be considered) when productive activity is expanding, and at the rate at which the expansion takes place. The internally generated flow of financial resources which, together with the additions made available by the external sources (if any), determine at each step the existing financial constraint, depends on how the economy evolves sequentially, which, in turn,

Money

essentially reflects the dynamics of productive capacity and of its effective utilization governed by the intertemporal complementarity of production processes.

In particular the resources in the hands of firms in each given period t can be written

$$M(t) = m(t-1) + h_d^f(t-1) + h_{nd}^f(t-1)$$

where $m(t-1)$ are the proceeds of the sales of final output in the previous period, which clearly depend on the existing productive capacity put to use, and h^f are the idle money balances carried over by producers, which can be desired (d) and are then the result of some kind of choice made in the past, or non-desired (nd), a sort of induced lacking that results from the way in which the sequence has actually developed. To these resources must be added the external resources $f(t)$ which usually depend on the choices of the monetary authority and/or the banks. These, in the modelization we are proposing, are either considered as exogenously determined and actually dealt with as a control variable, or determined endogenously in view of the specific economic policy followed (see Section 6.3 below).

An intra-period sequence[16] can now be added to the inter-period sequence sketched out by the intertemporal complementarity of the production process.

At the beginning of each period producers, on the basis of the existing constraints,[17] decide the amount of resources to devote to their own consumption $c(t)$, and h_d^f, that is, what they want to keep as idle balances; what remains is devoted to finance the workers employed in the production processes to be carried out, in other words it makes up the wage fund $\omega(t)$[18]

$$M(t) + f(t) = \omega(t) + c(t) + h_d^f(t).$$

Within the period current production takes place, and at the end of it, the output obtained is sold. The constraint on final demand, under the

---

[16] Let us define an elementary period as the span of time required to obtain a round of final output from the existing productive capacity, and within which decisions concerning the determination of all relevant economic variables cannot be changed.

[17] In a Neo-Austrian context a human resource constraint must also be taken into account, besides the financial constraint. This will be dealt with in particular in Chapter 3.

[18] Current production, that is, the degree of utilization of the inherited productive capacity, may be made to depend on the expected final demand within the period; what remains of the wage fund will be used to finance investment, that is, the construction of new processes.

simplifying hypothesis that wages are entirely spent on consumption goods, can then be written

$$y(t) + h_d^h(t) = \omega(t) + c(t) + h_d^h(t-1) + h_{nd}^h(t-1)$$

where $y(t)$ is the money value of current demand for final output, and h^h are the households' idle balances, desired (d) or non-desired (nd).

In equilibrium, when the economy has settled down to a smooth and regular pattern and production is synchronized so that not only construction and utilization but also investment and consumption and supply and demand of final output are harmonized over time (see Section 1.4 above), there is no need for idle balances to be held (or for physical stocks to pile up). Whether the economy is in a stationary state or steadily growing, no disturbance to its productive structure (but only its gradual expansion) is envisaged, and the complementarity relation between liquidity and productive activity is fully assured.

It is qualitative change, whether actually undertaken or simply envisaged, that implies the appearance of idle balances. Qualitative change, as defined in Section 1.5 above, is characterized by a structural modification which, except in very specific cases, implies a distortion of productive capacity.[19] Now, the piling up of idle money balances, be it the result of an intended 'hoarding' or of an induced 'lacking', is the physical expression of the dissociation of investment from *ex ante* saving, and of demand from supply, that always characterizes a distortion of productive capacity.[20] Thus the appearance of idle balances, whether voluntarily or involuntarily accumulated, reflects the intention to pursue a qualitative change that implies a structural modification which cannot be instantaneously realized.

In particular, voluntary idle balances reflect the intention of waiting for the moment when this change will actually be undertaken, but none the less result in a distortion of productive capacity which 'is itself' in the nature of a structural modification. The willingness to undergo a qualitative change may be seen on the other hand as the result of a change in long-term expectations, that is, of a change in the degree of confidence in the existing state of affairs as represented by a given structuring of the interacting patterns of production and con-

---

[19] This, we have already stressed in Chapter 1, is also true when we remain in an *ex post* perspective, as in the case of a speeding up of the growth rate; but, of course, is all the more true when, in an *ex ante* perspective, we pass from a problem of allocation of resources to one of creation of resources, as with a thorough innovation process.

[20] Dishoarding, that is, drawing on financial reserves accumulated in the past, has a similar, although sometimes opposite, dissociating effect.

sumption. This can be rendered by a change in the value of the parameters (call them ϱ and σ) which represent the fractions of the financial resources available to producers and households, respectively, voluntarily held as idle balances,[21] so that the resources actually used up for production and consumption will be

$$\omega(t) = [1 - \varrho\,(t)]\,[M(t) + f(t) - c(t)]$$
$$y(t) = [1 - \sigma(t)]\,[\omega(t) + c(t) + h^h\,(t-1)].$$

Non-desired balances, on the other hand, reflect a lacking induced by disequilibria brought about by the sequential evolution of the economy. Thus, for example, producers are forced to pile up idle balances when the resources they intend to devote to productive activity cannot actually be invested because of a human resource constraint (full employment), that is,

$$h_{nd}^f(t) = \omega\,(t) - \hat{\omega}\,(t)$$

when $\omega(t) > \hat{\omega}(t)$ and where $\hat{\omega}$ is the wage fund constrained by the available human resource. On the other hand consumers are forced to accrue liquidity when current supply of final output $s(t)$, at the going price $p(t)$ which is fixed within the period, cannot satisfy the current demand for it $d(t)$

$$h_{nd}^h(t) = p(t)[d(t) - s(t)] > 0.^{22}$$

In both cases, idle balances are a sign of disequilibrium.

The advances with respect to Robertson's analysis as regards the role of money in a sequential context made possible by the explicit consideration of a time articulated production process are now evident. Consideration of an inter-period financial constraint not only on final demand but also on investment brings to light the essential complementarity relation in time between liquidity, production, and investment due to the dissociation of inputs from output. The sketching out of an intra-period sequence that the consideration of the time dimension of production also implies, on the other hand, makes possible the appearance of flow disequilibria which result in the piling up of (real or

---

[21] These parameters will thus be equal to zero in equilibrium, when there is full confidence in the existing state of affairs. They (or one of them) will instead take up a positive value when the perception of the possible exploitation or structuring of new productive options and/or saturation of demand for the existing commodities will shake this confidence—the lower the values the greater the fall in confidence.

[22] The piling up of physical stocks $o(t)$ obtains instead when there is an excess supply of final output, that is

$$o(t) = s(t) - d(t) > 0$$

monetary) stocks that create complementarity problems.[23] In conclusion, when a qualitative change is attempted a change that implies a structural mutation and hence cannot be instantaneously realized, idle balances make the distortion of productive capacity no longer suited to the old productive structure and not yet adjusted to the new one come to the surface. In this case the role of money is 'to make visible a real phenomenon': the distortion of productive capacity.[24] But there is more to it.

2.6. FINANCIAL DECISIONS AND REAL CHOICES

A different balance between production processes in the phase of construction and processes in the phase of utilization end up being the result of the intended structural change, but the economy must actually go through the phase of construction of a different productive capacity before this happens. In particular cases, which require specific assumptions, the existing productive structure is gradually transmuted into a new one as resources are gradually freed and invested in the building of the latter, and the equilibrium between supply and demand is maintained in each moment of the process through which the change is brought about.[25] Money is not essential in a similar process; it can be there, but just as a 'veil'.

More generally, however, the immediate result of the intended change is a true disruption of economic activity, that is, the scrapping of some production processes not planned beforehand, the abrupt disappearance of a part of the existing productive capacity, and hence a sudden mismatch between supply and demand.[26] These imbalances, given the intertemporal complementarity both of the production process and of the decision process, are handed over from one period to

---

[23] E.g. through a reduction of the wage fund which strengthens the financial constraint on production.

[24] The money we are referring to here is money coming out of production. As a matter of fact we do not strictly need its presence for the distortion to arise. Barter economies can also experience structural disturbances, if we make the assumption that excess supplies can be stored and can pile up in surplus stocks; stocks of physical goods as well as stocks of money may be the expression of distortions of productive capacity.

[25] The often mentioned analysis of the Traverse is one such case.

[26] As already mentioned in Section 1.4 above, the fact that construction and utilization become out of balance also implies that investment and consumption, and supply and demand, are no longer harmonized over time.

the next. Thus the initial distortion stimulates an out-of-equilibrium process which, via expectations, may become cumulative, so that its very viability may be hampered. The problem, then, is to bring to light the conditions for viability, that is, what is required to re-establish the consistency over time of the relevant interacting magnitudes of the economy.

While, as we have just seen, the piling up of money stocks is not strictly necessary for a disruption of economic activity, money (now the fact that it is being used up instead of being kept as idle balances) is essential for harmonizing construction and utilization (and hence investment and consumption, and supply and demand) over time. It is essential because it represents the bridge that links inputs and output and costs and proceeds, dissociated by the distortion of productive capacity and remaining out of balance throughout the out-of-equilibrium process which must be undergone for the intended change to be realized. We shall see[27] that it is indeed the availability of financial resources at the right moment during this process—additional money which must be looked at as a true control variable—that determines the viability of the process itself; and this emphasizes the fact that, out of equilibrium, 'real choices cannot be separated from financial decisions.'

In the sequential monetary economy sketched out—in which the time articulation of decisions and of effective transactions matters— the central role of the financial constraint is the expression of a theory of money that focuses on transaction and precautionary motives and on their interaction.

In order to better understand this aspect we can refer again, reinterpreting it, to Hicks's distinction between, on the one hand, real and financial assets, and, on the other, running, reserve, and investment assets. This classification makes it possible to clarify the relations between different assets. Running assets, in the first place, appear as a bundle of complements, and money—cash in hand or at the bank—is one, and an important one, of these complements. So what we have stressed in the above modelization is precisely the fact that, given the productive capacity inherited from the past at time t—the vector of processes

$$\mathbf{x}(t) = [\mathbf{x}^c(t); \mathbf{x}^u(t)]$$

[27] In the analyses developed in Part II of this book.

the economy needs complementary financial assets to carry on current production and real investments. Now, at the heart of economic change there are necessarily complementarity failures. As a matter of fact, out of equilibrium there is no reason to expect a constancy in the ratio of money to real running assets (i.e. to the number of production processes). Moreover, uncertainty calls for reserve assets: thus idle balances contribute to determining the financial constraint. Idle balances reflect a precautionary motive: when information about the future is incomplete firms (and households as well) look for more liquid positions. Of course if firms know that they can obtain funds when they need them, no liquid assets will be held as reserves.[28]

Whatever the source of liquidity firms have access to, 'liquidity is not a property of a single choice, it is a matter of a sequence of choices, a related sequence' (Hicks 1974, p. 38). In this perspective, too, reserve assets belong to a bundle of complements. Firms need reserve assets to realize their choices and carry out production processes—that is, for financing current production and investment. In some sense reserve assets and real assets also appear as complements: they are complements over time. And this complementarity relation is essential for rendering viable a process of change out of equilibrium.

There is no reference to the rate of interest in this analytical framework. Investment does not depend on the interest rate; rather, it depends on available financial resources (and on long-term expectations which determine the amount of idle balances, or the amount of unused overdraft).[29] This is consistent with the fact that in a dynamic context the profitability of each investment (at each given moment) depends on the undertaking of other investments in time. Each investment belongs to a bundle of complementary investments over time, and it would not be rational for a firm to drop it only because the interest rate increases at a given moment of time (Hicks 1989, p. 119).

The interest rate is crucial within a perspective of substitution between financial and productive assets, when it determines the convenience of holding one or the other. But within a perspective of complementarity, where liquidity appears as a bridge linking inputs

---

[28] It will in fact always be possible to take advantage of agreed overdrafts. In the modelization proposed this can be rendered by making the external financial resources dependent on the demand for money from firms.

[29] External financial resources are considered net of the interest charge and after reimbursement.

and output over time, financial constraints, not the interest rate, represent the true dynamic link between financial decisions and real choices, in that they establish interactions over time between them.[30] Thus, the age structure of productive capacity affects the time profile of the wage fund and hence the complementarity relation between liquidity, production, and investment; this in turn, determines the changes in the age structure, with the consequence that the constraints themselves are continuously changing, as the result of the sequential evolvution of the economy.

This process unveils the true nature of the complementarity relation between financial and real assets. The essence of it is the relation between the liquidity brought about by productive activity, and hence generated within the economy, and the additional liquidity required step by step (net credit furnished by the bank system or the running down of existing idle balances). The sequential evolution of the economy, and the viability of the out-of-equilibrium process of change undertaken, depends on the actual articulation of this relation.

2.7. THE INTEREST RATE AND THE TIME STRUCTURE OF ECONOMIC ACTIVITY

What we have just said might give the wrong impression that the essence of monetary analysis comes down to whether to put the accent on the interest rate or on the amount of available financial resources. This is not so: what really matters is to take properly into account the intertemporal dimension of economic activity. Leijonhufvud's interpretation of Keynes, whether we accept it or not, helps us to grasp the point.

According to Leijonhufvud the true object of monetary theory is to explain 'what goes wrong with relative values in macroeconomic fluctuations.' (1968, p. 343). This leads to a focus on an aggregative structure of the model of the economy which distinguishes between investment goods on one side and consumer goods on the other, that is, 'between goods with a relatively high and a relatively low interest-

---

[30] In this sense what Robertson wrote on the rate of interest more than fifty years ago, still maintains all its topicality: 'If I have a personal heresy in these matters, it is that in recent years, alike in academic, financial and political circles, we have heard rather too much about that entity in connection with the processes of trade recovery and recession' (1940, p. 148).

elasticity of present value.' (ibid. p. 41). Within this perspective the analysis of economic fluctuations becomes an analysis of the distortions between investment and consumption. Whenever the marginal efficiency of capital decreases, and the rate of interest for whatever reason does not follow suit, a 'false' relative price between investment goods and consumer goods prevails, and as a consequence recovery is no longer possible. This is Leijonhufvud's interpretation of Keynes's doctrine, an interpretation which clearly shows a Wicksellian heritage with a reference to the Austrian tradition. So is not by chance that this interpretation relies on the same analytical ingredients as Hayek's theory of fluctuations,[31] as stressed by Leijonhufvud himself:

> In Hayek's theory the boom was caused by a market rate held below the natural rate, and consequently involved over-investment. The crisis would arrive when it is no longer possible to maintain the low ratio (in value terms) of consumer goods to investment goods output. When consumption demand 'breaks through' asset demand prices fall as market rate *rises* to the level of natural rate, whereas Keynes' crisis arrives when market rate starts to lay behind the *decline* of natural rate (ibid. p. 345).

In both cases the essential aspects are the arising distortion between investment goods and consumer goods, on one side, and the rigidity of the money interest rate, due to the behaviour of banks and speculators, on the other. Lack of adjustment of the interest rate, both for Hayek and for Keynes on Leijonhufvud's interpretation, implies a distortion of productive activity which is exactly the expression of the fact that the economy is out of equilibrium.

This kind of approach 'combines the difficulties of capital theory and of disequilibrium analysis'(ibid. p. 43), a theory and an analysis which are intrinsically linked when qualitative change is involved, as often stressed in the preceding pages. However, it is important not to reduce the distinction between investment goods and consumer goods to a simple horizontal classification of industrial sectors, which would imply denying *de facto* the time dimension of productive activity (see Hicks 1973, p. 5). The central problem, when the focus is rightly put on this time dimension, is co-ordination of long-term production plans (investment plans) and consumption plans.

It is the failure of an incomplete market mechanism to reconcile the implicit

---

[31] The reference is Hayek's *Prices and Production* (1931).

values of forward demands and supplies—particularly in the fairly distant future—that is the source of the trouble. Unemployment of labour and other resources is a derivative phenomenon, albeit the depressed level of current income is the most striking manifestation of the wealth effects of a disequilibrium vector of perceived intertemporal values (Leijonhufvud 1968, p. 276).

The time dimension of productive activity is thus at the centre of the stage, together with the dissociation of costs and proceeds that it implies.

This time dimension is dealt with by referring to wealth effects which bring about changes in the interest rate; and the problems then depend on not being able to obtain the 'right' wealth effects. The point, however, is not whether the explanation based on wealth effects is convincing or not. What really matters, and what the aggregative structure of the model proposed by Leijonhufvud makes it possible to pin down, is the articulation over time of investment and consumption. Other aggregative structures serve the same purpose; in particular, of course, that of the Neo-Austrian model which we have chosen to refer to, and which focuses on the distinction between the phase of construction and the phase of utilization of production processes. In this latter case the key element of the monetary analysis is the amount of money (of financial resources) available rather than the interest rate. Nevertheless, the mechanism at work is not much different from the one evoked by Leijonhufvud. Where a fall in the rate of interest brings about an increase in investment, a greater amount of available financial resources allows a greater rate of starts of production processes and hence an intensification of construction activity. Where speculation does not allow a fall in the interest rate, the piling up of idle balances prevents the increase in the financing of production, with the same effects on the relation between investment and consumption. In both analyses the relation between monetary phenomena and the time structure of production is at the heart of the dynamics of the economy. The difference is that the Neo-Austrian model, by focusing on the effects of the intertemporal complementarity of production rather than on wealth effects, makes it possible to follow step by step the sequence of events instead of being confined to looking at what happens at a given moment in time: in other words, it is more suited to dealing with the analysis of processes of change.

In any case, the interest rate is not completely absent from the analysis carried out by means of a Neo-Austrian model. Rather what comes to be stressed, out of equilibrium, is once again the Wicksellian distinction between the natural rate of interest and the market rate of interest: and the first one has certainly a role to play in this analysis. Thus behind investment decisions, constrained by available financial resources, we can see the own rate of profit of the production process,[32] which determines the amount of resources that the firms actually intend to invest (in particular, in the modelization proposed, by determining the idle balances voluntarily held). The market rate, a monetary price, does not affect real investment decisions.

2.8. MONETARY CONTROL

'Money ... is a device which facilitates the working of markets' (Hicks 1989, p. 2). It is needed for all markets: the commodity and service markets as well as the labour market. Financial intermediaries then appear as the agents in charge of the management of this device, with the aim of achieving improved functioning of markets.

What does this actually mean? Out of equilibrium, where we have seen money to be essential, it means not allowing too strong and/or erratic fluctuations of prices and wages, or cumulative processes of increase or decrease of prices (either hyperinflations or strong depressions), which—also due to their effects on output, incomes, and investment—might affect both the allocation and the creation of resources in such a way as to hamper the viability of the economy. It follows that the specific role of financial intermediaries is to manage financial resources, and in particular money, so as to prevent or damp down the above-mentioned fluctuations or cumulative processes.

Robertson, as we have mentioned above, had already stressed that the aim of monetary policy 'should surely be not to prevent all fluctuations in the general price-level, but to permit those which are necessary to the establishment of appropriate alterations in output and to repress those which tend to carry the alterations in output beyond the appropriate point' (1926, p. 39). In the more complex sequential

---

[32] Which is certainly very difficult to calculate and changes from one period to the next, but is none the less present in the mind of investors as the expression of their more or less confident expectations.

context that we have considered—strongly characterized by the intertemporal complementarity of production—this means in particular preventing excessively strong distortions in the structure of productive capacity, in order not to over-affect the balance between construction and utilization and hence between investment and consumption. On the other hand, we have seen that this balance depends on a complex interaction over time between financial and real variables; it cannot therefore be dealt with by simply referring to bilateral relations between firms and banks.

As a matter of fact the approach followed by financial intermediaries must be a global one. They have neither to focus only on the short term nor on the long term, but to secure the right articulation between the one and the other. This point was also stressed by Robertson, although with particular reference to his analytical framework: 'We have to take account of the complementary nature of long and short lacking, and of the obligation which rests upon the banking system to preserve some sort of balance between them' (1926, p. 91).

This can only be obtained if the adjustments in the productive structure of the economy are not too sudden and abrupt. Hence the importance of reserve assets and of being able to get credit on the part of both firms and households. On the other hand, it is not the better knowledge of future events but rather that of the erratic changes in prices and quantities—that is, their global perception—that allows financial intermediaries, and in particular banks, to smooth out these adjustments. As Hicks pointed out when discussing Thornton's contribution to banking policy,

> though the financial system had no sure means of maintaining an 'equilibrium', it did have means of correcting excessive departure from it. There was no doubt that it was possible for leading banks by acting together to prevent 'overheating' . . . Violent swings, as experience showed, were damaging: but if the remedial measures were promptly and adequately taken, the swings would be damped down and so made less harmful. That however implied that there was someone, or some body, that was in a position to take the action required. In that crucial sense the system needed to have a *centre*. (1989, p. 98).

Thus reference to money and monetary policy throws light on another essential complementary interaction over time of out-of-equilibrium processes of change: that between the market and the organization: this will be analysed in detail in Chapter 4.

But what would monetary control actually amount to, out of equilibrium? Qualitative change, and paramount the creation of resources, is associated with structural modifications which imply a distortion of productive capacity such as to hamper the viability of the process of change undertaken. Dissociation of inputs from output and costs from proceeds is the real threat to viability, as it means the appearance of sunk costs which, by definition, cannot be dealt with by the proceeds of current productive activity or by means of the renewal of old credit contracts. 'Additional' liquidity (money reckoned as 'promise of payment') is then required to build the bridge through time at the heart of the production process destroyed by the distortion of productive capacity: and this can only be the outcome of an 'external' intervention. The aim of this intervention is to re-establish consistency over time of construction and utilization, investment and consumption, supply and demand. It must therefore itself be articulated over time so as to properly interact with the modification in the structure of productive capacity which is taking place sequentially; which means, in particular, being harmonized with the time profile of internally generated financial resources during this process.[33]

The accent on the complementarity between real and financial assets, on the other hand, raises the question of the implication of the exogenous or endogenous character of money supply. Thus, the fact that the monetary authority can control the total stock of money also implies that money supply can equally be a factor of the perturbation or the viability of the economy. As a matter of fact, consideration of the money supply (or of part of it) as a control variable (as in the modelization proposed in Section 2.5 above) renders the economic system partially 'decomposable' in the sense proposed by Loasby (1991). It allows, that is, a decoupling of the system from its environment, to reduce system integration, so as to also reduce the impact of external (or internal) events. 'Loose coupling is a means of providing reserves at the system level. It allows some of the elements to change, either in response to pressures of various kinds or by their own initiative, without disturbing the balance of the system to which they belong' (ibid. p. 47). However, it is also true that this control cannot be exerted in a systematically optimal

---

[33] Various out-of-equilibrium processes and the specific financial interventions (and intermediaries) required to secure the viability of the same processes will be analysed in Part II of this book.

Money 59

way, and that it may happen that the exogenous modifications of the money stock as they result from the decisions of the monetary authority bring about real shocks which affect the viability of the economy. This ambivalent character of the control exerted through exogenous changes in money supply draws attention to the concept of 'monetary regime' (Heymann and Leijonhufvud 1994), and on its possible developments. According to the authors 'by a monetary regime we mean, on the one hand, a system of expectations on part of the public that governs their decisions and, on the other, that pattern of behaviour on part of the monetary authorities that sustains these expectations' (ibid. p. 24). Thus a monetary regime postulates a certain coherence between the behaviour the of monetary authorities and the expectations of economic agents; and the state of these expectations determines the actual impact of a given monetary policy on production, employment, and prices.

The concept of monetary regime can be introduced into our analytical framework and extended to take into account the coherence of the behaviour of the monetary authorities within the time structure of productive capacity. It is in fact clear that, in the perspective proposed in this book, the time structure of productive capacity, together with expectations, is a main determinant of the impact of monetary policy on production, employment, and prices over time. When we focus, as we are doing, on economies undergoing out-of-equilibrium processes of change, we are naturally led to figure out a totally discretionary monetary policy aimed at re-establishing full co-ordination over time of construction and utilization, investment and consumption, and supply and demand. In principle, this is always possible, but only at the cost of ignoring two essential things: that monetary authorities do not have perfect knowledge of the time structure of productive capacity, and that 'volatile policies create a very difficult environment for decision-makers in the private sector' (ibid.) because they have incomplete information. In these conditions we need rules which render more reliable the interactions between monetary authorities and economic agents. These cannot be mechanical rules, nor can they focus on a specific and unchangeable target, like for example complete price stability; but they must exist.[34] 'A measure of accomodation by the banking system in response to real cyclical growth impulse is appropriate. But there is no easy criterion for exactly what measure

---

[34] This point will be dealt with more fully in Section 4.8 below.

of accomodation is appropriate' (Leijonhufvud 1988, p. 18). Within our out-of-equilibrium perspective this criterion is represented by a degree of distortion of productive capacity which cannot go beyond a certain threshold without hampering the viability of the process of qualitative change undertaken.

In conclusion, financial resources—both as stocks and flows according to the interpretation put forward in this chapter—are an essential element in the shaping of the 'constraints–decisions–constraints' sequence through which out-of-equilibrium processes evolve and qualitative change actually takes place. They are not the only essential element, though; together with financial resources and dynamically interacting with them, human resources—also as both stocks and flows—must be considered. Being out of equilibrium implies being confronted with imbalances over time, and hence with gaps to be filled, links to be established, and sunk costs to be covered. In determining these imbalances, and likewise in helping to resolve them, human resources play a role which is in many aspects the mirror image of the role played by financial resources.

3
The Human Resource

3.1. LABOUR INPUT, HUMAN CAPITAL, AND THE HUMAN RESOURCE

A pendulum between its interpretation as 'human capital' and as a 'labour input' characterizes the way in which the human factor has been dealt with by economic theory. These interpretations offer in turn the *ex post* or the *ex ante* perspective.

Labour has mainly been dealt with as human capital (in modern parlance) by classical economists, in the sense that it can be accumulated in the same way as physical capital and is perfectly complementary to it. This is the case with Smith's 'productive labour', the fraction of the existing labour force put to production by gross investment and increasing (or decreasing) with the latter. Behind this approach there is an *ex ante* vision of capital as the force that makes production possible rather than as specific productive assets.[1] Capital thus viewed adapts perfectly to labour with which it moves in parallel in the course of a production process based on the accumulation of complementary factors. In the classical vision, labour is a homogeneous flow that 'works on land *through* capital, not on capital nor with capital' (Hicks 1974, p. 156).

Another implication of this analytical framework is that growth is endogenous. The rate of accumulation depends on the amount of resources devoted to investment, and the complementary nature of these resources excludes a resource constraint stemming from accumulation itself. This is exactly the result which modern endogenous growth theories arrive at, as we shall see in particular in Section 5.3 below.

The whole scene, and the character of the actors involved in it, changes completely with the emergence and the definitive establishment of the neoclassical theory of production as epitomized by the production function. The *ex post* viewpoint behind this theory shifts the focus from the production process to productive capacity which is

---

[1] See the distinction between capital as a stock and capital as a fund stressed by Hicks (1974).

the physical counterpart of a given productive option (see Section 1.1 above). This results from the assembling of generic inputs, that is, resources that can be employed in different production processes without loss of productive value and hence matter only for the amount in which they are available. Capital is no longer looked at as a sum of values which activates production but as a physical input in the same way as labour, and the two become perfectly substitutable for each other, so that different production processes (techniques) can be defined exactly in terms of different ratios of the one to the other input. However while capital can be accumulated, labour cannot. This is a resource constraint which brings about diminishing returns to capital, and is the reason why the growth theory based on this analytical apparatus—a theory capable of explaining the levels but not the rates of change of the relevant economic magnitudes—is obliged to rely on exogenous sources of growth, namely, demographic and technological parameters (see Section 5.2 below).

In an attempt to endogenize the explanation of growth while remaining within a neoclassical framework the so-called 'new growth theory' (Romer 1986; Lucas 1988; and the subsequent vast literature on endogenous growth) features a return to the interpretation of labour as human capital, following the line sketched out much earlier by Uzawa (1965). Human capital is reckoned to be able to be accumulated in the same way as physical capital, there is no longer a resource constraint, and complementarity prevails. We are thus back to the classical vision according to which growth is endogenous in that it depends on how much we intend and are able to push the accumulation process.

We have stressed in Chapters 1 and 2 that the standard theory does not allow us to deal properly with qualitative change, that is, with change characterized by structural modifications, as this is in the nature of an out-of-equilibrium process resulting from distortions in productive capacity which can only be brought to light by focusing explicitly on the time articulation of the production process. This is so even when we consider changes (like the speeding up of the growth rate) which do not imply a movement from an *ex post* to an *ex ante* view of production, but where we cannot abstract from consideration of the phase of the construction of productive capacity and the intertemporal complementarity of the production process, with the resulting dissociation over time of inputs and output and of costs and proceeds while the change is being brought about. And, of course, this is much more so when we actually pass to an *ex ante* viewpoint and interpret construction as creation anew and focus on the learning process and on its dynamic implications.

The return to the concept of human capital in the new growth theory seems at first sight to allow us to take into account the need to consider of a phase of construction of productive capacity—which we have just stated to be essential for analysing a process of structural change—and to do it precisely with specific reference to labour. This is now characterized by skills and competences which accrue as the result of a process of accumulation. In Lucas's 1988 model the accumulation of human capital depends on the fact that the existing labour force can employ its time either working or studying, whereby studying means skills acquisition and hence is synonymous with human capital accumulation. This is a clear hint at the fact that skills and competences, before being used (working) must be constructed (studying). But in the model, any time that is not spent working results automatically in an increase in human capital. The process of production of human capital is synchronized so that the phase of construction actually disappears, in the same way as in the production of physical capital in standard models. Thus the implications of taking the time articulation of the production process and its intertemporal complementarity into account explicitly are not brought to the fore. This depends not so much on the *ex post* perspective which characterizes neoclassical models, whether of the old or of the new brand,[2] as on the hypothesis of equilibrium which draws attention to the utilization moment of production while pushing into the background the underlying productive capacity and its construction.

Reference to human capital that can be accumulated[3] is not a significant step forward, in the analysis of processes of qualitative change, with respect to the concept of labour input looked at as a given generic resource in traditional models. For such an analysis to be properly carried out we require both a thorough sequential context and the status of being out of equilibrium (see Section 1.4 above).

---

[2] We have seen in Section 1.5 that even in an *ex post* context it is possible to focus on the dissociation over time of costs and proceeds which characterizes a process of qualitative change.

[3] Although it is important for rendering endogenous the long-run growth rate of the economy, since accumulation depends on the value taken by preference parameters which determine the extent of the allocation to growth of some kind of resource (time, in the example given above—see Section 5.3 below).

Then a richer concept is also needed, that of the human resource which, together with financial resources, appears as an essential element in the sketching out of both an intra- and an inter-period sequence—where the one depends on, and at the same time determines, the other—through which the process of change takes place out of equilibrium. Within this context the concept of the human resource differs both from the concept of labour input and from that of human capital. It features an *ex post* as well as an *ex ante* character, and its greater richness depends both on the time perspective from which we look at it and on whether we are choosing an *ex post* or an *ex ante* viewpoint. At each given moment in time the human resource, looked at as a complex mix of skills, qualifications, and competences, appears as a state variable of the economy, one of the constraints on the decisions to be taken. Over time processes take place—learning processes—which represent the construction phase of the production of skills, qualifications, and competences, which will characterize the human resource state variable in each successive period. Although remaining within an *ex post* perspective there is already more here than in the characterization of human capital in equilibrium models: construction, as just stressed, is explicitly dealt with.

But there is another and more interesting dynamic level to which the analysis can be raised when the *ex ante* aspect of the concept of the human resource is highlighted. We have already considered learning in the sense of the acquisition of specific (higher) skills and qualifications. But there is another, more generic form of learning which constitutes the real essence of processes of qualitative change: learning that concerns the process of change itself, what it is and how it takes place. Learning, therefore, which is not related to specific elements, given once and for all, but rather to mechanisms aimed at stimulating the change and mechanisms of adaptation to it. The main analytical problem when we are dealing with out-of-equilibrium processes of change, as we have stressed in the previous chapters, is the viability of the processes themselves. The concept of the human resource in the above sense helps us to understand the functioning of the organizational and market mechanisms which make (or do not make) these processes viable. Within this perspective the human resource, in its relevant aspect, appears as a complex structure of knowledge and associated behaviours which is the expression of a potential capacity to manage the change.

3.2. THE WAGE RATE IN EQUILIBRIUM AND OUT OF EQUILIBRIUM

In the standard theory prices reflect the relative scarcity of given generic resources which can be substituted for each other and which price changes allow to be combined in optimal proportions. In particular, wage-rate differences are the expression of different endowments of a homogeneous labour input,[4] and hence wage changes have the role of contributing to bringing about the efficient allocation of resources that characterizes the equilibrium solution of the model. Within this context prices and quantities are determined simultaneously.

In the new version of the standard theory represented by endogenous growth models, where it is no longer substitution but complementarity that prevails, different wage rates are the expression of the weaker or stronger increasing returns which, however, are assumed in the model in the same way as the existence of given endowments in the traditional version (see Section 5.3 below). Labour mobility (now meaning not generic labour but specific qualifications) from the sectors (countries) characterized by weaker increasing returns and hence lower wage rates to those with stronger increasing returns and higher wage rates appears as a substitute for wage changes in determining the efficient allocation of resources. However, the way the notion of externality is dealt with ends up by cancelling the interesting aspect of the concept of human capital—that is, its being something 'brought about by a process' characterized by increasing returns. This is because increasing returns, as already mentioned, are of the same nature as an endowment. Workers with a given level of qualifications who move from a less productive to a more productive sector (or country) immediately acquire, simply by being there, the higher skills due to the higher existing increasing returns (Lucas 1988). This, as already mentioned in the preceding section, means that the problem of the construction of skills through a process in time, evoked by the concept of human capital, is actually dispensed with.

The equilibrium context within which the new growth models are sketched out is the reason why the change from a substitution to a complementarity approach does not imply essential changes in the analysis (except, of course, allowing for the possibility of endogenous

---

[4] Different wage vectors are the expression of different endowments of heterogeneous labour inputs.

growth). As a matter of fact in equilibrium the real differences between the hypothesis of substitution and that of complementarity, as concerns their analytical implications, are hidden.[5] These differences come back to light out of equilibrium. Complementarity reveals its true meaning when a process is involved where co-ordination problems arise.

On the other hand, as already mentioned, in equilibrium price and quantities (of labour) are determined simultaneously, in the sense that they determine each other at the same moment and by means of the same analytical mechanism. Out of equilibrium, however, there is a sequence of determination moments; and this, we shall see, implies the existence of reaction lags and constraints which may have different implications and bring about different developments. The situations to which prices and quantities have to adapt may not only differ greatly but are likely to change over time, and these changes are themselves in part the result of what has been happening to prices and quantities along the way. Within this different perspective the wage rate is no longer the crucial element of the analysis but only one of its elements: it fades into the background in the same way as, out of equilibrium, the interest rate has been shown to fade away in the preceding chapter.

An attempt to move from a simultaneous to a sequential determination of price and quantities of labour, albeit still within an equilibrium context, was developed by Hicks in 'Wages and Interest: The Dynamic Problem'(1935*b*). A sequential context is introduced into this analysis by means of the consideration of finite periods of time and of transactions which take place discontinuously, at the beginning of each period (the Monday of the 'week' which was to be made famous by *Value and Capital*).[6] Everything which takes place before that beginning is a datum. The economy dealt with is wholly engaged in the production of a single homogeneous commodity, call it bread, by means of homogeneous labour and (non-homogeneous) capital goods. Production plans concerning a series of outputs in successive weeks, together with a series of inputs of labour necessary to obtain

---

[5] No complementarity problems can arise in equilibrium since the required complementarity relations are assured by the very definition of equilibrium.

[6] 'We are accustomed to thinking of economic magnitudes as continuous "flows", but the convenience of this is limited to the static case, when the flows are constant through time. A flow which varies through time is very difficult to handle. Consequently it seems better to cut the varying flows into short sections, each of which can be treated as constant. We can do this by supposing changes to take place, not continuously, but at intervals' (Hicks 1935b, p. 270).

The Human Resource 67

those outputs, are considered. Out of the various possible plans (not an unlimited variety, since this is conditioned by the capital goods existing at the beginning of each period which, together with the amounts of initial bread and of initial debts, are the result of what has gone before and hence are all data) the one chosen in each period will be the one that maximizes the present value of the entrepreneur's net assets. Plans are implemented by hiring, and paying, labour, and by making loans (only for the current week) under perfectly competitive conditions. Two prices—a rate of wages and a rate of interest, both reckoned in terms of bread—have to be determined in each period at the level which will equate the demand and the supply for labour and for loans respectively, in the same period.

The analysis developed consists in investigating what will be the effects on the level of output and on the demand for labour (at the current date and at future dates) of a change in the current rate of wages or in the rate of interest. These are hypothetical changes, of course, since the equilibrium method only allows us to consider which different production plans would have been adopted if prices had been different. Abstracting from the specific answers given to the question,[7] it is to be stressed that the analytical context sketched out already contains most of the sequential ingredients of the Neo-Austrian framework developed almost forty years later by the same Hicks and of which extensive use has been, and will be, made in this book. However, we cannot yet talk of a thorough sequential determination of the variables involved. As a matter of fact, in the equilibrium analysis carried out the sequence of periods considered is taken into account as a whole, so that, although a change in the rate of wages determines a series of quantities of labour in the successive periods, these are actually all determined simultaneously at the moment the price itself is set.

In any case there are interesting hints in the analysis. In particular, a constraint appears which is in the nature of a wage fund: a different wage fund from that originally conceived by the classics with reference to their interpretation of the production process, though. It is

---

[7] In particular, a fall in the current rate of wages, whether accompanied or not by a fall in the expected rates of wages, is shown to reduce the marginal cost of output at all dates and hence to lead to an expansion of output and to an increase in the demand for labour (although how this increase will be divided between current labour and future labour cannot be determined a priori). Much the same is the case with a reduction of the rate of interest.

important, at this point, to suspend the discussion and focus on the concept of the wage fund. This is a concept, as we shall see in what follows, that, adequately revised, helps to bring to light the relation between human and financial resources—in particular the interaction between the human and the financial constraint—which appears as an essential element in the sketching out of the sequence through which a process of qualitative change takes place out of equilibrium.

3.3. THE WAGE FUND

The classics looked at the wage fund as at the economic beginning of a production process 'considered . . . in the context of the reproduction of final goods (national revenue) and, therefore, in the context of a one-way (but circular) avenue going from the consumption goods exchanged for labour at the beginning . . . to the final . . . goods returned by labour at the end' (Meacci 1994). Within this vertically integrated view of production the wage fund appears exactly as a fund, a 'sum of values' (Hicks 1974) which makes it possible to start off and to carry out the production process by being invested in a type of capital which presents itself as circulating capital (fixed capital being nothing else, in this perspective, than capital whose circulation requires a span of time longer than the single period).[8] Hence the idea that, with a given labour force, the wage fund determines the wage rate; while with a given wage rate it determines employment.[9]

---

[8] 'The notion of the classics is best rendered by Jevons's observation that one should not say "a railway is *fixed capital*, but that *capital is fixed in the railway*" (1871, p. 264): a remark which invariably points to the wage fund as the typical form of capital at the beginning of its transformation (free capital)' (Meacci 1994).

[9] However, the wage rate is not necessarily pegged to a subsistence level, that is, to the level just above starvation which keeps the supply of labour constant, in which case the wage fund automatically determines the demand for labour and hence also appears as a theory of employment. Apart from this specific case, and given the level of productivity, the wage rate can take any value between a floor represented by the subsistence level and a ceiling corresponding to a level which reduces the return on capital to zero (or to a minimum, if this is required to keep the supply of capital constant). In the interpretation of the wage fund theory proposed by Hicks and Hollander (1977) an equilibrium wage rate is actually determined, *together and simultaneously* with employment, as the rate at which 'the growth rates of labour and of capital would be the same, so that a steady state, of uniform expansion, would be possible.' (Hicks 1979, p. 51). Thus in an equilibrium context, it must be stressed, the idea of constraint and of the associated sequential determination of prices and quantities hinted at by the wage fund concept sketched out by the classics goes by the board.

Misunderstanding as to the concept of the wage fund and its use in economic analysis arises when we abandon the vertically integrated view of the production process stressed by the classics. This is typically the case with a recent paper by Paul Samuelson (1994), whose argument depends on his having in mind the horizontal structure of the production process that is highlighted light when we look at production in an *ex post* perspective and which he wrongly attributes to the classics. Within a similar perspective capital no longer appears as free capital, a fund of resources with which to carry out production in general, but as a stock of physical goods into which free capital has been already embodied and which are divided into fixed capital goods (structures and machinery) and working capital goods (which include wage goods).

Samuelson maintains that the 'classical fallacy', according to which the introduction of machinery, by diminishing the wage fund, results necessarily in a reduction in employment or in a decrease of the real wage rate, is based on the wrong idea that the demand for labour derives from circulating capital alone. A simple calculation points to the fact that since expenses on machinery are dissociated from expenses on wage goods, the introduction of machinery can only be at the expense of employment or of the real wage. However

> in any minimal production period, the outlay advanced on direct wages will be only a fraction of the total outlay that entrepreneurs must advance on all inputs. The wage fund that they advance . . . is thus much less than the total Kuznets-measured capital in the economy . . . It is one part of all capitals . . . The wage fund is not to be confused with the totality of 'circulating' capital . . . and it is not a *causal* determinant of the real wage in any meaningful long run, intermediate run, or short run . . . (ibid. p. 629). The 'wage fund' is just another name for the 'wage bill' . . . It is a fatuity to say 'Wages are high because the wage bill is high' (ibid. n. 5).

It is then easy for Samuelson to show that, in a context where a horizontal integration is stressed so that fixed capital is combined with working capital for the production of final goods, there is no simple and one-way relation between the composition of capital and employment or the real wage rate. But this is not the context that the classics had in mind. Samuelson's criticism is directed at the wrong target and depends on the confusion that he makes between what the classics, by referring to a vertically integrated view of production, actually intended by wage fund—the whole capital of the economy seen as a fund, as free capital which will circulate through the reproduction process—and what he seems to believe the classics had in mind but actually they did not: the wage fund as the working part of the existing physical capital, on which alone the demand for labour was made to depend.

Focus on the horizontal structure of production, and on its horizontal integration, actually leads us back to a simultaneous determination of prices and quantities, within the equilibrium context of which a similar structure is the expression. And together with a sequential determination the idea of constraint which is inherent in the wage fund concept disappears.[10]

3.4. TOWARDS A MODERN THEORY OF THE WAGE FUND

The Neo-Austrian model, as we have seen (Section 1.4 above), by stressing the time structure of production, its vertical integration, and its intertemporal complementarity, makes it possible to sketch out a thorough sequential analytical context within which to analyse transition processes between equilibria. Unlike in the original Austrian version, fixed capital is dealt with, but not explicitly shown in the model: this allows a return to the idea of capital as a fund, as free capital. This blend of Austrian and classic analytical ingredients also restores the concept of the wage fund as a constraint emerging from and impinging on a transition process characterized by a sequential determination of prices and quantities. This wage fund is no longer identified with circulating capital, though, as is the case within the context of a process of production interpreted as circular reproduction in the long-run perspective stressed by the classics.[11] A shift in focus from the long run to a transition process in fact implies an emphasis on intertemporal complementarity of production. And the consideration of fixed capital, although this is not explicitly shown, is clearly behind the time articulation of the relation between the construction and the utilization of productive capacity which, in a Neo-Austrian perspective, appears as the backbone of a sequential

---

[10] In other words, the wage fund becomes 'the malleable *result* of the equilibrium process and not the *causal* determinant of the level of the real wage' (Samuelson 1994, p. 629).

[11] A case, we have seen, in which circulating capital also re-absorbs fixed capital.

The Human Resource

process of change. This, by the way, is the shift in focus which is behind the famous numerical example put forward by Ricardo in his chapter 'On Machinery' which he appended to the third edition of his Principles and which shows how unemployment is necessarily associated with the introduction of a more mechanized technique while this is taking place (see Section 5.5 below). This example can only be understood if we consider the effects of the intertemporal complementarity of the production processes which come to the surface during a transition.

In the barter model dealt with by Hicks in his analysis of the Traverse (1973), the wage fund, in each given period, is determined by current final output, once 'taken out' the parts of it devoted to consumption out of profits and unproductive consumption. It is therefore the result of past investment decisions and it is used, in turn, to finance labour employed both in the construction and in the utilization of productive capacity, that is, to accumulate both fixed and working capital. Out of equilibrium, the conditions which determine the allocation of the wage fund between construction and utilization, and hence its step-by-step dynamics, also determine the evolution path of the economy.

This version of the wage-fund theory does not allow us, by itself, to trace out simultaneously the time profiles of employment and of the real wage rate. This is why Hicks deals with the performance of the economy under the alternative hypotheses of a fixed real wage rate and of the full employment of a labour force the supply of which grows at an exogenously given rate. With a fixed real wage rate, the assumption of Full Performance—according to which all output which is not consumed is invested, except for a constant take-out—makes it possible to endogenize the rate of starts of new production processes and hence investment, thus tracing out the time profile of employment. Alternatively, the rate of starts is determined in such a way as to secure the full employment of the exogenously growing labour force, and then the course of wages, given the assumption of a constant take-out and of no saving out of wages, will be the same as the course of productivity. In any case, either employment or the wage rate must be fixed exogenously.

We intend now to move a step forward along the path opened up by Hicks, by rendering the time profile of both employment and the wage rate endogenous. As a matter of fact, as already stressed in Section 1.7 above, in the modelling of an out-of-equilibrium process everything can be considered as given at a certain moment in time, but everything becomes endogenous over time.

To obtain this result we have to dissociate the determination mechanisms of the two variables. This requires us to pass from a barter to a monetary economy, like the one depicted in the preceding chapter where exchanges are made and wages are paid in money terms and the resources required to carry out production are financial resources, not physical output. In a sequential monetary economy, where all decisions are taken at the junction of one period and the next, the determination of prices and quantities is no longer simultaneous; their dissociation in time, out-of-equilibrium, is made tangible by the appearance of idle money balances. We thus have two different mechanisms, one regulating the wage rate, the other the wage fund and the level of employment, which contribute to determining the allocation of resources between the phases of construction and utilization of productive capacity. The coupling of these mechanisms, which involves the sequential determination of prices and quantities of resources and final output, generates a complex dynamic that, as we shall see, may hamper the very viability of an out-of-equilibrium process.

However, a revision of the wage-fund theory in order to render it fully consistent with a proper out-of-equilibrium analysis also requires a revision of the notion of human capital.

We have seen human capital as a homogeneous magnitude with the status of a flow in the vision of classical economists. We have seen it revamped as a stock in the new growth theories, enriched by the consideration of changing skills and competences,[12] but still a stock with the same analytic status as the labour force in the traditional production function models. Whatever the specific process through which the accumulation of skills and competences is envisaged to take place in different endogenous growth models,[13] it is not to the process itself that attention is drawn[14] but to its result. This result, as we have already mentioned, in Lucas's model depends on the number of hours devoted to education which affect in a multiplicative way the number of hours worked, so that a stock of human capital can be obtained by a summation in each given period.

---

[12] It is exactly the consideration of the qualifications and competences of workers that earns for labour the attribute of 'capital' (Becker 1964; Lucas 1988).

[13] This problem is dealt with more extensively in Section 5.3 below.

[14] This is usually synthesized in a formula chosen in such a way as to guarantee the regularity and endogeneity of growth.

Within this context the main agent of the economic process, the human resource, is downgraded to a simple stock that can be accumulated (or decumulated) freely, to an efficiency index determined by the time devoted to formation. The introduction of the consideration of different 'qualities' of labour has wider analytic implications than simply focusing on the quantitative results of a process of accumulation, though, implications which come to light when we shift the focus from the result of the process of accumulation to the process itself. This shift of focus also entails passing from the consideration of human capital looked at as a whole and reduced to a homogeneous magnitude to that of a heterogeneous human resource which does matter because of the structure of skills and competences that reflects its 'specific' character. In this different light the human resource steps forward to the centre of the stage and becomes the main actor of the evolution of the economy. It does so in different but related ways, depending on the time perspective from which we look at the sequential process through which the economy evolves. Thus at each given moment the human resource appears as a state variable, a constraint which, together with the financial constraint, binds all decisions concerning production processes. The specific nature of this constraint, on the other hand, is the result of what has been happening in the economy in the past, the inheritance of processes which have been taking place and, most of the time, are still going on, and which concern in particular the human resource itself. When we focus on these processes the human resource also appears as the engine of the evolution of the economy: the main engine when there is no destination known beforehand (as, for example, a productive capacity shaped according to a given superior technique to which the economy gradually adapts, as in the analysis of the Traverse). This is true whenever a qualitative change is involved, a change that, as already stressed in Section 1.7 above, is in the nature of an out-of-equilibrium process which comes down essentially to a creation of specific resources.

3.5. THE HUMAN CONSTRAINT

Dealing with the human resource in a Neo-Austrian model implies in the first place passing from a homogeneous to a heterogeneous labour force. Labour supply, in each given period t, can then be written as

$$\mathbf{L}_s^S(t) = [l_1^S(t), l_2^S(t), \ldots l_s^S(t)]$$

where $\mathbf{L}_s^S(t)$ is the vector whose elements represent the different skills,[15] inherited from the past, which are the expression of the specific character of the existing human resource. We may think of the different skills as ranked according to their level: skill 2 is superior to skill 1, and so forth. The process through which the skills themselves accrue and hence the human resource is actually shaped—a thorough creation process—will be discussed in detail in the next section.

The demand for labour at t, on the other hand, can be written

$$\mathbf{L}_s^D(t) = [l_1^D(t), l_2^D(t), \ldots l_s^D(t)]$$

and it is determined by the activity of construction and utilization of productive capacity, that is

$$\mathbf{L}^D(t) = \underline{\mathbf{A}}^c \mathbf{x}^c(t)' + \underline{\mathbf{A}}^u \mathbf{x}^u(t)'$$

where $\underline{\mathbf{A}}^c$ and $\underline{\mathbf{A}}^u$ are the matrices whose elements represent the quantities of the different types of labour (skills) required in the successive periods of the phases of construction and utilization, respectively, and $\mathbf{x}^c(t)$ and $\mathbf{x}^u(t)$ are the intensities with which the production processes in these different phases are carried on.

Current productive activity, in turn, is determined by the financial resources which make up the wage fund in the current period—resources that come, at least in part, from the proceeds of the sales of final output in the preceding period[16]—and by the wage rate(s) fixed for the whole current period.

However, a human constraint stronger than the financial constraint can appear when the demand for labour, given the constancy of the wage rates within the period, is limited by the supply of labour. This can depend either on a full employment barrier or on a mismatch due to the lack within the labour force of certain skills and competences required by productive activity. Unlike in the original version of the wage-fund theory, as well as in its Hicksian revisitation, here it is employment that determines the wage fund (the part of it which can

---

[15] The term 'skill' must be taken in a wider sense as referring to all the relevant characteristics of the human resource: those intrinsic to it (qualifications, competences, etc.) and those concerning its relations with the productive environment with which it interacts (mobility, organizational capabilities, institutional features etc.).

[16] Idle money balances possibly carried over by producers and external financial resources can be added to the wage fund, thus making the existing financial constraint less stringent, as shown in the preceding chapter.

The Human Resource 75

be actually used up), not vice versa. It is no longer the activity of construction and utilization of productive capacity, as allowed by available financial resources, that determines the demand for labour; it is the demand for labour, constrained by a supply whose level and structure is for the greater part inherited from the preceding period, that determines productive activity. In this case

$$\hat{\omega}(t) = \mathbf{w}(t)\,\hat{\mathbf{L}}^D(t)'$$

where $\hat{\mathbf{L}}^D(t)$ is the demand for labour that is 'constrained', $\mathbf{w}(t)$ the vector whose elements represent the current wage rates for the different types of labour, and $\hat{\omega}(t)$ the 'constrained' wage fund.

Wage changes—it might be objected—would eliminate this human constraint. But this is not so. It is certainly not so when the constraint depends on the fact that skills and qualifications are required which are not present, that is, when the problem is not a different allocation of existing resources (which can be obtained through price changes) but the creation of new and different resources. But also when this is not the case, the assumption that prices (including wages) cannot change within each given period but only at the junction of one period and the next will necessarily make an imbalance between supply and demand appear in the current period. This fixed price assumption, on the other hand, cannot be removed, unless we want to cancel the sequential context which is essential for the analysis of out-of-equilibrium processes, thus going back to a simultaneous determination of prices and quantities in equilibrium. In order not only to preserve but also to stress the sequential character of the model, we have opted in the first instance for the extreme hypothesis of a supply of labour completely inelastic to the wage rate.[17]

However, the focus which cannot be placed on wage changes in the traditional sense can be shifted on to different wage regimes, that is, to different modes of determination of wage changes 'between periods'; these are the expression of the different ways the labour market may function and represent different mechanisms of adjustment which have an important bearing on the actual evolution of the economy.

In particular wage regimes may be considered that reflect market rules. This may be rendered by writing

---

[17] This hypothesis will be partially relaxed so as to widen the analytical reach of the model in Part II of this book, where different types of out-of-equilibrium processes will be investigated.

76   *Out of Equilibrium*

$$g_w(t) = v\psi(t-1)$$

where changes in wage rates depend on supply and demand conditions (as rendered by the vector of excesses of demand for the different types of labour in the preceding period $\psi(t-1)$), and the value of the reaction coefficient v stands for different regulating mechanisms (thus $v = 1$ is the case of fully market-determined wages, which clear the respective markets, while values of v lower than one announce the existence of the filter represented by mediators—trade unions and the like). On the other hand, we may consider institutional regimes, which can be rendered by specific indexation rules (on prices, on revenues, and so forth).

3.6. WAGES AND EMPLOYMENT

Wages have a double analytical status: they are a component of income and an element of cost. Thus, although an increase in wage rates sustains the demand for final output, it also implies a stronger financial constraint, thus affecting both the bias in utilization and the bias in construction of productive activity. While the neoclassical viewpoint stresses mainly the cost effect of wage changes and the Keynesian viewpoint stresses the (direct and indirect) effects on demand, an out-of-equilibrium analysis requires that both effects are taken into account and that their interaction over time is considered in a sequential context. The viability of out-of-equilibrium processes in fact depends on the harmony over time of the activities of the construction and the utilization of productive capacity (which also concern, as we shall see, the re-shaping of the human resource involved in the production process).

We have already mentioned that the mechanisms determining the wage rates and the quantities of the different types of labour demanded and offered (which interact with the mechanism of the determination of output[18]) bring about a complex dynamic. Employment is the result of this dynamics, of which wage rates represent only

---

[18] Wage changes, which will affect final output through their effects on the construction and utilization of productive capacity, are themselves the result, e.g., of excesses in demand (or supply) of labour due to decisions concerning the activity of the construction and/or utilization which represent reactions to the imbalances in the market for final output in the preceding period.

one element. No specific trajectory of wage rates and employment towards a given state of the economy and its productive capacity can then be sketched out beforehand 'out of equilibrium', where the point of arrival is rather the outcome of what happens on the way, and hence is itself, at least in part, the result of the step-by-step dynamics of wages and employment. Co-ordination problems arise along the way; wage regimes do matter because they contribute to determining the kind of interaction that is actually realized. However we cannot say *ex ante* what is the right kind of interaction—that is, the interaction leading to harmony over time between construction and utilization. What may be stressed in any case is that this harmony depends essentially on the sequential interaction of the human and the financial resources—in particular, on the setting and the relaxing of human and financial constraints that this interaction brings about sequentially. Feedback mechanisms are at work which involve real and monetary variables.

To illuminate this discussion we need numerical simulations. There is, however, a conjecture about the relation between the dynamics of wages and employment and the viability of out-of-equilibrium processes that we can already advance. Wage rates—we have already mentioned and we shall see in particular when dealing with specific out-of-equilibrium processes—can go up or down during the processes themselves, and this, due to the double nature of wages, can entail increases or decreases in employment, along the way, depending on the actual development of the sequence through which these processes take place. What we can say, in any case, is that any change in wages—through its double effect on costs and final demand, and hence on the activities of construction and utilization—is a factor causing a distortion in the age structure of productive capacity, other things remaining equal. Fluctuations in wage rates—which, as we shall analyse in detail in Chapters 6 and 7 below, are one aspect of the fluctuations that characterize out-of-equilibrium processes of change—are thus likely to bring about increasing distortions of productive capacity, which explain persistence and fluctuations of unemployment and, more generally, represent a threat to viability. If this is true, damping down fluctuations in wage rates is favourable to viability, whether this is the result of the way in which wages react to prevailing conditions of supply and demand of labour, or of quasi-institutional mechanisms on which the working of labour markets depends (trade unions, market segmentation, or the relation between more or less established forms of employment.[19]) But this, as we shall see, may be equally true for all magnitudes involved in the process of change.

3.7. LEARNING

The specific character of the human resource, the structure of skills and competences which characterize it at each given moment, is the result of a process which has two main aspects. On the one hand there is the *upgrading*, the passage from a lower to a higher skill out of the existing ones, as the result of 'on the job training'. This implies a sort of circulation of the elements of the supply vector $\mathbf{L}_s^S$ within the vector itself, that is, a movement from the one to the other position in the vector. Thus the supply of each given skill $\tilde{l}_h^s > l_h^s$, ($h = 1, 2, \ldots s$), at time t can be written

$$\tilde{l}_h^s(t) = l_h^D(t)(1 + \xi) \text{ if } l_h^S(t) \geq l_h^D(t)$$

$$\tilde{l}_h^s(t) = l_h^D(t)(1 - \xi) \text{ if } l_h^S(t) < l_h^D(t)$$

where the function $\xi(t)$ ($\lim_{t \to \infty} = 0$) gives the additions to and the subtractions from skill h in period (t).

On the other hand qualitative change most of the time also bring about new productive options and structures which imply the appearance of altogether different and higher skills, that is, a thorough creation of a human resource. This can be rendered by the appearance of one (or more) new elements ($s + 1, s + 2, \ldots$) in the labour supply vector as the result of some kind of ongoing process.[20] Thus out-of-equilibrium learning, just like the existence of human reserves or the inflows of human resources made possible by the establishment of external relations at local or international level (such as immigration), helps to relax the existing human constraint. In the same way as, on the other hand, financial reserves (idle balances or the like) help to relax financial constraints.

The analysis of learning as a creative process, that is the analysis of

---

[19] See the distinction between *solid* and *fluid* employment proposed by Hicks (1989, p. 35).
[20] In a previous book (Amendola and Gaffard 1988) we considered this creation to be associated with the upgrading of the human resource, and made both depend on the intensity of the innovative activity carried on in the economy, that is, on the number of innovative production processes (as distinct from routine processes) actually carried on.

what it depends on and through which mechanisms it comes about, is a flourishing branch of economic theory, and one which draws heavily on interdisciplinary contributions. However, this is not what we want to focus on here, as it is rather the implications of the consideration of the learning process on an out-of-equilibrium analysis that we want to bring to light. Whatever the specific process through which it takes place, learning essentially concerns 'employed' labour. This had already been stressed by Phelps (1972), according to whom the persistence of unemployment is mainly explained by the fact that unemployed workers lose their chance to improve their skills through on-the-job training. The argument has been revived in recent contributions (e.g. Blanchard 1989, 1991) where the hysteresis of employment is explained in terms of a shifting of the wage—employment relation, that is, of a modification of the labour-market equilibrium which those outside the market do not contribute to determining and, in turn, are not concerned by. As time goes by real wage rates, for a given level of employment, go up, due to the improvement in the quality of employed labour. Although within a more sophisticated analytical context, it is still the traditional idea that real wage rates determine the level of employment which prevails.

We maintain instead that, out of equilibrium, we must focus on the intertemporal complementarity of production and on the related co-ordination problems rather than on equilibrium relations referring to an activity of exchange, in order to understand the dynamics of employment at a structural level. Only conjectures, as already mentioned, can be advanced here. The first is that distortions of productive capacity, the natural consequence of the attempt to bring about qualitative changes, are the expression of an imbalance between the activities of construction and utilization, which implies the appearance of mismatches between the demand and the supply of labour at the aggregate and/or at a sectoral level, and hence a fall in employment. There is thus a slowing down of the learning process (unemployment means less on-the-job training) which implies, in turn, a strengthening of the human constraint and, through the existing interactions, of the financial constraint as well.

The co-ordination problems which characterize out-of-equilibrium processes reflect not only imbalances due to the intertemporal complementarity of production but also, as we shall see in particular in Section 4.8, problems of the transmission of information which interact with the appearance and the amplification of these imbalances.

The human resource plays a crucial role in this process, in which it appears not only as a physical constraint to production but also as a carrier of knowledge and information. We are referring not only to the knowledge intrinsic in its skills; much more relevant, in this context, is the knowledge stemming from the relations that the conduct of productive activity requires to be established with the environment. Thus it is certainly true that the excesses in demand or supply of the different skills and the adjustment mechanisms induced in terms of changes in wage rates and of upgrading procedures are essential aspects of the acquisition and transmission of knowledge and information. However, as regards the crucial problem of the viability of the process of change involved, it does not automatically follow that a strong and quick acquisition of skills is a good thing (in the same way as we cannot say that an increase in the saving rate is unquestionably favourable, in terms of viability). This is because the way in which the process of the acquisition of knowledge and information takes place, and the conditions under which it occurs, matter more than the results in terms of the number and level of skills acquired.[21]

Once we have shifted the focus to learning that concerns the process of change itself, that is, to a learning process related not so much to specific elements, given once and for all, as to mechanisms aimed at stimulating change and mechanisms of adaptation to it, the organizational aspects which represent the essence of these mechanisms are highlighted. To these aspects we shall devote our attention in the next chapter.

---

[21] In the same way the relevant aspect of an increase in wage rates is not so much the inducement it represents (to migration or to an increase in the supply of the corresponding qualifications) as the processes that it stimulates. As a matter of fact an increase in the wage rate as a reaction to an excess demand also implies a modification of the structure of productive capacity: the effect on final demand associated with the effect on production cost introduces a bias in the time structure of production (as is the case with an increase in the credit granted to investment or to consumption).

4
The Market and the Firm

4.1. INSTITUTIONS AND THE PROCESS OF CHANGE

A proper analysis of qualitative change relies on a clear understanding of the interpenetration of markets and firms in relation to the production process interpreted in the wider sense mentioned in Chapter 1.

Complementarity between (real and financial) inputs at successive stages is the crucial aspect of production processes. Therefore co-ordination issues are the essential issues. The main problem that firms and markets have to deal with is how to co-ordinate supply and demand (of processes and commodities) over time, so as to avoid excessive imbalances which might hamper the viability of the changes undertaken.

In the first place, the intertemporal complementarity of both the production and the decision process, and the co-ordination problem that it entails, implies the need to pay more attention to the different kinds of external relations (between firms, between firms and institutions, and so forth). These can be pure market relations or organizational relations, that is, competitive or co-operative relations, which arise in the attempt to carry out effective co-ordination in the context of strong uncertainty and of bounded rationality within which changes actually take place. This co-ordination is successful when it allows a smooth working of markets period after period; that is, as stressed by Robertson (see Section 2.7 above), without excessive disequilibria between supply and demand which might generate excessive fluctuations of prices and industrial output.

Interpreted in a wider sense, co-ordination actually comes down to creating viable productive systems of which both markets and firms are active constituent elements. In this perspective investment in market development 'is not simply an aid to equilibration in response to external change' (Loasby 1993a, p. 8). It is rather the means to make a process of continuous change viable. As a matter of fact 'markets are one of the forms of organization which aid knowledge—not only the knowledge required to negotiate an efficient set of contracts, but the knowledge required to improve the choice set on which contracts can be based' (ibid. p. 9). This statement, which draws clearly on Marshall (1920), makes much more sense if we do not confine an enlargement of the existing choice set to knowledge acquisition, as hinted at by Loasby, but interpret it more properly as a 'construction' process bringing about a wider gamut of productive options. That is, if we put production, together with information, at the centre of the stage. When the focus is on information alone, as is usually the case in modern theory, we cannot in fact get hold of the irreversibilities which can only be brought to the surface by enlarging the focus to encompass production, with its intertemporal complementarity.

Within this different perspective, markets and firms are to be looked at as institutional structures which channel processes of change. They can appear as substitutes, and they are partially substitutes. But 'it is no less important to recognize that they are also complements.' (Loasby 1993b, p. 8). The role of markets is 'that of providing options for future contracts rather than contracts for future options' (Loasby, ibid.). If the term 'option' is not confined to the activity of exchange but more properly interpreted as a productive option associated with the appearance of a particular productive capacity, this role is to contribute to the viability of construction processes aimed at structuring new productive options rather than to the optimality of an intertemporal allocation of resources. And, as often stressed in the previous chapters, complementarity over time (of resources, assets, decisions etc.) is the most important aspect of some such processes.

On the other hand, shaping out markets, as well as constructing a new physical productive capacity, implies bearing sunk costs, as we have seen in Chapters 2 and 3. These are in some sense transaction costs. But 'this emphasis on the capital element in transaction costs . . . is surprisingly rare in transaction cost analysis, which is primarily directed towards a comparison of the transaction costs of operating within alternative governance structures: the cost of creating these structures rarely receives explicit attention' (Loasby 1993a, p. 10). A distinctive aspect of the out-of-equilibrium analysis we intend to carry out—we shall see in detail in Section 4.6 below—is precisely to focus on the 'capital element in transaction costs'.

However, the sunk costs implied by a qualitative change must be dealt with without having complete information about the economic environment. A lag in the transmission of information is a distinctive aspect of this process: a lag that interacts with the construction lag which implies the appearance of sunk costs. Market connections may help to acquire the relevant information for investment decisions. But uncertainty can never be fully dispensed with. A need for adaptability persists, which leads to a focus on the role of reserves and learning capabilities in out of equilibrium strategies. The viability of a process of qualitative change—as opposed to efficiency at a point in time which calls for full employment of resources—requires holding reserves and having learning capabilities. Reserves allow us to fill gaps over time and to deal with unanticipated contingencies; learning capabilities prevent us from having to face bad contingencies (or bad states of nature) by providing conditions for a harmonization over time of supply and demand.

Learning capabilities can be structured inside the firm or in the market, in the sense that we can learn the behaviours and commitments of others through market connections. These may, for example, assure investors that their investment will not be rendered unprofitable by an excess supply.[1] In any case it must be stressed that 'forms of organization which are best fitted for one environment may generate knowledge which makes them less appropriate' (Loasby 1993*a*, p. 18). Thus changing organizational arrangements, in the same way as changing technology, is a theme at the heart of an out-of-equilibrium analysis of markets and organization. And in both cases we have to deal with the co-ordination problems associated with these changes rather than with optimal forms of organization, or choice of best techniques, as is the case with standard theory.

4.2. MARKET FAILURE AND ORGANIZATIONAL CO-ORDINATION

In modern economic theory the organizational problem has been interpreted as the problem of drawing the optimal frontier between the firm and the market, and this was first mentioned in connection with the problem of the endogenization of technology.

In the traditional representation, as we have stressed in Chapter 1, technology is actually dissociated from production and appears as an exogenously determined constraint. The modern developments of the theory of technical progress are characterized by the attempt to endo-

---

[1] An example of this kind of connection are the agreements which establish technology consortia (see Baumol 1993).

genize technology. However endogenization, in these developments, reflects the standard approach: as already explained in Section 1.7 above, it is obtained by explicitly considering in the model a behaviour aimed at the production of technology. The principle is the same as that of the traditional representation, although it is no longer technology but the form of the behaviour function, and its coefficients, that now fall from the sky.

In particular, starting with Arrow (1962), endogenization of technology is obtained by means of the introduction of a new commodity and a corresponding market. This commodity, in a world characterized by uncertainty, is information, and hence invention is interpreted as a process directed towards the production of information. This interpretation of technology clearly goes in the direction already taken by Arrow (see Section 1.2 above), of dealing with problems by means of an extension of the list of commodities and of markets.

In this context the main problem is not so much the characterization of the process of production of this new commodity as the possibility of realizing an optimal allocation of resources in view of the properties of technology classed as information. As a matter of fact 'information is a commodity with peculiar attributes, particularly embarrassing for the achievement of optimal allocation.' (Arrow 1962, p. 112). It is in fact indivisible and (at least partially) inappropriable. Its value is difficult to assess and therefore it is not easy to trade. Then 'a downward bias in the amount of resources devoted to inventive activity is very likely.' (ibid.), with the result that a competitive market may not lead to an efficient allocation of resources. Organizational co-ordination is hence required to make up for this market failure and replace market transactions. This is how, in this context, organization steps on to the stage, but Arrow shows that even this can result in a distortion in the allocation of resources from a social viewpoint. As a matter of fact

> market failure, the inefficient allocation of resources with markets, can occur if there are too few markets, non-competitive behaviour, or non-existence problems. Many suggested solutions for market failure, such as tax-subsidy schemes, property rights assignments and special pricing arrangements are simply devices for the creation of more markets. If this can be done in a way that avoids non-convexities and ensures depth of participation, then the remedy can be beneficial and the new allocation should be efficient. On the other hand, if the addition of markets creates either non-convexities or shallow participation, then the attempts to cure market failure from too few

markets will simply lead to market failure from monopolistic behaviour (Ledyard 1989, p. 189).

4.3. OPTIMIZING STRATEGIES OF FIRMS

In this new view, in which technology is considered as a produced resource, production appears as a linear process made up of a succession of separate activities that do not interact. Research, by means of which innovation is pursued, is completely disconnected from manufacturing and characterized by a production function of its own.[2]

A series of models which refer to technology or information in the above sense introduce the problem of modifying the production possibility frontier (given in the standard approach) through research and development activity (R&D) seen as a strategic variable. This strategy is analysed mainly by means of game theory. The most important aspect of the analysis is summed up by one of its main contributors: 'Modern non co-operative game theory is a language of strategy and equilibrium; that is, it provides an equilibrium framework in which to examine individuals' strategic behaviour' (Reinganum 1984, p. 61[3]).

The equilibrium character of this analysis is primarily responsible for the essential timelessness of strategies that imply a production process of technology or information whose costs and proceeds are analytically contemporaneous, and that come down to punctual or intertemporal allocations of resources.

This is immediately evident in 'auction-type' models (see, for example, Dasgupta and Stiglitz 1980[4]), in which a particular innovation is sought simultaneously by a number of symmetrically or asymmetrically placed potential investors, and where what matters is to get there first, as patent protection is assumed to be perfect. A strategy for

---

[2] In Arrow's modelling of technological change—it should be stressed—what is at the heart of the debate about incentives to innovation is the structure of the market for the products which make use of the results of inventive activity. This means that what matters from the analytical viewpoint is the way in which a new technology (a new productive capacity) is 'used' rather than the way in which it is 'constructed'.

[3] Within this type of framework strategies are the expression of a co-ordination *ex ante* which implies consistency of individual plans but does not necessarily bring about a Pareto optimum. This is the meaning of co-ordination failure in this context.

[4] For a survey of models along these and similar lines see Reinganum 1989.

a firm i is defined as a bid x_i to which a date of completion of the innovation $T_i = T(x_i)$ is associated, and where $T(\cdot)$ is decreasing and convex; hence, postponing the date of invention allows the firm to reduce its invention costs, but at a decreasing rate (and vice versa). A Nash equilibrium is then defined as a vector of bids having the property that no firm wishes to change its bid unilaterally. No dissociation of costs and proceeds is possible in this context, since it is explicitly postulated that no real resources are expended until the winner is determined. Only the winning firm spends the amount of its bid and actually develops the innovation.

In other models, where the object of the strategy is no longer a lump sum expenditure x_i but the time trajectory of a flow of expenditure, effective commitments are considered, that is, situations in which all firms, whether winners or not, actually spend the sums they have decided to invest in order to affect the environment, namely the conditions in which the oligopoly game takes place. Thus commitments can be seen as the expression of a particular form of organization, aimed at co-ordinating strategies rather than at curing market failure as in Arrow's original interpretation. But even in this case, when effective commitments seem to dissociate costs from proceeds, these are actually set against results that will be obtained (certainly or with a certain probability) in the future but are already known, as they represent the solution of the game. Nobody will make a commitment unless the result of the market game is already known; the commitment still retains the nature of a bid. Thus either firms expend only *when* they participate to the market game (bids) or they expend only *if* the results of the game are known (commitments). In any case there is analytical contemporaneity of costs and proceeds over the time period over which strategies are defined: costs are not 'sunk' in the sense of implying a finance constraint, as they do not come before proceeds in an essential way.[5]

In this intertemporal equilibrium context the time articulation of the strategy is actually re-absorbed, due to the *ex post* perspective that implies taking into account the strategy over time as a whole, whether

---

[5] This is common to fixed-cost models and flow-cost models, to models with a simultaneous-move structure and with a leader-follower structure, to models where a certain degree of approbriability is introduced by relaxing the assumption of perfect patent protection, and to models that no longer consider a single innovation but a sequence of innovations; that is, to all the models of this kind.

the game is one shot or extending over a succession of periods.[6] An essentially timeless production process, in the nature of an (intertemporal) allocation of resources, is behind this. The logic of substitution, and exchange, prevails in this view of the process of production of technology.[7] No surprise then that, looking from this exchange vantage-point, authors like Dasgupta and Stiglitz (1980), Gilbert and Newbery (1982), and Vickers (1986) in their analyses of R&D strategies end up by focusing on the market, namely on market structure in the traditional sense of number of firms that make up the market. This, on the other hand, will differ according to the characteristics of the behaviour functions of the agents that determine the solution of the game, and hence according to the R&D strategy followed. The logical connection between organization and market failure is thus blurred as the very notion of market failure fades away. This is defined in fact in relation to an optimal configuration of the market which is the only one that leads to an efficient allocation of resources. The above analysis shifts the focus to the different market forms that, although no longer Pareto optimal, are still brought about by optimizing behaviour mechanisms in different information contexts.[8]

In this kind of analysis the point is that the agents form rational expectations, that is, they know the characteristics of the post-entry game, which obviously cancels any disequilibrium co-ordination problem. As Eaton (1987) has stressed, this is a desirable feature of any concept of equilibrium. However, the fact is that 'there may be no agreement about the rules of the post-entry game, and there may be periods of disequilibrium before any order is established. Financial positions of the firm may then acquire an important role' (Dixit 1980, p. 95). This is when co-ordination problems arise, and we have already seen in Chapter 2 how much, and in what sense, this is true.

---

[6] This is quite similar to what we have seen happen in the analysis of the Traverse where, notwithstanding the explicit consideration of the time structure of production and of costs that are actually dissociated in time from proceeds, particular assumptions reduce the Traverse to a sequence of steps determined beforehand, and hence keep the analysis in an *ex post* perspective. We shall go deeper into this point in Section 4.8 below.

[7] Clearly, here an innovative strategy is not associated with the construction of a new productive capacity, which would imply instead a focus on intertemporal complementarity.

[8] Going to the extreme Fischer (1989) points out that this kind of model has produced a taxonomy of particular cases which refer to various assumptions about behaviours and which fail to provide a robust analysis of real situations. 'The principal result of theory is to show that nearly anything can happen.' (ibid. p. 117).

4.4. THE FIRM AND THE MARKET AS SUBSTITUTES

Two slightly different but similar interpretations of the meaning and the role of organization have come up in the last two sections in connection with different attempts to endogenize technology: organizational co-ordination to replace market transactions in view of market failure, and commitments to co-ordinate strategies, always aimed at obtaining an optimal allocation of resources. It is therefore within the context of the analysis of technology that a certain concept of organization has been evoked.

The modern theory of the firm, however, goes beyond technology to focus directly on organization. And this, we shall see—not taking properly into account production and technology—is exactly the main limitation of this theory.

Coase (1937) is generally acknowledged as the starting-point of the modern theory of the firm, and of the interpretation of the latter as an organization. Information is still at the centre of the stage, but the problem now is deciding which form of organization is best suited to the prevailing information structure. There are two main lines of development of this analysis. The first, as stressed by Coase himself, goes back to Knight and focuses on the asymmetric attitudes towards risk of employers and employees. This directly evokes the Arrovian asymmetry of information which is explicitly behind this line and leads to principal-agent models and to the analysis of opportunistic behaviours (e.g. moral hazard and adverse selection).[9]

The other line of development of this analysis, that of the 'incomplete contracts' (see, for example, Grossman and Hart 1986) originates from Coase himself, when he stresses the particular nature of the employment contract, whose object (what the employee is required to do) cannot be precisely specified: it will depend in fact on the situation in which the firm will find itself, and this, in an uncertain context, cannot be predetermined. It is the nature of this contract—not to specify a unique course of action but just to set an agreement that frames the relationship between the parties—that forms the basis of the *raison d'être* of the firm. This is the aspect of Coase's analysis developed by the theory of incomplete contracts. No asymmetry of information is postulated here; both the principal and the agent are

---

[9] Credit rationing (Stiglitz and Weiss 1981, 1992) and efficiency wages (Stiglitz 1982) are some of the most interesting problems dealt with in this context.

unable to determine what the content of the contract will be in the future.

Reference to the impossibility of describing a priori the totality of the states of nature and hence of stipulating contracts in relation to all possible future contingencies seems to place the incomplete contracts theories of the firm in an *ex ante* perspective. It seems to evoke, in a way, the problem of the construction of a productive capacity the final configuration of which we are not able to forecast, that is, to go in the direction of interpreting production as a process of the creation of resources as stressed in Section 1.7 above. However, this is not so. As a matter of fact in these models the basic problem remains that of allocation; not so much of allocation of resources, though, as of residual decision rights in case of the occurrence of a bad state of nature. A normative vision prevails: the object of the analysis is to prescribe the best possible behaviour in the context of expected indeterminacy, which means to stipulate in the contract who will have control when the state of nature reveals itself.[10]

Reference to incomplete contracts should have led to a reconsideration of the concept of efficiency had it been considered that the revision of strategies along the way implies a transaction cost. What about transaction costs, another Coasian heritage, in the light of the above two characterizations of the theory of the firm? According to Coase, different transaction costs between the firm and the market determine the boundaries of the former. Thus transaction cost economics (Williamson 1985, 1989) assesses hierarchical organizations in terms of their efficiency at economizing on the costs that emerge in the process of allocating resources.

When the focus is on the asymmetry of information the idea is that asymmetry, due to opportunistic behaviour, implies a cost of acquiring information. Transaction costs subject to *ex post* opportunism will then benefit if appropriate safeguards are devised *ex ante*, and this justifies particular kinds of contracts (leading e.g. to vertical restraints or vertical integration).

The interpretation of transaction costs within the incomplete contracts perspective is more interesting. In a way this recalls the Hicksian

---

[10] This is actually what is behind Aoki's analysis of different financial systems for the firm (Aoki 1990). In the Japanese case it is the Main Bank—the manager of a loan consortium—that will retain the residual control rights and hence will decide what to do if and when there is a crisis (a bad state of nature), while in a market system it is the market that will actually attribute the power of control in such a case.

interpretation of transaction costs,[11] which evokes a sequential analytical framework. However, no true sequence—that is, a sequence of periods that from the analytical and the accounting viewpoints do not collapse into a unique period—is actually contemplated in incomplete contracts models. The economic calculus on control rights, in the same way as that related to R&D strategies, is actually carried out within an intertemporal equilibrium context. Allocation, though of control rights, is still the issue; production remains in the background, and it is always production in the sense of exchange. Transaction costs refer to intertemporal correlated choices, but these always concern 'substitution' problems.[12] Thus the truly interesting idea behind the concept of sequence—intertemporal 'complementarity'—is not perceived. And as a consequence the capital element in transaction costs cannot be properly taken into account.

What does all this depend on? First of all, on the idea that markets and organizations have to be looked at as different institutions in the sense of alternative means of co-ordination. But that is not all. 'A fundamental feature of the new institutional economics is that it retains the centrality of markets and exchange . . . [and that] all phenomena are to be explained by translating them into (or deriving them from) market transactions based upon negotiated contracts.' (Simon 1991, p. 26). Now a theory of the firm aiming to understand processes of qualitative change (and all the more if these imply the creation of resources) must give up the idea of looking at things from the vantage-point of the exchange. It must go beyond the consideration of co-ordination issues in the restricted sense of an intertemporal substitution of resources to focus on the intertemporal complementarity which is the essence of production interpreted as the construction of new productive options.

4.5. ORGANIZATIONAL DESIGN

We have shown in Chapter 1 that intertemporal complementarity, the backbone of a process of change, comes to the fore when the 'definition'

---

[11] Hicks (1935a), as is well known, was the first to stress the implications of the consideration of the cost of making transactions.

[12] As a matter of fact this is as far as Hicks himself goes. His analysis of liquidity (Hicks 1967, 1974), originating from the earlier consideration of transaction costs, in fact leads to a definition of liquidity itself as the matter of 'a related sequence of choices', that is, as a means of intertemporal substitution of assets.

moment of a productive option is explicitly taken into account. This is typically (albeit not exclusively) the case when we look at production and technology within an *ex ante* perspective. Modern analyses of the firm, however, as stressed above, essentially abstract from the very consideration of the production process.

The analysis of the firm proposed by Aoki (1984, 1988, 1990) is an important although an intermediate step in the right direction. Production comes back explicitly onto the stage, thus making it possible to evoke problems like growth and learning. However, although Aoki's analysis contains most of the ingredients relevant for a study of the process of economic change interpreted as a *creation* of resources, it is still carried out within an allocative framework that stresses *substitution* in an intertemporal equilibrium context. In particular (1990) the analysis is aimed at comparing the efficiency of different organizational structures of the firm in terms of their abilities to compensate for mistakes and the occurrence of uncertain events.[13] It is while carrying out this comparison—namely between a vertical and centralized structure which mimics the American ('A') type of firms and a horizontal and decentralized structure which represents the Japanese ('J') type of firms—that the step towards coming back to the consideration of production is made. While in fact in the 'A' firm co-ordination and production still appear as completely separate functions, co-ordination is explicitly related to the production process in the analysis of the organizational design of the 'J' firm, where intershops, horizontal communication provides the basis for the adjustment of the centralized general production guideline to external shocks. This kind of co-ordination, on the other hand, helps to bring about learning in the form of on-the-spot knowledge and rapid problem-solving, and hence is behind the growth capability of the firm.[14]

However, all this is not (and cannot) be translated into an effective analysis of the process of the creation of resources. This is because the theory of the firm underlying Aoki's analysis is that of a complex system of intra- and inter-firm relationships. In particular a firm is characterized by a coherent organizational design that results from combining a given mode of co-ordination (vertical or horizontal) with

---

[13] Efficiency, with respect to the firm, is defined in terms of the cost of organizing particular activities.

[14] It is important to stress here that Aoki's analysis focuses on a firm involved in a growth process, thus shifting from a static context (still prevailing in the modern analyses of the firm) to a dynamic one.

a scheme of incentives (market-oriented contracts or rank hierarchies). This coherent organizational design, according to Aoki, tends to favour innovative processes, namely to generate learning processes which bring about specific quasi-rents. These are organizational quasi-rents, that result from the mutual commitments of employers and employees within the firm, and relational quasi-rents, group-specific economic returns arising from the co-operation between firms (1984, 1988).

Organizational quasi-rents are defined as total proceeds net of prime costs. They are devoted in the first place to financing growth expenditures. What remains is divided between dividends to shareholders and employees' premium earnings through a process, portrayed as a game, which converges to an equilibrium position that reflects the relative bargaining power of shareholders and employees. It appears that in this sort of process the arguments of the utility functions of the players have a crucial role. As a matter of fact 'the organizational equilibrium is the state in which neither of the game players (the participants of the firm) can raise its utility without risking a higher expected loss of utility owing to the possible withdrawal of cooperation by the other players' (1984, p. 73). In particular, the consideration of investment as an implicit variable in the bargaining process (on the growth rate of the firm) implies that the employees can derive benefit from growth because their intertemporal utility function includes as an argument the present value of their future earnings. As a consequence, in a steady state the coalitional firm pursues a higher growth rate than that which a short-run price maximization would warrant. The main conclusion of this equilibrium analysis is that the differences in the preferences for growth explain the differences in the growth performances.

At the heart of Aoki's model there are thus given intertemporal utility functions on which both the incentive system and the coordination mode are based. This is consistent with an image of the firm solving problems of *allocation* (although intertemporal ones) in an equilibrium perspective, not with that of a firm dealing with out-of-equilibrium processes that endogenously *create* knowledge[15] and resources over time. Sunk costs, typically associated with a learning process, are considered, yet are taken care of by means of an inter-

---

[15] As a matter of fact the learning process considered comes down to an acquisition of information from an exogenously changing environment.

The Market and the Firm 93

temporal redistribution which once again is clearly in the nature of a reallocation of resources. Thus in the case of the 'J' firm workers are required to share these costs and to accept lower wages, and less consumption, today, in order to insure the growth of the firm and hence greater advantages tomorrow (claims for seniority payments, retirement compensation and so on). If we were looking for them we would have found in this model the microfoundations of endogenous growth theory.

In conclusion, the novelty of Aoki's analysis is that he does not focus on the firm as a substitute for the market. He is interested, rather, in differences among firms looked at as production systems, in characterizing and comparing different systems whose efficiency is analysed in relation to given characteristics of the environment, namely the level, variety, and volatility of external final demand. However—although 'being in relation to' rather than 'being a substitute for' is thus stressed—no analytical link is established between the organization of production, as reflected by the firm, and the functioning of the market, and hence no interaction between the firm and the market is worked out. Once again the co-ordination problem is confined to the transmission of information in view of an intertemporal allocation of resources. The reason for this is the equilibrium nature of the model underlying an analysis still focused on steady-state solutions. For the above-mentioned link to be brought to light a truly dynamic analysis of the firm is needed that matches the dynamic context evoked by the analytical ingredients already present in Aoki's analysis.

4.6. THE CO-ORDINATION OF PRODUCTION

The analysis of a process of qualitative change implies passing from the consideration of the 'utilization' moment of the production process to that of its 'definition' moment, i.e. passing from the consideration of the production decisions of the firm concerning the utilization of a given productive capacity, as in Aoki's analysis, to the consideration of investment decisions in the sense of construction of this productive capacity.

Transaction costs are intrinsically associated with these kinds of investment decisions, provided they are properly redefined. As already mentioned at the beginning of this chapter, they are in fact an important aspect of investment in the sense of 'construction', a phenomenon characterized by a sequential structure and intertemporal complementarity.

The relation between transaction costs and a sequential context has already been mentioned. As a matter of fact

> as soon as transaction costs are taken into account attention can no longer be concentrated solely on the next decision point, but we have to consider the pattern of investment over several periods not taken separately; and we are faced with a sequential context where considerations of timing come in, related to the occurrence of emergencies, or the appearance of opportunities, whose date of arising cannot be exactly foreseen (Amendola 1991, p. 335).

Within this context transaction costs acquire the character of investment and disinvestment costs. This is the aspect of transaction costs stressed by Hicks who, however, looks at investment in the perspective of a choice between real and financial assets. The problem then is that this choice may reveal itself in time as a bad one which can only be undone at a cost. Liquidity is the way to deal with this kind of cost: 'it gives time to think' and to wait, and hence allows 'that the form of investment should be wisely chosen' (Hicks 1974, p. 57), so as not to incur in investment and disinvestment costs. In this analysis, as we have already mentioned in Section 4.4, we are dealing with intertemporal correlated choices that still concern substitution problems.

Intertemporal complementarity comes to the fore instead when investment is no longer interpreted as choice between given assets, and hence between given options, but as the creation of (new) options. Transaction costs are then no longer the costs of making transactions in the sense of exchange (even if it be intertemporal exchange) but the costs referred to a sequential process of production interpreted as structuring anew.

> Not only does the innovative organization make strategic choices concerning the types of 'transactions'—that is, products and processes that are generally referred to as 'technologies'—in which to invest, but by definition, an innovative strategy requires that the organization also *develops* the productive resources that it controls. Insofar as the innovative organization is successful in developing, as well as maintaining control over, its productive resources, it will come to possess 'organization specific' assets, both human and physical, with unique productive capabilities (Lazonick 1991, p. 217).

Investment and disinvestment then acquire a different meaning. In the development process just mentioned costs are dissociated in time from proceeds[16] and hence are 'sunk' costs. In a way all kinds of investment entail some sunk cost, but the sunk costs associated with a process of qualitative change are a different thing from the costs of reversing a choice which comes down to simply moving from one asset to another, and raise different problems. The sunk costs of the investment in a process of creation of resources will only be recovered when (and if) the process itself is actually established.[17] The cost of disinvestment is then the vanishing of the whole process if this proves not to be viable. Liquidity is once again required to deal with these costs; not, however, because it makes it possible to 'think' before making an investment decision but because it makes it possible to actually carry out an investment decision. As has been shown in particular in Chapter 2, it is the transaction function of liquidity, not the precautionary function, that now matters.

This interpretation of transaction costs, whose Hicksian derivation has already been stressed, has little to do with Williamson's transaction cost approach, which, as Lazonick (1991) rightly points out 'puts forth a theory of the adaptive organization and ignores the role of the business enterprise in the innovation process'. An adaptive organization 'merely tries to minimize its cost or maximize its profit on the basis of existing productive resources.' (ibid. p. 197); while an innovative organization, as we have just seen, in order to contribute to the process of economic development, 'must develop its productive resources in order to produce a superior product at competitive cost (product innovation), a salable product at lower cost (process innovation), or both.' (ibid. p. 199). A process of creation of resources and new productive options is clearly the business of an innovative organization, and in this case, we shall see in what follows, what is critical to economic performance is how the organization deals with 'relations', not how it deals with transactions.

---

[16] This is the distinctive feature of investment in fixed capital, the typical 'construction' investment. To pretend to pass from a circulating capital model to one that considers investment in long-lived physical capital and to assume at the same time that 'input costs and output revenues are contemporaneous in each subperiod' (Greenwald and Stiglitz 1989, p. 10) is nothing but an analytical trick.

[17] This means not only taking into account the whole period of construction of the new productive capacity—which is likely to have a considerable length as, before construction in a proper sense, it implies experimenting, pilot plants, and so forth—but also going beyond that point, until the stream of receipts from the new output has reached a certain size. That is, until the entrepreneur 'reaches calmer waters . . . in sight of his big output and can begin to have confidence (of which he can persuade his banker) in his ability to go on selling it.' (Hicks 1989, p. 119).

4.7. THE MARKET AND THE FIRM AS COMPLEMENTS

The main connecting lines of an analysis of the relation between market and organization within the perspective of a process of qualitative change are derived from Kaldor's paper of 1972 on 'The Irrelevance of Equilibrium Economics'. In exploring the main implications of increasing returns on economic progress Kaldor stresses that markets stand at the core of economic processes in so far as they are considered as instruments for 'transmitting impulses to economic change' (ibid. p. 1240). He also stresses that equilibrium analysis is not suited to dealing with economic change. In this context in fact, in contrast to what Say's Law maintains, supply does not generate a demand of an equal amount. Every reorganization or restructuring of productive activities is the source of further changes which can be characterized by persistent differences between production and demand.[18] This evokes the 'creative' functions of the market. As a matter of fact 'the pattern of use of resources at any one time can be no more than a link in the chain of an unending sequence, and the very distinction vital to equilibrium economies between resource-creation and resource-allocation loses its validity.' (ibid. p. 1245).

In this light a complementarity relation between the market and the main actor of the process of change, the firm, becomes all the more clear. This kind of relation was originally at the centre of the analysis of the classical economists but, unfortunately, it very soon dropped out of sight. As McNulty (1984) has pointed out,

> economics emerged from the hands of Adam Smith as an analytical blend of firm and market forces. But it was not a balanced blend. The analytical core of his work was in the operation of the pricing system, and this became, with the subsequent development of economics, increasingly the focus of the theory ... With J.B. Clark the concept of production was explicitly narrowed to exchange and distribution (ibid. pp. 239–41).

This meant that only the role of the firm in the pricing system would be considered. Now, when production is reduced to exchange and distribution it loses its essential time dimension, that is, it loses the perspective within which the complementarity relation between market and firm can be perceived. This kind of relation, in fact, is the

---

[18] The analyses carried out by means of the model expounded in Part II of this book will make it possible to furnish a rigorous basis for this statement.

The Market and the Firm

backbone of a process that takes place over time. To remain with Kaldor, this can be seen with reference to increasing returns, provided these are not considered the result of the degree of utilization of a given productive capacity, as Kaldor considers them, but are associated with the production of processes rather than of commodities (see Section 1.3 above). This is a point which had been clearly understood by Smith, as stressed by Richardson. 'In the *Wealth of Nations* competition is given more to do than equate demands and supplies within the context of a given industrial structure and a given technology; the invisible hand has also to adapt both structure and technology to the fresh opportunities created by expanding markets.' (Richardson 1975, p. 353).

Behind the complementarity relation in time between the market and the firm there is the complementarity relation of productive resources within the firm, at each point of time and over time. 'The neoclassical contribution was to eliminate the concept of the wages fund and, with it, the idea of fixed factors proportion, by conceptualizing the firm as the institution through which capital and labour would be efficient substitute for each other in the production process.' (McNulty 1984, p. 243). Thus, by focusing as we do on the firm in its capacity to organize production processes and to make production factors complementary, we come back in a way to a pre-neoclassical approach.

We have already stressed that production of processes is in the nature of a change, and that it appears as a sequential process by which productive options come about and, possibly, new resources are created. The structuring of new production processes over time, on the other hand, implies that inputs come before output in an essential way, so that production costs in each period cannot be set against corresponding proceeds. What happens in each period, and not what happens over the whole sequence of periods, then comes to the fore. This points to a problem of sunk costs in the form of a lag between the time profile of output (proceeds) and that of inputs (expenditure) as the result of the crucial time dimension of production.[19] In this context costs appear in a different light and raise different problems. How to deal with the sunk costs implied by out-of-equilibrium processes of

---

[19] Learning and specific assets always imply sunk costs. Thus in an *ex ante* perspective, where production appears mainly as a learning process bringing about new specific resources, the problem is even more complex.

change is what now matters. The standard efficiency problem—choice of the optimal allocation in order to minimize costs—is no longer relevant.[20]

The traditional image of the firm identified with a production function defined by the technology obviously fades away. Technology appears in fact as the outcome of a process which must be organized and carried out: organization leads technology. The task of the firm is then still co-ordination, but no longer in the sense of allocating given resources, rather in that of organizing a process of qualitative change, which often entails the creation of resources so as to make it viable.[21] This is the specific task of the firm interpreted as an organization. Dealing with the sunk costs of a process of change which implies learning requires establishing a wide range of co-operative relationships over time (not only internally but also between different firms, between firms and banks, and so on) as well as market relationships over successive periods; and this is all the more true when the change undertaken implies learning. This different image of the firm also implies a different relationship with the environment. As long as we keep looking in an *ex post* perspective at a firm whose boundaries are defined by a given technology and which must relate to a given market to carry out its allocative task, we stick to the idea of environment as an exogenous constraint, of which technology and the market are specific expressions. But when we move the attention to a process of change that the firm itself must organize, and that most of the time involves learning and structuring anew, the environment necessarily becomes a strategic variable, to be moulded according to and as a functional part of the strategy pursued (Amendola and Bruno 1990).

We thus come to an image of the firm that overcomes both the distinction between a micro and a macro definition and that between the firm itself and its environment. Organizing and implementing a

---

[20] As a matter of fact this is a problem that in an *ex ante* perspective cannot even be properly defined, not only because production and cost functions canot be specified, but also because the mere presence of resources 'in excess', which are a necessary condition for the firm to be able to undertake a creation process, prevents the firm itself from being efficient in the short term.

[21] A hint at this exclusive role of the firm in organizing a process which implies a modification of resources and not only their efficient allocation was given by Alchian and Demsetz (1972) who define the firm as 'a device for *enhancing competition* [emphasis added] among sets of inputs resources as well as a device for more efficiently rewarding the inputs' (ibid. p. 795).

process by which new productive options (and technology) are brought about also entails simultaneously redefining intra- and inter-relationships which make the firm change its configuration and articulation within a context that itself becomes modified and redefined together with the firm.[22]

In this interpretation of the relation between market (the environment) and organization (the firm) the latter is no longer regarded as the elementary analytical particle, but is already in a way an aggregate of elements which exhibit different relations among them. The nature of these relations is at the heart of the analysis of processes of change, an analysis which has thus an essential macro aspect.

This means that we can only make a dynamic analysis—concerning growth, learning, and the creation of resources—by referring to aggregation processes, whereby these are read as restructuring processes. If we stick to the analysis of the elementary analytical particle, the changes considered are reversible. It is only through the consideration of relations which are structured into different aggregations that we introduce irreversibility, real time, and hence true dynamics.[23] This blurs the distinction between micro and macro in the analysis of market and organization, and at the same time stresses their interaction in structuring coherent innovative systems, that is, their nature as 'complements' in a process of change.

4.8. OUT-OF-EQUILIBRIUM STRATEGIES

Modern theories of the firm—as we have seen—are mainly concerned to define organizational forms that aim at sketching out optimal frontiers between the firm and the market, whether this means finding the optimal number of firms in a given market or explaining different (weaker or stronger) forms of integration. This comes out as the result of rational behaviours in incomplete and asymmetric information

---

[22] This is what Schumpeter was actually hinting at with his famous sentences 'add as many stagecoaches, you will never get a railway' and 'in general it is not the owner of stagecoaches who builds railways' (Schumpeter 1954, p. 66). Along the same lines see Morishima (1992 p. 140).

[23] The organizational structure that successfully implements an innovative strategy *extends the bounds of the organization's rationality* and *alters the behavior of those who participate in the enterprise*. In effect, when an organization puts in place an organizational structure to implement an innovative strategy, it does so in order to manage its economic environment' (Lazonick 1991, p. 224).

contexts. A historical perspective à la Chandler (1977, 1990, 1992) would focus instead on how organizational forms change in time, and on the processes through which they adapt to exogenous or endogenous changes in the environment. However, adapting to change is only one aspect of the more active and complex role of the firm in a process of qualitative change. This role is to make viable the out-of-equilibrium process through which the change itself takes place.

A process of change is in the first place a process of acquisition of information, of knowledge. According to Marshall (1920):

> Knowledge is our most powerful engine of production; it enables us to subdue Nature and forces her to satisfy our wants. Organization aids knowledge; it has many forms, e.g. that of single business, that of various businesses in the same trade, that of various trades relatively to one another, and that of the State providing security for all and help for many (ibid. p. 115).

The statement that organization aids knowledge shifts the focus from information in itself to the conditions under which the process of the acquisition of knowledge (learning) takes place; from the 'production of commodities' to the 'production of processes', in Georgescu-Roegen's parlance (see Section 1.3 above). The 'construction' of organizations in Marshall's sense, that is, of organizations which carry out processes of creation of information, is then highlighted. So is the consideration of the interaction of these processes with the intertemporal complementarity of the phases of construction and utilization of a new productive capacity, which is the physical expression of a qualitative change.[24] This construction is itself in the nature of an out-of-equilibrium process: what matters is the sequence of attempts and mistakes which sketch it out rather than its result. Co-ordination over time of this process so as to make it viable is then the crucial problem. Not an intertemporal co-ordination over the sequence taken as a whole, though, but one carried out step by step, a sort of adaptive control of the process of change.

But when and why does a co-ordination problem actually arise in this context?

For a process of change to take place investments must be decided and actually undertaken which, after a phase of construction, will

---

[24] Information is obviously incomplete when a qualitative change is considered. Organizations and institutions—including of course the market—are there to provide the supplementary information required for the process of change to be actually undertaken.

result in a new productive capacity to be matched by a corresponding demand for final output. Organizational strategies which involve both competitive and co-operative relations are required for this purpose. As Richardson (1990) puts it, the profitability of any investment project depends on the setting up of a satisfactory amount of both complementary and competitive investments along the way. The volume of competitive investment must not exceed a critical limit set by the demand available, and the volume of complementary investment has to go beyond a minimal threshold for the investment project considered to be feasible. Of course if entrepreneurs immediately had complete information on all existing investment projects no co-ordination problem would arise as eventually there would be no imbalance between supply and demand on the market for final output. However,

> it seems more reasonable to assume that entrepreneurs will generally learn of the investment commitments of others only after a certain period of time which, for convenience, will be called the 'transmission interval'. The duration of this interval, it seems safe to presume, would not be greater than the gestation period, after which the extra flow of goods would have themselves felt on the market, but could be shorter than this, where entrepreneurs were able to obtain evidence about the amount of construction under way. (ibid. p. 51).

A specific co-ordination problem would then be involved, a problem that becomes much more complex if we also take into account another lag: the construction lag which characterizes the production process. This problem would then arises at the junction of these two lags: the phase of construction of productive capacity—which entails sunk costs—and the delay of transmission of information—which implies uncertainty. Both lags must be taken into account in the analysis, because cancelling one of them also cancels the co-ordination problem. Thus absence of the latter lag in the Hicksian analysis of the Traverse—which relies essentially on the existence of a construction lag—guarantees the equilibrium between supply and demand in each period of the sequence through which a superior technique is adopted by the economy (see Section 5.5 below). Meanwhile overlooking the lag represented by the construction phase, even in presence of incomplete information leading to mistakes in investment, allows not only a revision of plans, but also for this to be instantaneous, so as to cancel imbalances at the very moment of their appearance.

Within this perspective modern theories of the firm are not much more effective than the traditional theory of the firm in a context of perfect competition. The game theoretic approach to firms' strategy already mentioned in Section 4.3 shares with Richardson's analysis the vision of investment as an irreversible 'commitment'; however, the focus is on intertemporal optimization behaviours which assume that nobody will make commitments unless the result of the market game is already known. This comes down to cancelling the delay of transmission of information and, together with it, the co-ordination problem. On the other hand the incomplete contracts' approach focuses on incomplete information and on the existence of a delay in the transmission of information which calls for stipulation of contracts contemplating the allocation of residual control rights (see Section 4.4 above). However, these rights authorize a reconsideration of strategies and investment choices, in relation to a new state of nature, without considering the irreversibilities and the time constraints implied by a phase of construction which thus is not actually taken into account. And this, once again, removes the co-ordination problem.

Out of equilibrium, when the two above-mentioned lags are properly taken into account and a co-ordination problem is then involved, this, as has often been repeated, must be dealt with in the light of the criterion of the viability of the process of change undergone. This means in the first place re-establishing the harmony between construction and utilization, disturbed by the structural modification implied by a qualitative change, so as not to have excessive imbalances between costs and proceeds and between supply and demand of final output on which viability depends in the end.

This is what the firm is required to achieve: a strategy that, we shall see, needs primarily implicit or explicit agreements with other firms—that is, market connections usually considered as market imperfections. However, these connections may still be interpreted as a means of having an equilibrium co-ordination, as they are aimed at equilibrating the different plans of the various agents. An out-of-equilibrium strategy, thus, cannot be confined to market connections but needs to take into account the existence of disequilibria to which the economy must adapt step by step. This calls for consideration of quantity adjustments besides the price ones. As a matter of fact price relations, the only market relations usually considered, give information on what exists, that is, they allow learning in the sense of getting to know what is already there, not learning in the sense of a creation of information, which is the distinctive aspect of an out-of-equilibrium process of the creation of resources. Price rigidity—as rendered for instance by a fixed-price hypothesis (Hicks 1985, 1989)—on the one hand allows disequilibria to come to the surface through the appearance of stocks, and on the other is the expression of a behaviour which, through the management of these stocks, tries to correct the sheer working of price adjustment mechanisms. In particular in the utilization phase, when the problem is the gradual harmonization of final demand with the existing productive capacity, the role of sales intermediaries is paramount as regards avoiding strong fluctuations in prices which would be a threat to the required harmony over time between supply and demand.[25]

Out of equilibrium, in a context without complete information and where bounded behaviours are relevant, constraints emerge at each successive step. A sequential strategy, by establishing new and changing relations with other subjects in order to deal with these constraints, appears as a tool for acquiring information and knowledge on the way.

Constraints, in a sequential process of change, are not only limits to the activity carried out but can also help to keep the economy within the boundaries of a stability corridor. The relevant constraints—not only financial and human constraints, but also established relations (such as, for example, collusive behaviours)—are inherited from the past, as brought about by the evolution of the economy shaped by technology and the prevailing forms of organization. However, these constraints can be strengthened or relaxed, or new ones can be brought about, as the result of deliberate choices aimed at structuring new and different connections and forms of organization. These choices reflect the need to deal with the problem of the sunk costs, which 'occurs because the production and sale of the enterprise's output occur neither instantaneously nor with certainty' (Lazonick 1991, p. 198). This is another way of evoking the problem of the existence of both a construction lag and a delay of transmission of information.

---

[25] Of course this kind of co-ordination is not required when a state of equilibrium prevails in the economy, that is, when each firm persists in the behaviour already adopted because it is aware that the behaviour of every other firm in the economy will not be altered since technology and customers' preferences are expected to remain unchanged. In this context the co-ordination role of the price mechanism is sufficient.

Different examples of dealing with these problems in different contexts can be mentioned, from the introduction of a multidivisional organization of the firm to the realization of vertical integrations or vertical restraints. However, unlike in the standard analysis, there is no optimal form of organization—that is, an optimal sharing of the task of co-ordination between the firm and the market—when we have to deal with an innovation process. Furthermore, as already stressed, 'forms of organization which are best fitted for one environment may generate knowledge which makes them less appropriate' (Loasby 1993a, p. 18). Thus changing organizational arrangements is the theme actually at the heart of the analysis of the complementary role of markets and organizations out of equilibrium, which has deep implications for the definition of appropriate strategic behaviour.

Standard strategic behaviour, aimed at choosing the best solution out of a given set, implies: (1) identifying an opportunity offered by the market, and (2) being able to mobilize the resources required in order to take advantage of this opportunity. Generic resources are considered within this context, a context which defines the finding of the optimal solution as an essentially timeless problem. Then if opportunities change, resources can be reassembled so as to obtain different (optimal) solutions, and drastic and immediate adaptations are possible. This is what the market sees to. When information failures induce market failures, organization is called in as a substitute for the market; however, the problem is still the immediate (re)adaptation through a (re)assembling of generic resources.

This is no longer so when strategic behaviour concerns a process of innovation involving the creation of resources. In this case there is neither the possibility of fully identifying an opportunity offered by the market nor the possibility of mobilizing whichever resources at whatever moment we need them. The opportunity is not there to be taken advantage of: it must be created, together with the resources that are intrinsic to it and hence help to define it. This can only happen through a process constrained at each successive step by the resources existing at that moment: specific resources, however, which are themselves the outcome of the process under way and that hence are constantly changing their character as the process itself goes on.

In this perspective profit maximization, at a given point of time or over time, becomes meaningless. In the first place because there is no consistency between short-term profit maximization and the long-term objective, and secondly, because out of equilibrium the evolution path is actually unpredictable and so no rational expectations can be formed. Thus an out-of-equilibrium strategy appears as something different from the immediate adaptation of standard strategies. A strategy that takes shape step by step, as does the one evoked by this process, is rather a strategy that assures flexibility, not in the usual sense of *response* and quick adaptation but in the more active and creative sense of a new and different *proposal*. The existence and the modification along the way of different types of constraints, particular organizational arrangements, stable price policies, and the holding of real and financial reserves are all elements of a strategy for the acquisition of information aimed at preventing excessive shocks from affecting the viability of the out-of-equilibrium process through which qualitative change takes place.[26]

This strategy will be that of the representative firm portrayed in the model which we shall use in Part II of this book to analyse at the macro level various processes of qualitative change. In this sense this chapter, which may have appeared as a wide digression, provides the microfoundations of the analytical framework underlying our modelling. Our model represents a completely different approach to the problem of the microfoundations of macroeconomics with respect to the standard approach focusing on a representative consumer who maximizes his utility function intertemporally.

---

[26] Along the same lines, although with reference to the specific problem of making the required amounts of competitive and complementary investments possible, see Richardson (1990, chapters 3 and 8).

5
Change

5.1. ECONOMIC DYNAMICS: METHODS AND PROBLEMS

It is a widespread opinion that dynamic analysis depends on using models that employ dynamic methods, which is clearly due to the fact that the distinction between statics and dynamics was not originally an economic distinction, but just 'an echo of a far older distinction in mathematical mechanics' (Hicks 1965, p. 4). Steady growth has been reckoned to be a dynamic method (Hicks 1965, chapter 12); the introduction of non-linearities is said to lead to dynamic models, such as chaotic models (Baumol and Benhabib 1989).

Reference to steady growth, non-linearities and the like, is not enough to define dynamic analysis, though; it might even have very little to do with it, as we shall see. Dynamic analysis, in economics, depends on dealing with issues which are in the nature of dynamic problems rather than on referring to supposedly dynamic methods. But what is a dynamic problem? It all depends, of course, on what we mean by 'change'; it is the consideration of change, we all certainly agree, that actually makes dynamics differ from statics. In the above-mentioned case of steady growth—an equilibrium over time which amounts to nothing other than a static equilibrium continuously inflated by multiplication by a scalar[1]—change has a sheer quantitative meaning. It means an increase in the level of activity of a productive structure whose essential features and ways of functioning remain untouched once its equilibrium analytical configuration has been defined. In a different way, but in the same perspective, the introduction of non-linearities is only aimed at making possible the definition of an equilibrium configuration of the path followed by the economy, although one different from regular growth. These are very reductive interpretations of change: surely it

---

[1] The only difference with a static equilibrium is that in steady growth it is no longer the basic economic magnitudes that are (exogenously) given, but the parameters which determine the movements through time of these magnitudes. Hicks himself changed his mind on this subject and came to consider steady growth 'on the edge between statics and dynamics' (1985, p. 9).

cannot be all we have in mind when we think of 'dynamics' as referred to economic phenomena.

The distinction made by Schumpeter between growth, explicitly defined as a quantitative phenomenon, and development, a 'discontinuous change that comes from within the economic process because of the very nature of that process' (Georgescu-Roegen 1976*b*, p. 245) helps us to grasp the point. That is, that qualitative change—a change that implies a 'structural modification' which can only be brought about through a process in real, irreversible time—is involved whenever a thorough dynamic problem is contemplated. Innovation, which implies the creation of new resources and construction of different choice sets, is the foremost example of qualitative change, but a speeding up of the growth rate or a simple change of the technique in use—as we have already seen in Chapter 1—also have the same nature. In all these cases, the previously existing productive structure is disturbed, its way of functioning is affected, and as a result a problem of 'intertemporal complementarity' arises which calls for 'co-ordination over time' of economic activity[2] to render the process of change undertaken viable. As a matter of fact new aggregates of elements that exhibit different complementarity relations among them have to be shaped to fit a different productive structure with its distinctive way of functioning. It is the nature of these relations, and the way in which they are created and established, that really matters. It is only through the consideration of relations which bring about different aggregations that we introduce real time, irreversibility, and qualitative change. Thus dynamic analysis essentially comes down to the analysis of aggregation processes, whereby these are interpreted as restructuring processes (see Section 4.7 above). Viability is the main problem associated with these processes, and interaction, complementarity, and co-ordination over time, which determine how the processes themselves are actually shaped, are the relevant issues for viability.

Is the equilibrium approach, which is behind most of the so-called dynamic methods, suited to deal with qualitative change and the analytical problems that it involves? In other words, can equilibrium models deal properly with dynamic issues in the above sense? This is the first question to answer, in order to clarify the relation between problems and methods in economic dynamics.

---

[2] A co-ordination which is assured by definition in an equilibrium state.

5.2. THE EQUILIBRIUM APPROACH

Not only regular growth, but also fluctuations can be interpreted as equilibrium phenomena; and in fact they are by mainstream theory. However, 'the equilibrium assumption looks distinctly different, according as it is used in one or another of the . . . branches of economic theory. . . . In Welfare Economics there is no problem; the equilibrium assumption is included in the way the theory is set up' (Hicks 1965, p. 17). This is because the social optimum is defined by a social welfare function, so that the economy is treated as if it consisted of a single individual and hence 'it is the equilibrium choice of that single chooser which *is* the optimum choice. . . . A welfare optimum has to be an equilibrium' (ibid.). Within a normative context, then, equilibrium dynamics is perfectly at ease, not in the sense of determining the actual path which the economy will follow, but in the sense of sketching out the optimum path, that is, the path that will best satisfy a given social objective. In this perspective, focus on individual optimizing behaviour points to intertemporal resource allocation mechanisms as the main determinants of dynamic paths. Various such paths are thus sketched out, including fluctuations, as is typically the case with real business cycles, which are the outcome of optimizing behaviour as an answer to exogenous real shocks (Kydland and Prescott 1982; Long and Plosser 1983; Lucas 1987; Plosser 1989).

It is true that some sort of structural change can be contemplated: whenever we consider a change in technique, for example, or a productivity shock as in real business cycle models, or, as we shall see better in what follows, an enlargement of the list of production goods (Romer 1990) or of consumption goods (Grossman and Helpman 1991). But these are changes that are only brought in to define a certain phenomenon. There is no attempt to bring to light the economic problems that these changes imply: namely, problems of the intertemporal complementarity of production and decision processes and the associated co-ordination problems. As a matter of fact co-ordination of economic activity is always assumed in normative models; this is, of course, by definition. Optimal models always imply an equilibrium over time, and over time co-ordination is assured because the equilibrium assumption implies that expectations are always fulfilled.[3]

---

[3] Intertemporal equilibrium is the natural habitat of normative models. But also in temporary equilibrium models, as we shall see, co-ordination is assured, when these models are supplemented with rational expectations hypotheses.

Positive economics differs from normative economics in a sense that is very relevant to our discussion. Behaviours can be assumed, in order to describe the evolution of the economy, that are not optimizing behaviours. This is typically the case with Solow's original growth model (1956), from which most of modern growth theory stems. The 'behaviouristic' version of growth that this model gives—as opposed to the 'optimizing' version developed later—immediately raises a problem which does not appear in a normative context, though. As the equilibrium assumption is no longer included in the very definition of the path followed by the economy, 'it is to be justified'. In other words the existence of the equilibrium must be proved, and 'even if the equilibrium exists, it has still to be shown that there is a tendency towards it . . . and even if the tendency to equilibrium exists, we must still have sufficient ground to justify the equilibrium assumption if the convergence to equilibrium is very slow' (Hicks 1965, pp. 18–19).

The problem of a 'transitional dynamics' is thus evoked in positive economics, and, in particular, in Solow's model. However, the distinctive analytical implication of a transition, that is, the emergence of a co-ordination problem, is not, and cannot be, considered by Solow. This is because, although stability is evoked, the focus is always on the problem of the existence of an equilibrium configuration of the economy. 'Stability' is strictly linked to 'existence'; as a matter of fact it is ancillary to it.

There is thus a sort of analytical contradiction which emerges: a problem is put forward which cannot be properly dealt with. The assumption of continuous full employment, in Solow's model, actually cancels out the problem associated with the transition hinted at by mentioning the existence of a stability issue: the problem, that is, of resources not being combined in the 'right' proportions.

This is a contradiction that the optimizing version of neoclassical growth theory wipes away. Instead of looking at the evolution of the economy as the outcome of the well-known differential equation

$$\dot{K} = F(K, N, t) - Nc(K, N, t)$$

where K is capital, N the labour force, c consumption per capita, and t, of course, time, under the full employment hypothesis

$$N = N_0 e^{nt},$$

the optimizing version (Cass 1965) focuses on a path of per capita consumption chosen so as to maximize

$$\int_0^\infty e^{-rt}\, u[c(t)]\, N(t)\, dt$$

that is, to maximize the integral of instantaneous utility u with the discount rate r under the technological constraint

$$N(t)\, c(t) + \dot{K} = F(K, N, t).$$

The 'optimizing' version of one-sector growth theory says that the economy behaves *as if* it was solving this problem. You see where the 'co-ordination problem' has vanished here: the production side of the economy just performs what is best for the household. Under favorable assumption, the unique solution to this problem is also the unique competitive equilibrium for this economy (Solow 1992, p. 3).

Thus in the optimizing version, in the same way as in the behaviouristic version, 'the steady state is approached asymptotically by any optimal path from any initial conditions: starting from arbitrary initial conditions the solution to the optimization problem converges to the saddle point' (Solow, ibid. p. 15). But while in the optimizing case the economy is always in equilibrium, not only at the saddle point but also along the path followed to reach it[4]—and this is why the movement along this path can be explicitly dealt with in the model—this is not so in the behaviouristic case, where the economy is in equilibrium only at the saddle point. This explains why out-of-equilibrium positions cannot be explicitly analysed by means of a model which relies on equilibrium assumptions.

5.3. ENDOGENOUS GROWTH

Traditional neoclassical growth theory, both in its 'behaviouristic' and in its 'optimizing' version, has come under fire for two main reasons. The first is that the long-run growth rate of the most important magnitudes of the economy is due to exogenous factors, namely, population growth and the rate of scientific discovery, and hence is not determined within the model. Thus growth depends on demo-

---

[4] As a matter of fact in some optimizing models, as in real business cycle models or in endogenous business cycle models (Benhabib and Nishimura 1979, 1985; Grandmont 1985), no steady state is actually approached by the economy, which keeps following cyclical equilibrium paths.

graphic and technological parameters, not on preference parameters. The latter, through changes in savings, can only affect the level of output (or of capital or consumption), not its growth. Without exogenous technical progress the economy will reach a steady state, in the long run, with a zero growth rate in output per head. This is certainly not a satisfactory conclusion, as it amounts to giving up the idea of actually 'explaining' growth. On the other hand, the theory also implies that all economies which have access to the same improving technology will converge to the same growth rate, at least in the very long run; and we all know that this is not what the evidence shows. The second reason, which is strictly related to the first, is that in this context, as just mentioned, there is no place (or a very marginal one) for economic policy.

Endogenous growth theory aims at removing these limits while keeping the distinctive features of the basic neoclassical model, that is, the equilibrium assumption and the optimizing perspective. The main features of this theory are: the endogenous determination of the long-run growth rate; the possibility of explaining a diversity of performances not only among economies endowed with different resources (that is, in the presence of different initial conditions) but also for those endowed with the same resources; and, finally, the return of economic policy to the centre of the stage.

How have these results been obtained? The specific conclusions of the original neoclassical model (in particular, the tendency to a zero growth rate of per capita quantities in the long run) depend essentially on a resource constraint which implies a falling marginal productivity of capital. We thus have to keep the marginal productivity of capital from falling as capital accumulates to avoid to coming to a standstill. Now, the marginal productivity of capital, in the original model based on a well-behaved aggregate production function equipped with Inada conditions, falls as a result of an increase in the capital intensity of production expressed by the ratio of capital to labour; and this happens because it is assumed that the one factor, capital, can be accumulated while the other, labour, cannot; and substitution between them is admitted. Thus, in order to obtain endogenous growth 'we have to drop the assumption of diminishing returns to capital, or of diminishing returns to any factor that can be accumulated' (Solow 1992, p. 33).

A first way out is to consider only factors which can be accumulated, and which are in a complementarity relation rather than in a substitution relation with each other. This is what is done by Jones and Manuelli (1990), who are able to relax the upper Inada condition—with the result that the marginal productivity of capital no longer tends to zero as the capital–labour ratio goes to infinity—by not considering primary (non-reproducible) factors at all. And, in a similar way, by King and Rebelo (1990), who consider two kinds of capital—physical and human capital—which reproduce themselves without diminishing returns as the primary factor, labour, has actually disappeared.

A second way out—the way actually followed in the papers by Romer (1986) and Lucas (1988) which started the endogenous growth literature—is to introduce increasing returns to scale, which, however, on the one hand are not strictly necessary to obtain endogenous growth,[5] and on the other, as clearly shown by Solow (1992), do not necessarily imply endogenous growth. In other words, increasing returns are neither a necessary nor a sufficient condition for endogenous growth.

Aggregative increasing returns to scale are induced by the external effects of human capital accumulation (Lucas 1988), or come about through an increase in the number of varieties of capital goods (Romer 1990) or of consumer goods (Grossman and Helpman 1991), or through an improvement in the quality of the existing varieties of capital goods (Aghion and Howitt 1992). In all cases they are the result of private decisions (the maximizing actions of individual agents) and not simply an automatic outcome, e.g. of past investment, as in the pioneering article by Arrow (1962) on increasing returns. Thus preference parameters, which did not play an important role in the traditional set-up, come now to the centre of the stage. As a matter of fact the growth rate is eventually made to depend on the rate of time discount and the elasticity of substitution between present and future consumption which determine the saving rate and hence the intensity of the accumulation of whatever factor in the model is reckoned to bring about increasing returns. However, once again, it is accumulation (under very restrictive conditions, as we shall see immediately) that does the trick, not increasing returns to scale, which are a consequence of the specific conditions under which the accumulation process must take place.

---

[5] We have just seen that to consider only reproducible factors equally does the job: and, we shall see in what follows, this is what in the end actually makes endogenous growth possible.

What *is* essential is the assumption of constant returns to capital (. . . interpreted as the whole collection of accumulatable factors of production). The presence of increasing returns to scale is then inevitable, because otherwise the assumption of constant returns to capital would imply negative marginal productivity of non-capital factors . . . It may not be generally recognized how restrictive this assumption is. There is no tolerance for deviation. Lucas emphasized in his 1988 article that a touch of diminishing returns would change the character of the model drastically, making it incapable of generating permanent growth. He did not notice that a touch of increasing returns to capital would do the same . . . The conclusion has to be that this version of the endogenous-growth model is very un-robust. It can not survive without *exactly* constant returns to capital. But you would have to believe in the tooth fairy to expect that kind of luck. (Solow 1994, pp. 49–51).

In Lucas's 1988 model, as just mentioned, increasing returns are brought about by an endogenous process of accumulation of the human capital H. Preference parameters, through the maximization of a utility function, determine the proportion of time u devoted to physical production and that subtracted from it $(1 - u)$ and devoted to the accumulation of human capital (learning and skill acquisition), which is thus governed by the differential equation

$$\dot{H} = \delta\, H\, [1 - u(t)]$$

where δ is a parameter which indicates how effective time spent learning is. Consider now an alternative formulation of this differential equation, that is,

$$\dot{H} = \delta\, H\, [1 - u(t) - l(t)]$$

where l stands for leisure. Solow (1992) shows that if you do that—and leisure enters the utility function whose maximization determines the path of the economy—Lucas's model reduces to the standard neoclassical model and it provides no endogenous growth at all.[6] Without leisure the whole of the labour force is always employed (either working or studying); complementarity between factors, which makes accumulation and endogenous growth possible, is assured by the externality that allows human capital to grow at the same rate as physical capital. Leisure breaks this complementarity relation and sets a limit to the process of accumulation in the same way as non accumulatable primary labour does in the standard neoclassical model.

---

[6] Solow mentions that this result was actually brought to his attention by two Italian economists, Paolo De Santis and Giuseppe Moscarini.

Thus it is the accumulation of complementary factors that eventually allows endogenous growth. However, the conditions of the process of accumulation, expressed by the value of specific parameters and coefficients in the different models, must be quite particular in order to obtain endogenous growth. The value of these parameters, in other words, must be such as not to affect the complementarity relation between factors, which, in particular, comes down to assuming the linearity of specific relations (e.g. between new varieties of capital goods and the amount of human capital allocated to research in discovering these new varieties (Romer 1990), or between the production of skill and the total stock of skills which enters the production function of the skills themselves (Lucas 1988), and so forth).

In any case, it is worth mentioning that all the essential analytical ingredients of endogenous growth theory were already present in Adam Smith's analysis of the process of accumulation. Hicks's modelization of this process brings this clearly to light (Hicks 1965, chapter 4). Thus we can see that, according to Smith, productive resources are complementary and hence fully accumulatable, that increasing returns come about as the result of the accumulation of resources, that the intensity of the process of accumulation depends on the fraction of resources devoted to 'gross investment' (which sustains 'productive' labour) and that, finally, equilibrium is assured at each successive step of the process by the equality between investment and *ex ante* saving. Which is exactly what endogenous growth is all about.

5.4. TRANSITIONAL DYNAMICS

Focus on endogenous sources of growth—whether an increase in the saving rate and hence in the fraction of output invested, as in the most simple models, or a diversion of resources into R&D so as to speed up the process of innovation, as in the most sophisticated ones—is the distinctive contribution of endogenous growth theory. However, the appearance of a productive capacity with a different structure or the production of a new technology are not simply the matter of a different input–output relation: allocation of resources is just the preliminary step of a process through which these changes will be brought about. 'The hard part is to model what happens then' (Solow

Change 115

1994, p. 52). And this is exactly what endogenous growth models cannot do for us.

As a matter of fact endogenous growth models are equilibrium models where the appropriate choice of the relevant conditions (the preference parameters, coefficients of the equations, and the like), guaranteed by perfect foresight, makes the economy jump immediately to its steady growth rate. This allows a comparative analysis of different endogenous steady growth paths (in the same way as with standard neoclassical models) but does not allow us to focus thoroughly on transitional dynamics problems.[7] No complementarity and/or co-ordination problems (which necessarily come about during a transition) can in fact 'actually arise' in economies which are always in equilibrium. Thus, notwithstanding 'that many endogenous growth models produce the characteristic result of coordination failures models: multiple suboptimal equilibria' and 'although the techniques of endogenous growth models have helped to uncover many coordination and adjustment problems, the theory is ultimately rooted in a conventional equilibrium analysis that assumes most of them away' (Howitt 1994, p. 764). The reason is that only the long period matters in equilibrium models; it is paramount in optimizing models, which are the most coherent equilibrium models. And conventional analysis identifies co-ordination problems with co-ordination failures that are confined to the short period, as evoked by Keynes's analysis of shortages of effective demand. Instead, we should bear in mind that 'when we turn our attention to long-run questions we aren't turning away from coordination and adjustment problems, we are simply looking at them from a different perspective'(ibid. p. 765).

In conclusion, endogenous growth models, like all equilibrium growth models, are aimed at identifying growth factors and measuring their respective contribution to growth, so as to be able to derive policy implications (in particular, as just mentioned, through a change in the value of preference parameters). However, there is no attempt to understand the working of the growth mechanism, which is assumed in the model.[8] The actual working of this mechanism may

---

[7] Although, of course, comparison is more interesting here than in the standard analysis, as the association of different growth paths with different preference parameters brings back into play policy interventions.

[8] An exception is the analysis of the way in which increasing returns are brought about; but, we have seen, increasing returns are not essential for endogenous growth.

have implications (including policy implications, as just shown) which have an important bearing on the viability of the economy.

On the other hand, the claim that endogenous growth models allow for a welfare analysis—in the sense that they make it possible to compare alternative policies and to select the best one, that is, the policy that secures the highest growth rate—also needs to be amended. As a matter of fact, within the equilibrium context considered policy interventions must be able to put the economy in the required conditions 'instantaneously' (which, as, we have seen, may be very restrictive due to the particular value that the basic parameters and/or coefficients of the model must take to assure endogenous growth). Meanwhile the shift of resources, automatically identified with the result that it should bring about, may instead generate a very complex dynamic that can even lead the economy to collapse, as we shall see in particular in Part II of this book.

The point can be grasped with reference to traditional optimal growth models—which share the same logic according to which once the best policy has been selected the new equilibrium path must be reached as quickly as possible—and to the Turnpike conjecture put forward in connection with the same models. The Turnpike theorem (Koopmans 1964) shows that all optimal paths that maximize an objective function and start from different initial conditions quickly converge to the steady state and stay close to this steady state for most of the time. However, the adjustment to the optimal path renders the existing initial conditions no longer adequate to what is going on. But the faster the transition, the quicker the transformation of the initial capital stock into a top-balanced stock and the greater the discarding of capital required: hence the greater the destruction of resources associated with the transition (Hicks 1965, chapter 19). The greater, in other words, is the threat to the viability of the change undertaken.

5.5. HARROD'S KNIFE-EDGE

Equilibrium growth models, whether the determination of the long-run growth rate is exogenous or endogenous, do not allow a thorough dynamic analysis. This is because, as already stressed, qualitative change is involved whenever a dynamic problem is dealt with, and qualitative change implies structural change, which is in the nature of an out-of-equilibrium process. In the analysis of a process, if this is properly looked at as the sequential building up of a new state of the economy, the separation between the short and the long period fades away, as there is interaction between short- and long-term phenomena. The effective backbone of a process, and at the same time the actual link between the short and long terms, is productive capacity, its creation and its utilization, with a focus of course on fixed capital in a wide sense. Thus investment activity, rather than the intertemporal allocation of resources in view of maximization over time of consumers' utility (as is the case in endogenous growth models where the production side of the economy is adjusted to comply with consumers' behaviour), is what actually shapes dynamic paths. Investment activity looked at as a time-structured process of creation of new productive options and resources and not as a (punctual or intertemporal) allocation of given resources, is likely to take the economy out of equilibrium, stimulating cumulative, erratic, or explosive processes which raise the problem of the viability of the path followed by the economy.

The true aim of Harrod's analysis—whose distinctive contribution is usually reckoned to be the formulation of the archetypal steady growth model—was exactly to deal with the behaviour of the economy out of equilibrium, with a focus on investment activity and, in particular, on fixed capital. As a matter of fact the breaking up of an equilibrium only creates a problem if the decisions which have brought about the disequilibrium cannot be immediately revised, which is the case if the mistakes made are somehow fossilized, in stocks of physical and/or human capital, thus creating irreversibilities. The disequilibrium is then passed down through successive periods between which links are established, primarily 119

the link represented by fixed capital. In Harrod's model (1939) the hypothesis of a fixed coefficients technology establishes a complementarity relation between factors whose accumulation depends on the saving rate. This renders accumulation and growth endogenous in the same way as in endogenous growth models, that is, in the sense that state parameters determine the rate of growth. However in Harrod's model the co-ordination of economic activity is not assured. This is because, unlike in endogenous growth models, the short period is explicitly considered as well as the long period, and the interaction between the two comes to the fore. Investment—unless along the knife-edge, where the economy can only be by chance—brings about a productive capacity (fixed capital) which is not harmonized with final demand. The original imbalance which results from an attempt to increase (decrease) the rate of accumulation, thus making the effective growth rate diverge from the warranted one, is fossilized into the existing capital stock, and carried on and amplified, period after period, by short-term expectations. The short and long terms interact through the multiplier-accelerator mechanism, which makes output and investment affect each other in turn, and stimulates an out-of-equilibrium process that becomes cumulative.

The process sketched out by Harrod is not necessarily explosive, though. A formalization of Harrod's model proposed by Hahn and Matthews (1964) makes it possible to realize that the fundamental instability of the model depends on the attempt of the entrepreneurs, who wish to increase the rate of accumulation, to bring the capital stock immediately to the new desired level, while at the same time forecasting a growth rate greater than the previous warranted growth rate. It is this very strong and abrupt attempt at adjustment—which implies investment behaviour bringing about a decrease in the ratio of the effective capital stock to income—that results in a succession of mistakes in forecasting and determines the instability.[9] As a matter of fact a dynamic path shaped out by adaptive expectations easily results in cumulative processes which hamper the viability of the path followed. To avoid that, adjustments must be not too rapid and lags must be introduced so as to produce a certain inertia (Heiner 1988). It is this inertia that establishes a link between the short and the long term, thus appearing as a factor of viability of the economy.

In conclusion, complementarity, which characterizes Harrod's model, is not necessarily associated with explosive behaviour, as the introduction of the hypothesis of substitution between factors made by Solow (1956) in order to assure the existence of a steady state seems to suggest. However, the essence of Harrod's message remains that steady state is a particular case, and that being out of equilibrium rather than being stable in the sense of moving always near an equilibrium path is the natural state of economies.

Within this perspective, the limit of Harrod's analysis is that the out-of-equilibrium process considered cannot be exhibited as a

---

[9] Along these lines Hicks (1965, chapter 11) suggests that this instability could be eliminated if savings increased with income in such a way as to avoid the fall in the ratio of the capital stock to income.

sequence and followed step by step. We remain half-way between a stability analysis, aimed at bringing to light stability (or instability) conditions, and the analysis of a thorough process taking place sequentially over time. The reason is that Harrod, although taking into account fixed capital and assuming complementarity between factors, has no theory of production as a time-structured process to deal explicitly with the intertemporal complementarity of the production process that makes up the effective backbone of an out-of-equilibrium process.

5.6. THE ANALYSIS OF THE TRAVERSE

The articulation over time of the production process is the distinctive feature of the Neo-Austrian model. In this model, we recall (see Section 1.4 above), production appears as a scheme for transforming a sequence of primary labour inputs into a sequence of homogeneous final output. The production process is fully vertically integrated, which makes it possible both to exhibit explicitly the phase of construction of productive capacity by bringing it inside the production process,[10] and to stress that it must necessarily come before the phase of utilization of the same capacity. Focus on the time structure of the production process, and on its intertemporal complementarity, makes it possible in turn to posit the transition between two different techniques (a Traverse) as a thorough process through which the transition itself takes place, and to analyse this process by following it in its sequential development (Hicks 1973).

The intertemporal complementarity of production is the main link between the sequence of periods along which the barter economy dealt with by Hicks in the analysis of the Traverse is made to move from the one technique to the other by means of the mechanism provided by the assumption of Full Performance. This implies that all the output not absorbed by consumption out of wages paid to workers engaged on existing production processes (whether still in the construction or already in the utilization phase) or by consumption of other kinds, is in fact used to start new production processes. The rate of starts, thus made endogenous, sketches out the path followed

---

[10] The 'machine' is regarded as an intermediate product of the production process which does not exist outside it and hence cannot be transferred.

by the economy, a fully predetermined path once the value of the parameters of the model are given.[11] Full Performance, on the other hand, also implies flow equilibrium in each period, both in the sense that final output is totally absorbed by existing demand and in the sense that investment is equal to *ex ante* saving. Thus the existing productive structure is smoothly transmuted into the one adapted to the new technique as resources are gradually freed and invested into the building of the latter. In this context there are no co-ordination problems; Full Performance allows us to dispense with them and with the imbalances which could otherwise arise from the strictly *ad hoc*, arbitrary saving function corresponding to the hypothesis of a constant, exogenously determined 'take out' (consumption out of profits). This is exactly the opposite of Harrod's model, where there are co-ordination problems but no intertemporal complementarity of production.

However, Full Performance only concerns final output; there is nothing of the sort in the labour market. This makes possible the thorough step forward represented by the analysis of the Traverse: that is the bringing to light of 'what happens on the way' (Hicks 1973, p. 10), in particular what happens to employment, as the result of taking explicitly into account the time structure of production in an out-of-equilibrium context. This allows important analytical insights, the most important being the demonstration of Ricardo's 'machinery effect', a highly controversial issue in the history of economic thought. As is well known, in the chapter *On Machinery*, which he added to the last edition of his *Principles* in 1821, Ricardo changed mind with respect to his previous opinion and, on the basis of a numerical example which has puzzled economists ever since, put forward the idea that technical progress could be detrimental to the interest of the working class because of the unemployment resulting from the introduction of machinery. Being pro or anti this conclusion has remained mainly an article of faith until 1973, when Hicks was able to prove beyond doubt the existence of the 'machinery effect' for the case of the introduction of a more mechanized technique (in Neo-Austrian terms, a more labour-intensive technique in the construction phase, and, of course, more than proportionately less labour-intensive in the utilization phase than the technique already in use—whether the new technique is characterized by a modification in the length of the phases of the production process n and/or N or not). The reason, which focus on

---

[11] We are clearly back to positive economics here.

Change   121

the time structure of the production process makes apparent, is the dissociation of inputs from output and of costs from proceeds during the Traverse,[12] resulting in a temporary fall in final output, and hence in the resources available to sustain employment,[13] with respect to the equilibrium state associated with the old technique in use.

As a matter of fact any attempt to change a given productive structure implies bringing back to the fore the time articulation of the production process—its having to go first through a phase of construction of a different productive capacity in order to be able to use it later for current production—that is obscured by the synchronization of production in equilibrium. This is what Hicks means when he writes, in what might appear at first sight a rather cryptic way, that 'Ricardo had learned to distinguish between investment at cost and investment of output capacity' (Hicks 1973, p. 98). But the fact that there is a dissociation of inputs from output and of costs from proceeds whenever a change in the structure of productive capacity is contemplated, also implies that Ricardo's 'machinery effect' is in fact much more general and takes place whatever the nature of the technical improvement considered, that is, whether the new production processes are more mechanized, the specific case stressed by Hicks, or not. This has been proved (Amendola 1972) with reference to processes of production with a more general time profile whose life can be shortened or lengthened as the result of an optimizing behaviour confronted with different values of the relevant economic variables (primarily, the value of the rate of interest in relation to the wage rate).[14] A fall in final output, and the unemployment associated with it, is then shown to be the result of a scrapping of production processes—

---

[12] This is a consequence of the change in the age structure of productive capacity resulting from the modification of the balance between processes in the phase of construction and processes in the phase of utilization implied by a change in the technique in use.

[13] The fall in final output ('gross produce') associated with the introduction of a more mechanized technique, is seen as the result of the conversion of circulating capital into fixed capital, implying a reduction of the Wage Fund and hence of sustainable employment.

[14] Hicks considers instead only production processes with a simple profile which 'retains the vital distinction between construction and utilization—but almost nothing else . . . a constant rate of input during the construction period, and a constant (but different) rate of input during the utilization period; zero output in the construction period, and a constant rate of output during the utilization period' (Hicks 1973, p. 82). This simplification implies that truncation of the production process is excluded, whatever the rate of interest.

as a consequence of the introduction of a new technique, whatever the nature of the technical improvement, in the specific case considered a neutral technical improvement—greater than in the equilibrium state associated with the old technique.

Here the arbitrary saving function considered by Hicks is essential. Optimal saving behaviour which took into account the intertemporal complementarity of production processes could possibly serve the purpose of maintaining full employment over time. But this[15]—in the same way as the hypothesis of flexible real wages would artificially conceal the problem of technological unemployment by instantaneously re-absorbing it—would only lead to the rejection of the idea that intertemporal complementarity of production matters. The theory that would emerge, then, would not be 'a sequential theory, of the kind we are here endeavouring to construct' (Hicks 1973, p. 56).

However, an analytical incongruity still besets Hicks's analysis of the Traverse (or its generalization): the assumption of Full Performance, which makes it possible to stick to an equilibrium approach (even when scrapping occurs, as it reflects an intended behaviour) in what is essentially an out-of-equilibrium context. This comes down to an assumption of co-ordination of economic activity in a context where productive capacity is not adapted and that hence denies co-ordination.

Still, being able to throw light on what happens on the way is a momentous achievement, and not so much for the specific analytical results obtained as for the change of analytical perspective that it implies. As a matter of fact although 'the way' considered is still 'the way to' a predetermined point of arrival, Hicks himself makes it clear that the problem of convergence to this point (which is in the end why the equilibrium structure is called in) is not really the important thing, and that what happens on the way may matter in itself

Convergence to equilibrium has been shown to be dubious, but it has also been shown to be unimportant. Even at the best, it will take a long time . . . and before the time has elapsed something new will surely have occurred. It is therefore of the first importance that something can be said . . . about the short-run and medium-run effects of an exogenous disturbance' (Hicks 1975, p. 316).[16]

---

[15] Even granted the possibility of actually being able to sketch out a time profile of saving coherent with an unbalanced structure of productive capacity.

[16] This change of perspective has not been perceived at all by those who have kept working along the line of proving the convergence of the Traverse, and this is the main reason for the substantial sterility of these attempts.

Hicks's analysis of the Traverse is certainly a piece of transitional dynamics, but it has two main limitations. First, it remains within an *ex post* perspective: the sequence considered is fully predetermined as it portrays the passage from one given technique (with the associated equilibrium state) to another. Secondly, the equilibrium approach followed does not allow co-ordination problems to arise: the assumptions that guarantee equilibrium imply that no decision process is actually envisaged. Removal of these limits, and more general assumptions than the specific ones made by Hicks, will make it possible to throw more light on the relation between technology and employment in the analysis of out-of-equilibrium processes of change which will be developed in Part II of this book (in Chapter 7).

5.7. PATH DEPENDENCE

Path dependence (Arthur 1988, 1989; David 1985, 1988, 1992) is a phenomenon associated with processes that take place in real, irreversible time. It represents an important step forward in the understanding of economic change in that it focuses on the fact that this change is in the nature of a true process; that is, not a predetermined trajectory towards a given point but something that builds up and takes shape and direction step by step.

The following ingredients make up the analytical context within which the phenomenon of path dependence comes to the fore. First, a 'sequential decision framework', which allows for actions to occur and economic choices to be made sequentially, in a process, and for the irreversibility of these choices to be stressed (sequential choices between alternatives which consist in different 'allocations' of resources are actually considered). Second, a 'stochastic model': a certain randomness must be allowed for history (small exogenous events) to influence the process in question. This is rendered by including in the dynamic equation which describes the process a stochastic component (a perturbation effect) as well as a deterministic component, and ensuring that the first, at the beginning of the process, is quantitatively more important than the second.[17] Third, a positive

---

[17] A further aspect of the stochastic character of the model is that the probability of the next action, rather than the state of the system, is what actually determines the next choice.

local feed-back', that is, increasing returns on the margin due to learning and co-ordination effects, which represent the backbone of the sequential processes modelled as above.

All this results in cumulative, self-reinforcing processes whose outcome is indeterminate, and which have a potential for multiple equilibria. Path dependence, in particular, focuses on the fact that small events, occurring early on the path, have great importance in selecting one or another among the set of stable equilibria (i.e. history matters). It stresses the externality of initial events, namely, the fact that decisions taken sequentially are affected by externalities produced by the decisions taken previously by other agents, especially when, with adaptive expectations, 'increasing prevalence on the market enhances beliefs of further prevalence' (Arthur 1988, p. 9).[18] The role of 'smaller ensembles of interacting decision agents when these remain isolated from external inference and their internal structure relations remain undisturbed' (David 1992, p. 16) in bringing about 'lock in' effects (convergence to indefinitely persisting equilibria) is brought into light, while large finite systems appear less likely to remain in an absorbing state and rather show a tendency to oscillate between opposite extremes. Interesting implications of the analysis for policy interventions, whose 'timing' assumes paramount importance, are also stressed. As a matter of fact, 'windows for taking fiscally and administratively feasible actions that could tip the system's evolution in one direction rather than another, tend to open only briefly ... The study of history ... would therefore be an integral part of policy analysis, inasmuch as it would help to anticipate and identify such propitious moments for action' (ibid. p. 37).

The emphasis put on networks, whichever way we look at them, and hence on policy interventions aimed at affecting their behaviour, naturally leads us to focus on the issue of co-ordination. But what kind of co-ordination? As a matter of fact path dependence, 'lock in', and so forth have emerged with reference to problems of the competitive diffusion of alternative technologies, which are typical problems with the allocation of resources; and allocation is perfectly at ease within an equilibrium framework. Now we maintain that reference to

---

[18] The typical example is that of a system that gets 'locked into' the choice of a technology which, for whatever reason, prevails in the early stages of an adoption process (David 1985).

an equilibrium framework is exactly the reason why path dependence analysis does not, and cannot, go all the way that the above-mentioned points raised by the analysis itself hint at, and that, in order to go all that way, reference must instead be made to an 'out-of-equilibrium' analytical framework.

When path dependence is considered within the context of out-of-equilibrium processes of change, the implications of the analysis acquire a different and deeper meaning. Let us consider, for one, the problem of co-ordination, which is actually at the heart of all thoroughly dynamic problems. Co-ordination with respect to the equilibrium solutions that represent efficient choices, with focus on competitive relations, is what matters when allocation of resources is envisaged. Co-ordination in view of organizing and making viable an out-of-equilibrium process of construction, with a focus on complementary activities, is rather the problem when a creation of resources is envisaged. Organizing a process of creation of resources and of new productive options in fact requires us to establish all kinds of co-operative relations over time; in other words, it requires the setting-up of an environment conducive to a common learning process.

When the structuring of an altogether new productive environment is what we are after, what matters is the organization of patterns of relations (how the environment is brought about) rather than the specific content of the relations themselves (the characteristics of the environment and its being more or less conducive to certain choices). That is, how relations are born and whether and through which process they are likely to change in time rather than what they are and are good for (Bruno and De Lellis 1993). Problems that, of course, cannot be dealt with within an equilibrium analytical framework.

Out-of-equilibrium processes of change require dynamic complementarities, that is, complementarities over time, aimed at making the processes themselves viable. As a matter of fact, as we shall see in particular in the following chapters, qualitative change is most likely to engender a complex dynamic which casts doubts on the very viability of the change undertaken. However, this analysis first requires us to sketch out a sequential context where the problems involved can first stand out at the analytical level and then be dealt with.

5.8. THE SEQUENCE 'CONSTRAINTS–DECISIONS–CONSTRAINTS'

The interaction between the short and long terms, as we have already stressed, is at the heart of a dynamic process defined as an out-of-equilibrium process. This interaction is apparent from Kaldor's analysis of the implications of increasing returns on economic progress (Kaldor 1972). In this analysis Kaldor does not consider a steady state characterized by the existence of positive externalities (as is the case with Romer, Lucas, and the other authors who have dealt with endogenous growth) but focuses on an out-of-equilibrium process of change, which he defines as such due to the 'imperfect' articulation between the working of the productive side of the economy, exhibiting increasing returns, and the working of markets for final goods. This imperfection, which is the expression of co-ordination failures, prevents the economy from systematically realizing a cumulative causation: that is, from actually implementing a growth mechanism.[19] As a matter of fact every change on the production side is a source of further changes which imply successive (very often erratic) disequilibria between supply and demand on the markets for final goods (see Section 4.7 above). At the opposite of what the 'optimizing' version of equilibrium growth theory assumes, the production side of the economy does not adjust to what is best for the demand side, and this is what brings about the above-mentioned disequilibria.

The interaction between the short and the long term which, following Kaldor's suggestion, we must focus on in order to understand the working of the growth mechanism of the economy, can be captured by sketching out both an intra- and an inter-period sequence, where the one depends on, and at the same time determines, the other. But to do so we have first to figure out a different relation between parameters and variables (between exogenous and endogenous magnitudes) with respect to standard analytical models—that is, as already made clear in Section 1.6 above, a relation based on the time perspective under which we look at economic magnitudes rather than on the specific character of these magnitudes. This different relation reflects a change in the analytical focus of the model considered—no longer aimed at singling out growth factors but at analysing a process of change—

---

[19] Thus Kaldor's out-of-equilibrium analysis shifts the attention from the identification and the measure of the contribution of growth factors, typical of equilibrium growth models, to the study of a growth mechanism.

which also implies a different structure of the model itself and a different use to which it can be put.

The effective link between the short and the long term in a sequential model are the state variables, which at each given moment represent the existing constraints but are themselves the result of what has been happening along the sequence of periods which has led to the present state of the economy. These state variables at time t, in an economy with a Neo-Austrian representation of production and where all exchanges are intermediated by financial assets, so that the resources required to carry out production and to sustain consumption are financial resources, not physical output, are

- Productive capacity, expressed by the vectors $\mathbf{x}^c(t)$ and $\mathbf{x}^u(t)$ of construction and utilization production processes (see Section 1.4 above), to which must be added the stocks of final output $O(t)$ (if any) accumulated in the preceding periods.
- Financial resources, that is, the money proceeds from the sales of final output in the previous period $m(t-1)$, and the idle balances of both firms and households $h^f(t-1)$ and $h^h(t-1)$ (if any) inherited from the past (see Section 2.5 above).
- Human resources, that is, the vector of supply of labour $\mathbf{L}_s^S(t)$ which portrays the structure of skills and competences available at time t (see Section 3.5 above).

These state variables, which constrain the decisions taken in period t, undergo a change during the period itself as the result of these decisions; they will thus take new values in the following period $(t + 1)$ when they will again constrain the decisions to be made in $(t + 1)$. 'Thus today's decisions, taken on the basis of today's constraints, go to modify the constraints that will affect tomorrow's decisions—and so on in the sequence 'constraints–decisions–constraints' (Amendola and Gaffard 1988, p. 49). This intertemporal complementarity of the decision process characterized by a lag in the transmission of information (see Section 4.8 above), interacting with the intertemporal complementarity of a production process characterized by a construction lag, determines how the economy evolves sequentially over time.

In this context decisions appear as reactions to changing constraints and oncoming disequilibria, and, at the same time, as a means for acquiring information (see Section 4.8 above). Unlike in equilibrium models, where the process through which decisions are arrived at is not dealt with, and hence a mechanism of acquisition of information is not considered,[20] here the sequential order of decisions matters, which calls for an adequate time articulation of the decision process.

5.9. THE DECISION PROCESS

How, and in what order, are decisions arrived at in each period of the sequence through which an out-of-equilibrium process takes place, given the existing constraints? The elementary period is defined here[21] as the length of time required to carry out a round of final production. This elementary period is also looked at as the decision period; thus not only decisions about final production but also those concerning price changes (the price of final output p and the wage rates vector $\mathbf{w}$) can only be revised at the junction of one period and the next.

This makes the model a discrete time model with a fix-price method, as opposed to the flex-price method of traditional equilibrium models[22] Dealing with discrete time or with continuous time is not indifferent to the kind of analysis we intend to carry on, though. A reduction in the length of the time span over which the elementary period extends, that is, gradual elimination of the inertia which characterizes the revision of decisions in discrete time sequential models, also tends to eliminate the irreversibility which is the essential feature of dynamic processes looked at as out-of-equilibrium processes. In the limit, in continuous time models the possibility of instantaneous revision of decisions implies that co-ordination of economic activity can always be maintained, thus hampering the disequilibrium implications of structural modifications from coming to the surface.[23] This, as already men-

---

[20] In these models imperfection of information is dealt with by means of *ad hoc* hypotheses—most often rigidity hypotheses—and the reactions to exogenous shocks actually depend on the equilibrium values of the behavioural parameters of the models themselves rather than on the state of information (Leijonhufvud 1983, p. 76).

[21] Following the tradition of Swedish sequential models (Lindahl 1930; Lundberg 1937).

[22] 'It is not implied by the description Fixprice method that prices are never allowed to change—only that they do not necessarily change whenever there is a demand-supply disequilibrium' (Hicks 1965, p. 78).

[23] On the other hand, once the possibility of instantaneous adjustment is cancelled by consideration of discrete time periods, different lengths of adjustment may become a means of controlling the sequential process, and hence the length of the elementary period can be dealt with in the model as a control variable.

tioned in Section 4.8 above, would be the result of the elimination of the hypothesis of a lag in the transmission of information.

Production decisions concern not only final output but also productive capacity (that is, its construction, not its simple utilization). Given the intertemporal complementarity of a Neo-Austrian production process, the effects of decisions concerning productive capacity extend beyond the period in which they are actually taken. While decisions concerning current final production $q(t)$, whose effects will be felt within the period, are driven by short-term expectations (namely, in the modelling proposed, expectations about the level of final demand in the current period), decisions concerning productive capacity are affected by long-term expectations, which reflect the degree of confidence in the existing 'model' of the economy (not only on the part of producers but also on the part of consumers) as represented by a given structure of the interacting patterns of production and consumption. In particular, producers' long-term expectations are expressed by the value of the parameter , which determines the amount of available financial resources that firms want to hold as idle balances (see Section 2.5 above). Changes in the value of , which result in an accumulation (decumulation) of idle balances, are a way of introducing into the model the intention of producers to (or not to) pursue a structural modification[24]—be it a change in the growth rate, an innovation, or whatever.[25] The remaining resources (the whole of the available financial resources if = 0), after a part of them is set aside by producers to be devoted to their own consumption, are used in the first place to sustain the activity of the utilization processes required to satisfy current final demand as determined by short-term expectations; what is left is fully used up to finance construction activity. A more complex explanation of the level of construction activity than this 'residual' determination is

---

[24] In other words, desired idle balances reflect the intention of 'waiting' for the moment when this modification will actually be undertaken.

[25] In the same way consumers' long-term expectations are expressed by the value of the parameter σ which determines the amount of households' available financial resources actually withheld from consumption (see Section 2.5 above). An increase in the value of σ is a signal of a change of tastes, of a dissatisfaction with the commodities offered on the market, and of the desire for something new and different, while a decrease in its value is the signal of the establishing of a given consumption pattern.

alternatively proposed in the full model expounded in Section 6.3 below.

Once, at the beginning of each period, available financial resources have been allocated in the way just mentioned (and a wage fund corresponding to the amount of resources devoted to productive activity has been distributed to households[26]), the production process takes place. At the end of the period a round of final production is obtained and at the same time a step forward is realized in the construction of new productive capacity.[27] Current final production is absorbed, fully or in part, by the demand sustained by households' available financial resources (a fraction $(1 -)$ of the wage fund distributed in the period, plus non-desired idle balances from previous periods, if any) to which must be added consumption out of profits. If the level of final demand thus determined is not such as to absorb at the going price (which cannot adjust within the period) the whole of current production, real stocks $o(t)$ are accumulated by firms which are not desired, and hence will be put on the market as soon as possible (in the next period). If, on the contrary, current production is not sufficient to satisfy the whole demand formulated, idle balances will be held by households which are not desired, and hence will go to accrue final demand in the next period. The fix-price method which is behind real and monetary stockholding in this modelling reflects the absence of perfect information that does not allow instantaneous adjustments and hence causes the appearance of disequilibria in the model (see Section 4.8 above)

In particular, supply of final output in real terms, at time t, may be determined in the following way

$$s(t) = [y^* (t)]/p(t)$$

where

$$y^*(t) = y(t - 1) [1 + g_m (t - 1)]$$

that is, the money value of final demand expected by the firms within the period, is obtained by extrapolating the change of money proceeds

---

[26] Producers may be obliged to accumulate non-desired idle balances if a more stringent human constraint does not allow them to actually use the whole of the potential wage fund (see Section 2.5 above).

[27] This may be the last step, in which case a certain amount of productive capacity—simply replacing part of the existing capacity or expanding it—appears on the market.

in the previous period. The demand for final output in real terms will be given by

$$d(t) = [y(t)]/p(t)$$

where

$$y(t) + h_d^h(t) = \omega(t) + c(t) + h^h(t-1).$$

Current final production will then be

$$q(t) = s(t) - \eta [O(t)]$$

where a value of η lower than one states the willingness to hold some real stocks. On this basis we determine the degree of utilization of existing productive capacity, that is, the vector $\mathbf{x}^u(t)$ and hence

$$\omega^u(t) = \mathbf{w}(t) \underline{\mathbf{A}}^u \mathbf{x}^u(t)'$$

that is, the fraction of the wage fund required to carry out the production processes in the utilization phase. The remaining funds will go to finance investment[28]

$$i(t) = \omega(t) - \omega^u(t)$$

thus determining the vector of production processes in the phase of construction $\mathbf{x}^c(t)$.[29] Total employment will then also be determined as

$$E(t) = \underline{\mathbf{A}}^u \mathbf{x}^u(t)' + \underline{\mathbf{A}}^c \mathbf{x}^c(t)'.$$

External financial resources $f(t)$, another control variable in the model, can relax the constraint represented by available financial resources; a constraint (if any) which, in each period t, results from the development of the sequence through which the economy evolves. The vision of the dynamic process behind the sequential analytical framework just sketched out differs from the leading dynamic analytical approach, namely, the approach according to which the evolution of the economy is the result of intertemporal optimization processes. In this approach perfect or rational expectations drive choices which are made in view of a point of arrival or a reference path, be it regular or irregular, determined beforehand. In this context we are not really interested in the way agents adjust or react to oncoming events, since the evolution path is already traced out once, given the optimizing

---

[28] Alternative ways of determining investment will be considered in Section 6.3 below.
[29] In determining $\mathbf{x}^u(t)$ and $\mathbf{x}^c(t)$ scrapping rules which depend on the specific criteria adopted have to be taken into account.

hypotheses, the values of the relevant parameters (technological and preference parameters) are given.

Out of equilibrium, the way we have defined it, the process in the making is instead at the centre of attention. A process is built up step by step, which implies that we must focus on the adjustments and reactions which, step by step, determine the evolution of the economy. This 'requires far more structure than does the equilibrium approach. Mechanisms that describe *how* agents make decisions, how prices are determined, and how exchanges can take place out of equilibrium must be specified' (Day 1993, p. 21). However, as there is not a given reference path, expectations cannot be derived from it. On the other hand expectations cannot be adaptive in the naïve and short-sighted sense of taking into account only recent past events. Dealing with a thorough process means having in mind the interaction between the short and the long run, as a process is actually the result of interactions and complementarities over time which involve sequentially related decisions. Expectations must thus be defined with reference to the mechanism shaping out the evolution path of the economy rather than to the (as yet undefined) specific time profile of this path. This, as we have already stressed, is a 'constraints–decisions–constraints' mechanism confronted with the co-ordination problems which result from the interaction between the construction lag of productive capacity and the delay of transmission of information.

Thus, if in the model proposed we considered a simple adaptive mechanism, it would be the case that the resources freed, for instance, by a scrapping of utilization processes due to a fall in final demand, would be instantaneously devoted to the construction of new processes, thus aggravating the distortion of productive capacity and bringing about stronger and stronger fluctuations, as will be shown in particular in Section 7.5 below. If, on the contrary, we took into account the problem of co-ordination over time of economic activity, which implies the interaction of the short and long run in terms of the structure of productive capacity, a mechanism for the formation of expectations consistent with this outlook would put viability at the centre of the focus and bring about interactions aimed at rendering the economy viable.

The 'constraints–decisions–constraints' mechanism that characterizes our model includes both the view (common, among others, to Marshall, Myrdal, Kaldor, and the path-dependence theorists) that stresses the role of history—in that past events set out the pre-conditions that drive the economy one way or the other—and the view that the key determinant of the evolution of the economy (in particular, of the choice among multiple equilibria) is expectations: 'that there is a decisive element of self-fulfilling prophecy' (Krugman 1991). In our model the two views interact. History looks through the time profile of costs and proceeds, as sketched out by the existing intertemporal complementarities, and the speed with which the process of structural adjustment is carried out. Expectations, on the other hand, whose role we have just defined, may embody a weaker or a stronger memory, implying less or more immediate adjustment processes.

PART II
ANALYSIS: PROCESSES OF CHANGE

6
Out-of-Equilibrium Modelling

6.1. THE SCOPE AND ROLE OF MODELLING OUT OF EQUILIBRIUM

Paul Krugman (1990) candidly admits that the bulk of what he terms the 'new' trade theory—that is, the idea that increasing returns could explain international trade even in the absence of comparative advantage—although well known to many economists, was left out of textbooks and trade courses until the 1980s because before that date nobody had been able to develop a clean and simple model making the point. 'Since economics as practised in the English-speaking world is strongly oriented toward mathematical models, any economic argument that has not been expressed in that form tends to remain invisible' (ibid. p. 3). Thus 'the role of increasing returns was legitimized as a concern of trade theory' and 'all forms of increasing returns were given greater respect' only when 'it proved possible to develop models of trade in the presence of increasing returns and imperfect competition that were not only illuminating but also simple and elegant.' (ibid. pp. 4–5).

This tendency towards a formalization often not required for a better understanding of a given problem has been recently criticized even by Frank Hahn, one of the economists who in the past has done most for the success of the tendency itself. With reference to the multiplication of endogenous growth models, he writes 'I have not found my understanding increased by the formalisation', and adds 'It would be interesting to see whether a stylised box model which does not stylise its main content away can be constructed' (Hahn 1994, p. 17). As is unfortunately the case with most of the dominant theory today, the modelling undertaken appears at its best as a price paid to the fashion, an optional extra which does not add anything to the analysis. In fact it even goes as far as implying the very canceling out of the economic meaning of the problem dealt with, which is sacrificed to formal elegance.

This is not the case in our modelling of qualitative change as a sequential process, though. As a matter of fact, the formalization of the inter- and the intra-period sequences through which an out-of-equilibrium process of change takes place is essential for both sketching out the analytical framework suited to deal with this process and actually carrying out its analysis. But it is a different kind of formalization that we are referring to. The nature of the economic phenomenon we are interested in—the process through which qualitative change occurs—does not call for a traditional type of model, that is, a model capable of generating a 'solution' in the sense of a type of behaviour of the economy (the attainment of a point or the following of a path) characterized by certain specific features (equilibrium, efficiency, optimality, and so forth).[1] What we are after, instead, is to follow the evolution of the economy—traced out step by step by a 'constraints–decisions–constraints' sequence, as we have seen in particular in Chapter 5—in order to investigate its viability.

Within the sequential context sketched out by the intertemporal complementarities of the production and decision processes, output, prices, and wages determination mechanisms carry over and probably amplify the imbalances (first of all that between construction and utilization) resulting from the original breaking up of the functioning of the economy due to the attempt to carry out a qualitative change. This stimulates an out-of-equilibrium process that causes fluctuations in output and prices, and hence in available financial resources and in investment, which make productive activity less and less consistent over time and hence undermine the viability of the path followed by the economy. The viability of this path then becomes the crucial analytical problem. The main point to be stressed, here, is that different kinds of interventions—aimed at regulating the working of the existing dynamic mechanisms (prices, wages, and output determination systems as affected by the control variables of the economy[2]) or, as we shall see, at providing other compensating mechanisms—are required to interact dynamically in order to correct both the bias in construction and that in utilization, thus re-establishing the consistency over time of productive activity and making the evolution of the economy viable. This mix of interventions, on the other hand, cannot be made once and for all but must be continuously modified, since the interventions are interventions over time that have to deal with a process affected by perturbations which take on different shapes

---

[1] As we shall see, a solution of this kind—in particular, a steady-state solution—will only be considered in order to test the analytical coherence of the model proposed.

[2] The external inflow of money $f(t)$ and consumption out of profits $c(t)$, in the modelization proposed in the preceding chapters.

Out-of-Equilibrium Modelling 139

and intensities in time. 'Such *viability creating mechanisms* are the analog of equilibrium "existence" proofs, but in the out-of-equilibrium setting. They are required to guarantee the existence of a continuing "solution" to the system in terms of feasible actions for all its constituent model components' (Day 1993, p. 39). This is the different way in which the concept of 'solution' must be intended when referred to an out-of-equilibrium process.[3] It calls for a monitoring of the process itself to bring to light its salient moments. This can only be achieved by means of numerical experiments, that is, by simulations that, under certain conditions (chosen so as to stress aspects relevant to the analysis) allow us to unveil what happens 'along the way'.[4]

The relevance of this analytical set-up for policy interventions is evident. As a matter of fact these interventions are most often devised

in response to economic pressures caused by unemployment, bankruptcy, poverty and other problems of inviability experienced by individuals and organizations. Models that can generate similar phenomena could provide a realistic environment for experiments with alternative policy strategies. They might provide better 'engines for discovering the truth' and they might help formulate more effective mechanisms for steering the economy away from precipitous hazards and along less bumpy paths (ibid.).

The analysis carried out in this chapter and in the following one will confirm this.

The intertemporal complementarities and the interactions that characterize a process of qualitative change trace out complex dynamic paths which call for an adaptive approach, though one of a particular kind, as stressed in Section 5.9 above. 'Obviously, however, the adaptive approach will, when pursued very far, lead to models of great complexity and variety' (Day 1975, p. 30). When confronted with this problem we can take two different stands. We can use simple models to try to reproduce complex evolution paths of the economy, as is the case with chaos theory.[5] Or we can build models that take into account the complexity of economic phenomena and of their interactions over time, and try to derive simple and clear evolutions

---

[3] It is evident that this has very little to do with the analytical solution which defines a steady state or, more generally, an intertemporal equilibrium.

[4] Model simulation, as already stressed in Section 5.6 above, 'can never yield general inferences from a given system of assumptions but can yield specific inferences of great variety and interest' (Day 1975, p. 29).

[5] 'The simplest and most common chaos model involves a nonlinear one-variable difference equation of first order' (Baumol and Benhabib 1989, p. 79).

from them, which is what, following on the analytical line developed in Part I of this book, we intend to do here. The reason for this choice lies in the way in which we interpret a model: namely, as a heuristic tool for exploring economic phenomena so as to have a better understanding of their essence—in our case, the phenomenon of change which is in the nature of an out-of-equilibrium process, that is, of a process that has in its developing its analytical relevance—rather than as a device for reproducing particular aspects of economic reality, in a descriptive, *ex post* perspective à la Lucas.[6]

6.2. THE GUIDING LINES

Standard theory seeks to explain and to predict the behaviour of economic agents from the external constraints, e.g. technology and preferences. This leads to a consideration of 'optimal' strategies in the sense that, given the constraints, all future consequences are taken into account by economic agents. This is the essence of the concept of equilibrium in the modern intertemporal version of the standard theory. Optimality of strategies thus defined, on the other hand, necessarily implies efficiency of production. Costs and proceeds always match over the equilibrium period dealt with. As a corollary, expectations are always fulfilled, plans are realized, and markets clear. The departure from standard theory leads instead to

algorithmic representation of both decision rules and learning procedures (including expectations formation) . . . But algorithms are, of course, procedures, and the focus on decisions procedures of this kind *avoids the traditional sharp distinction in economics between "given" preferences and preference formation, between technology and technological change, between equilibrium and learning or adapting.* (Leijonhufvud 1993, p. 5).

Institutional structures and behavioural conventions are thus stressed, structures and conventions that 'emerge in society to make it possible for people to interact with reasonable confidence in the predictability of the result of their actions' (ibid.).

---

[6] 'a "theory" is not a collection of assertions about the behaviour of the actual economy but rather an explicit set of instructions for building a parallel or analogue system—a mechanical, imitation economy. A "good" model, from this point of view, will not be exactly more "real" than a poor one, but will provide better simulations' (Lucas 1980, p. 697).

In this context we propose to substitute a sequentially articulated strategy, as defined in Sections 5.8 and 5.9 above, for the optimizing behaviour of standard theory. As just mentioned, the modelling of a similar strategy 'can be based on a frequently encountered principle of algorithm construction which is the incorporation of more or less *ad hoc* rules that limit the distance succeeding steps taken in a sequence of trial choices' (Day 1986, p. 61). This is exactly the way in which we have been proceeding in this book, and it is certainly a particularly useful perspective when dealing with out-of-equilibrium processes of change, where what matters is what happens on the way and the viability of the path followed becomes the paramount issue.

The first implication of focusing on sequentially articulated strategies in an out-of-equilibrium context is that markets can no longer be represented as auctions or bidding games, in the sense that instantaneous price adjustments allow the markets themselves to clear systematically. Their functioning now obeys stock–flow mechanisms which mediate transactions among agents using periodic price adjustment rules. In Hicks's terminology markets are 'fix-price', not in the sense that prices do not change but in that there are forces at work represented by intermediaries (e.g. wholesalers) or by the producers themselves which could in principle stabilize the market but that can also operate in the opposite direction. These mechanisms show to what extent there are co-ordination failures. One could expect that buffer stocks and liquid assets make the system more stable, but this is only a conjecture and it is difficult to validate. As a matter of fact things are much more complicated: disequilibrium forces are much less dependable than equilibrium ones. All we can do, then, is to consider specific working rules and calculate the behaviour of the resulting model, keeping in mind, however, that 'such calculations are of illustrative value only' (Hicks 1985, p. 87).

Besides, and behind, these sequential price mechanisms, an out-of-equilibrium context leads us to stress the role of constraints which derive from the intertemporal complementarity of the production process. As a matter of fact the actual evolution of the economy does not depend only on the cognitive abilities of decision-makers but also on the complexity of the phenomenon of production.

The technical intertemporal complementarity of fully vertically integrated processes of production ... creates irreversibilities that establish links between what is required (and what can be done) today (and, to a certain extent, what will be required and what it will be possible to do tomorrow) and what happened yesterday—by determining the spread over time of the human and of the financial requirements of the choices made at each moment and the lags in the effects of such choices . . . Thus the decisions of a given period imply the setting in of irreversible processes that call for other related decisions in the future and, at the same time, set constraints on them (Amendola and Gaffard 1988, p. 48).

The complementarity over time required to render a process of change viable, rather than intertemporal efficiency, is the relevant aspect of production in a thoroughly dynamic context.

Finally, a proper out-of-equilibrium analysis has an essential monetary aspect. The reason why money is called to play a crucial role—as we stressed in Chapter 2—is that out of equilibrium the time structure of production comes back to the fore. The phase of construction and the phase of utilization of productive capacity can no longer be considered as synchronous: a bridge through time must then be launched to link them, and this is what money is called up to. Out of equilibrium real choices cannot be separated from financial decisions: as a matter of fact, the availability of financial resources at the right moment determines the viability of the evolution of the economy.

6.3. A SEQUENTIAL MODEL

We shall now present a model that, following the main lines just stressed, gives structure to the theory expounded in Part I of this book, and which embodies the analytical approaches proposed each time in relation to the various issues considered as relevant to the analysis of out-of-equilibrium processes of change. The rationale behind the various equations, or groups of equations, of the model can thus be traced back to the different chapters in Part I of the book. In particular, reference to these chapters (namely, Sections 5.8 and 5.9) is essential for understanding the intra- and the inter-period sequences sketched out by the model.

The Production Process (Chapters 1 and 3)

Production is carried out by means of production processes of a Neo-Austrian type which use a heterogeneous human resource characterized by s different skills to obtain m different commodities. An elementary process of production j is defined by the input matrix

$$\underline{\mathbf{A}}_j = [a_{i,h}]_j; j = 1,2, \ldots m; i = 0, \ldots n + N; h = 1,2, \ldots, s \quad (1)$$

whose elements represent the quantities of the different types of labour (skills) required in the successive periods of the phase of construction c (from 0 to n) and, following it, of the phase of utilization u (from $n + 1$ to $n + N$) of the productive capacity of commodity j, so that

$$\underline{\mathbf{A}}_j = [\underline{\mathbf{A}}_j^c; \underline{\mathbf{A}}_j^u]$$

and by the output vector

$$\mathbf{b}_j = [b_{n+1}, \ldots, b_{n+N}]_j \quad (2)$$

When a homogeneous labour input is considered, the input matrices become vectors

$$\mathbf{a}_j = [a_0, a_1, \ldots, a_{n+N}]_j$$
$$\mathbf{a}_j^c = [a_0, a_1, \ldots, a_n]_j \quad (1a)$$
$$\mathbf{a}_j^u = [a_{n+1}, \ldots, a_{n+N}]_j$$

At each given moment t the productive capacity of commodity j is represented by the intensity vectors

$$\mathbf{x}_j(t) = [\mathbf{x}_j^c(t); \mathbf{x}_j^u(t)]$$
$$\mathbf{x}_j^c(t) = [x_0(t), x_1(t), \ldots, x_n(t)]_j \quad (3)$$
$$\mathbf{x}_j^u(t) = [x_{n+1}(t), \ldots, x_{n+N}(t)]_j$$

each element of which is a number of elementary production processes of a particular age, still in the construction phase or already in the utilization phase.

On the other hand, as a consequence of ageing and of scrapping, the actual number of production processes of type j of different ages carried out at the same moment t is such that

$$x_{(i)j}(t) = \hat{x}_{(i)j}(t) - u_{(i)j}(t); i = 1, \ldots n + N \quad (4)$$

$$\hat{x}_{(i)j}(t) = x_{(i-1)j}(t - 1); \hat{x}_{(0)j}(t) = u_{(0)j}(t) \quad (5)$$

where $u_{(0)j}(t)$ is the rate of starts of new processes of type j and $u_{(i)j}(t)$ is the number of processes of the same type which have been scrapped.

Scrapping of production processes occurs when human or financial resource constraints are so stringent as not to allow all the processes inherited from the past to be carried on. As an alternative to scrapping we can consider a partial use of utilization processes, which, however, also implies a cost. We can then write

$$\check{b}_{(i)j}(t) < b_{(i)j}(t); \ i = n + 1, \ldots, n + N \tag{6}$$

where $\check{b}_{(i)j}$ is the output resulting from a partial utilization of the production process, and

$$\check{a}_{(i,h)j}(t) < a_{(i,h)j}(t); \ \check{a}_{(i)j} = a(\check{b}) \tag{7}$$

is a cost which can be made a function of the degree of utilization. It can be a different function, if we like, according to the type of labour and/or the particular commodity considered.

The 'productive structure' of the economy can then be defined in terms of the age structure of its productive capacity. It has a horizontal dimension, expressed at time (t) by the vectors of elementary production processes of the various commodities at different stages of their life—still in the phase of construction $\Sigma_j \mathbf{x}_j^c(t)$ or already in the phase of utilization $\Sigma_j \mathbf{x}_j^u(t)$—being carried on. This also implies a vertical dimension: the time pattern of production associated with this age structure of productive capacity. These, in equilibrium, must be consistent with each other. Then, together with construction and utilization, investment and consumption and supply and demand of final output are also harmonized, at each given moment of time and over time. An equilibrium age structure of productive capacity also implies a given and stable relation between the relevant economic magnitudes.

The Financial Constraint (Chapters 2 and 3)

We consider two classes of agents: firms and households. All exchanges between them are intermediated by a financial asset, call it 'money', which is the only one considered in the model; the resources required to carry out production and to sustain consumption are therefore financial resources, not physical output. These resources, for both producers and consumers, come from their participation in current productive activity. External financial resources (that is, resources that do not come from productive activity: fiat money, overdrafts etc.) are required when productive activity is expanding, and at the rate at which this expansion takes place. These resources (call them $f(t)$) usually depend on the choices of the monetary authority and/or the banks. They can be determined exogenously and actually dealt with as a control variable, or they can be determined endogenously, that is, can be made to depend on some economic variable (see equations (41) below).

In each period the firms' level of activity is constrained by available financial resources or, alternatively, by labour supply. Let $m(t-1)$ be the money proceeds from the sales of final output in the previous period, $f(t)$ the external financial resources, $\omega(t)$ the wage fund—that is, the resources devoted to finance labour employed in production processes of all kinds—$c(t)$ the 'take-out', that is the resources (consumption by producers, transfers, and so forth) withheld from the financing of production, and also dealt with as a control variable in the model, $h^f(t)$ the idle monetary balances held by firms (desired $h_d^f(t)$, and undesired $h_{nd}^f(t)$). Then the firms' finance constraint which determines $\omega(t)$ can be written

$$\tilde{\omega}(t) = m(t-1) + h^f(t-1) + f(t) - c(t) - h_d^f(t) \qquad (8)$$

with $\omega(t) \equiv \tilde{\omega}(t)$ if firms are not constrained in their activity by human resources. Otherwise $\omega(t) \equiv \hat{\omega}(t)$ where $\hat{\omega}(t)$ is the wage fund 'constrained' by lack of human resources. In this case we have the appearance of non-desired idle balances

$$h_{nd}^f(t) = \max\,[0,\,\tilde{\omega}(t) - \hat{\omega}(t)] \qquad (9)$$

that is, the amount of available financial resources which it was impossible to actually use up in production because of the existence of a human constraint.

Desired idle balances are defined as

$$h_d^f(t) = \varrho(t)\,[m(t-1) + h^f(t-1) + f(t)] \qquad (10)$$

and appear when the function $\varrho(t)$, which represents the fraction of available financial resources that firms intend to withhold from production because of a loss of confidence in the existing state of affairs (see Section 2.5 above) takes a positive value.

Total expenditure by households in period (t) also depends on financial resources available to them, that is, on wages received at the beginning of the period $\omega(t)$, and on the idle balances $h^h(t-1)$ (desired h_d^h and non-desired h_{nd}^h) carried over from the preceding period. If we add consumption out of profits we obtain the money value of current demand for final output $y(t)$, that is

$$y(t) = \omega(t) + c(t) + h^h(t-1) - h_d^h(t) \qquad (11)$$

Desired idle balances, as with producers, pile up when there is a loss of confidence in the existing state of affairs and the function $\sigma(t)$ takes a positive value in the expression

$$h_d^h(t) = \sigma(t)\,[\omega(t) + c(t) + h^h(t-1)] \qquad (12)$$

where we assume that producers behave like households when acting as consumers, and hence include $c(t)$ on the RHS of (12).

Within the sequential setting considered, all prices, including wage rates, are fixed within each given period and can only change at the junction of one period and the next.

As a consequence we have

$$m(t) = \sum_j \min\,[p_j(t)s_j(t);\; p_j(t)d_j(t)] \qquad (13)$$

that is, money proceeds are determined by the minimum between the value of the current demand d and that of the current supply s of final output, which can differ since we cannot count on price changes to bring demand and supply back into balance within each given period.

Real and monetary stock changes are a substitute for the price changes which cannot take place within each period. Thus excess demand for final output (if any) results in the appearance of undesired idle balances for households

$$h_{nd}^h(t) = \sum_j p_j(t)\,\max[0,\,d_j(t) - s_j(t)] \qquad (14)$$

while excess supply results in an accumulation of undesired stocks o by firms

$$o_j(t) = \max\,[0,\,s_j(t) - d_j(t)] \qquad (15)$$

The Human Constraint and Learning (Chapter 3)

Total labour supply, in each given period t, can be written

$$\mathbf{L}_s^S(t) = [l_1^S(t),\, l_2^S(t),\, \ldots\, l_s^S(t)] \qquad (16)$$

where $\mathbf{L}_s^S(t)$ is the vector whose elements represent the different skills, inherited from the past, which are the expression of the specific character of the existing human resource. With a homogeneous labour-force this vector, of course, becomes a scalar.

We assume that the supply of labour, given the growth rate of population, depends on changes in wage rates.

In particular, each element of the supply vector is determined as follows

$$l_h^S(t) = l_h^S(t-1)\,(1 + \iota)(1 + \lambda) \qquad (17)$$

where ι is the rate of growth of population and λ is a function of the rate of change of the wage rate for skill h. In the simulations carried out we have used a hyperbolic tangent function

$$\lambda = \lambda_1 \tan h[\lambda_2 g_{w_h}(t)]$$

where λ_1 and λ_2 stand for the amplitude and the speed of adjustment, respectively.

Total demand for labour, on the other hand, will be

$$\mathbf{L}_d^D(t) = [l_1^D(t), l_2^D(t), \ldots l_s^D(t)] = \sum_j \mathbf{L}_j^D(t), j = 1, \ldots, m \quad (18)$$

where the demand for labour employed on production processes of commodity j, $\mathbf{L}_j^D(t)$, is determined by the activity of construction and utilization of productive capacity of type j, that is

$$\mathbf{L}_j^D(t) = \underline{\mathbf{A}}_j^c \, \mathbf{x}_j^c(t)' + \underline{\mathbf{A}}_j^u \, \mathbf{x}_j^u(t)' \quad (19)$$

The intensity of productive activity, in turn, depends on available financial resources (the wage fund $\omega(t)$) and on the wage-rates vector $\mathbf{w} = [w_1, w_2, \ldots, w_s]$, whose elements are fixed for the whole current period, as are all prices. When, due to full employment in the case of homogeneous labour or to scarcity of at least one essential skill (that is when $l_h^S < l_h^D$ for some $h = 1, \ldots, s$) with a heterogeneous human resource, labour demand is limited by labour supply, a human constraint stronger than the financial constraint can appear. In this case productive activity is determined by a 'constrained' wage fund which is given by

$$\hat{\omega}(t) = \mathbf{w}(t) \, \hat{\mathbf{L}}_d^D(t)' \quad (20)$$

where $\hat{\mathbf{L}}_d^D(t)$ is the 'constrained' demand for labour.

The human constraint, due essentially to the specific character of the human resource, is relaxed by the learning process, which affects the labour supply vector $\mathbf{L}_s^S(t)$ (see Section 3.6 above). This can come about through an upgrading—the passage from a lower to a higher skill out of the existing ones—as the result of some activity of formation or of 'on-the-job training'. The supply of each given skill $\bar{l}_h^S$ at time(t) [7] can then be written

$$\bar{l}_h^S(t) = l_h^D(t)(1 + \xi) \text{ if } l_h^S(t) \geq l_h^D(t) \quad (21)$$
$$\bar{l}_h^S(t) = l_h^D(t)(1 - \xi) \text{ if } l_h^S(t) < l_h^D(t)$$

where the function $\xi(t)$ ($\lim_{t \to \infty} = 0$) gives the additions to and the subtractions from skill h in period(t).

---

[7] At each given time the vector is scaled in order to take into account the growth of the population.

Out of Equilibrium
Consumption, Production, and Investment Decisions
(Chapter 5: Section 5.8)

The demand for commodity j at time(t), in real terms, can be written

$$d_j(t) = [y_j(t)/p_j(t)] \qquad (22)$$

where

$$y_j(t) = \delta_j\, y(t); \quad \sum_j \delta_j = 1 \qquad (23)$$

and where δ_j is a utility index.

The supply of commodity j at time (t), in real terms, is determined as follows

$$s_j(t) = [y_j^*(t)/p_j(t)] \qquad (24)$$

where

$$y_j^*(t) = y_j(t-1)\,[1 + g_m(t-1)] \qquad (25)$$

is the money value of final demand expected in the current period, obtained by extrapolating the trend of money proceeds from the sales of final output in the previous period.

Current final production of commodity j will then be

$$q_j(t) = s_j(t) - \eta\,[O_j(t-1)]; \quad 0 < \eta < 1 \qquad (26)$$

where η represents the fraction of total real stocks O (if any) actually put back on the market. Moreover

$$q_j(t) \leq \sum_{i=n+1}^{n+N} b_{(i)j}\, x_{(i-1)j}$$

Thus we determine the vectors of production processes in the phase of utilization $\mathbf{x}_j^u(t), \forall_j$, given the scrapping rule, and the fraction of the wage fund required to finance the carrying out of these processes, that is

$$\omega^u(t) = \sum_j \mathbf{w}(t)\,\underline{\mathbf{A}}_j^u\,\mathbf{x}_j^u(t)'. \qquad (28)$$

The resources available for financing construction processes will then be

$$i(t) \equiv \omega^c(t) = \omega(t) - \omega^u(t) \qquad (29)$$

and these resources, given the scrapping rule, will determine the vectors of production processes in the phase of construction $\mathbf{x}_j^c(t)$, $\forall_j$, that is

$$\omega^c(t) = \sum_j \mathbf{w}(t) \, \underline{\mathbf{A}}_j^c \, \mathbf{x}_j^c(t)'$$

In determining $\mathbf{x}_j^c$ and $\mathbf{x}_j^u$ for the various commodities the processes scrapped must also be taken into account. This, in each period, depends on the magnitude of final demand as concerns the utilization processes and on the available financial resources as regards construction processes. In other words, there is never a voluntary scrapping of construction processes, which only occurs as a result of a lack of financial resources; while the scrapping of utilization processes is the result of decisions taken on the basis of given expectations. When there is a final demand constraint the first processes in the utilization phase to be cut are the older ones; when there is a financial constraint the first to be cut is the rate of starts of new processes, then the processes still in the construction phase (first the more recent, then the older). This reflects a flexibility criterion that focuses on expected final output (both in its amount and in its nearness in time), and hence on expected profits, as an index of a less stringent expected finance constraint.

The above is a sort of 'residual' determination of investment in construction processes, given the available financial resources[8] and the long- and short-term expectations of producers which determine the fraction of those resources kept voluntarily as idle balances and the fraction devoted to finance utilization processes, respectively. This reflects an adaptive mechanism according to which—as already mentioned in Section 5.9 above—the resources freed by a scrapping of utilization processes are automatically shifted to finance the construction of new production processes, thus resulting in a sudden increase in the rate of starts, with all that this implies over time. Producers, in other words, do not actually take into account the information represented by current market disequilibria. This is a rather odd assumption if all producers are assumed to be alike in the activity they carry out and the information they have access to. It is much less so in a world where the plans independently formulated by a plurality of different agents who have access to different information are not necessarily consistent with each other.

As an alternative we may consider an endogenous determination of the rate of starts, and hence of the demand for additional financial

---

[8] However, not all existing financial resources will be available for production if a stronger human constraint exists.

resources to be confronted with the current supply of external financial resources as given by $f^S(t)$ (see below). One way to proceed is to determine the rate of starts of new production processes by referring to the current growth rate or, better, to an average of past growth rates (g^*). This is a Harrodian way of endogenizing investment, which depends on current demand for final output whether a lag exists or not; and this is a source of instability. In order not to distort the age structure of productive capacity too much the rate of starts may then be determined by referring to a constant growth rate (the natural rate g^{**}). The rate of starts for each production process of type j can then be written

$$u_{(O)j}(t) = \hat{x}_{(n)j}(t) [1 + g_j^*(t)]^{n+1} \qquad (31a)$$

or

$$u_{(O)j}(t) = \hat{x}_{(n)j}(t) [1 + g_j^{**}(t)]^{n+1} \qquad (31b)$$

Given the rates of starts of the various types of production processes and the number of the same processes still in the phase of construction inherited from the past we determine $\omega^c(t)$ and hence the total wage fund $\omega(t)$. The demand for additional financial resources will then be

$$f^D(t) = \omega(t) + h_d^f(t) - m(t-1) - h^f(t-1) \qquad (32)$$

and the external financial resources actually supplied to the economy

$$f(t) = \min[f^D(t), f^S(t)] \qquad (33)$$

Finally, total employment at time t will be

$$E(t) = \sum_j [\underline{A}_j^c \mathbf{x}_j^c(t)' + \underline{A}_j^u \mathbf{x}_j^u(t)'] \qquad (34)$$

which results from current production and investment determined as shown above.

Key Variables

The evolution path followed by the economy put out of equilibrium by the attempt to carry out a qualitative change is actually determined by the behaviour of the control variables $f(t)$ and $c(t)$ and by the adjustment mechanisms represented by price and wage changes.

Prices and Wages

Let the operator g be defined by

$$g_z(t) = [z(t) - z(t-1)]/z(t-1) \quad \forall z(t) \tag{35}$$

Then market-determined wage rate changes can be written

$$g_{w_h}(t) = \nu_h \, \psi_h(t-1) \tag{36}$$

where

$$\psi_h(t) = [l_h^D(t) - l_h^S(t)] / l_h^S(t) \tag{37}$$

is the rate of excess demand for the h type of labour, and ν a reaction coefficient which can be different for different skills. As an alternative, we can consider an indexation rule, e.g. of the kind

$$g_{w_h}(t) = \alpha \, g_{\bar{p}} \, ; \, 0 < \alpha < 1 \tag{38}$$

where $\bar{p}$ is the general price level.

On the other hand market-determined price changes can be written

$$g_{p_j}(t) = \kappa_j \, \phi_j(t-1) \tag{39}$$

where

$$\phi_j(t) = [d_j(t) - s_j(t)] / s_j(t) \tag{40}$$

is the rate of excess demand for the j commodity, and κ is a reaction coefficient that can differ for the different commodities. Different values of the coefficients κ and ν stand for different regulating mechanisms which can be made to represent alternative market organizations. So, while $\kappa, \nu = 1$ is the case of fully market-determined prices (and wage rates), values lower than 1 for these coefficients represent more institutionally determined prices and wages, or the existence of the filter represented by mediators (merchants or trade unions) in the respective markets. Values greater than one represent non-institutionalized markets which are likely to lead to excessive variations in prices and wages and hence possibly to strong fluctuations of the economy.

Money supply

Money supply is alternatively determined as

$$f^S(t) = f^S(t-1)[1 + g_m(t-1)] \tag{41a}$$
$$f^S(t) = f^S(t-1)[1 + g_m(0)] \tag{41b}$$
$$f^S(t) = f^S(t-1)[1 + g_{fS}(t-1) - \chi \, g_p(t)]; \, \chi > 0 \tag{41c}$$

that is, its growth rate is set equal to the current growth rate of the economy or to the original steady growth rate, or is determined in such a way as to prevent fluctuations in the price level.

Finally, it can also be determined by the demand for money.

Take-out

The 'take-out'—which, in a broader sense, includes not only consumption out of profits but also the consumption of public bodies and the resources withheld from production for whatever reason—is alternatively determined as

$$c(t) = c(t-1)[1 + g_m(t-1)] \tag{42a}$$
$$c(t) = c(t-1)[1 + g_m(0)] \tag{42b}$$
$$c(t) = c(t-1)[1 + g_m(t-1)\,\varepsilon^{t-t_c}], \mu \geq \bar{\mu} \tag{42c}$$
$$c(t) = c(t-1)[1 + g_m(t-1)], \mu < \bar{\mu} \tag{42c*}$$

that is, its growth rate is set equal to the current growth rate of the economy or to the original steady growth rate, or is determined in such a way as to gradually increase the amount of resources devoted to finance the construction of new production processes. In the last case the reduction in the growth rate of the 'take-out' which begins at the date t_c goes on until the fraction of resources taken out reaches the value of $\bar{\mu}$.

6.4 THE COHERENCE OF THE MODEL

Let us now test the coherence of the above model in the mathematical sense of finding values for the parameters which generate a regular type of behaviour of the economy. In the first place, given suitable values for the parameters, this model is capable of producing a steady state (a stationary state or balanced growth) characterized by a constant growth rate, say g, of the number of production processes of each age, which is also the general growth rate of the economy. In steady state relative proportions remain constant. We can thus consider an economy where a *homogeneous* final output is obtained from a *unique* primary input (a type of labour) without affecting the generality of the conclusions. The rate of starts of new processes can then be written

$$u_0(t) = x_{t-i}(t)\, G^i, i = 1, \ldots, n + N$$

where $G^i = [1 + g]^i$. This allows us to maintain the equilibrium

Out-of-Equilibrium Modelling

relation between construction and utilization processes, and the right balance over time between investment and consumption guarantees equilibrium both on the labour market and between the supply and demand of final output. Thus there is no reason for physical stocks to pile up or for idle balances to be held—be them undesired, the result of a disequilibrium, or desired, the sign that agents are not satisfied with the existing state of affairs.

If, following Hicks (1973), we now consider a production process with a 'simple profile', that is, with output coefficients such that

$$\mathbf{b} = [b_i]; \ b_i = b, \ i = n + 1, \ldots n + N$$

and input coefficients such that

$$\mathbf{a}^c = [a_i^c]; \ a_i^c = a^c, \ i = 0, \ldots n$$
$$\mathbf{a}^u = [a_i^u]; \ a_i^u = a^u, \ i = n + 1, \ldots n + N$$

the value of supply with no stocks carried over

$$pq(t) = p\mathbf{b}\mathbf{x}(t)'$$

which in equilibrium will be equal to the value of demand, can be written

$$y(t) = pbx_o(t)[G^{-(n+1)} + \ldots + G^{-(n+N)}]$$

while the wage fund

$$\omega(t) = w[\mathbf{a}^c \mathbf{x}^c(t)' + \mathbf{a}^u \mathbf{x}^u(t)']$$

can be written

$$\omega(t) = w\{a^c x_o(t)[1 + G^{-1} + \ldots + G^{-n}]$$
$$+ a^u x_o(t)[1 + G^{-(n+1)} + \ldots + G^{-(n+N)}]\}.$$

The non-wage demand–supply equilibrium will be

$$c(t) = \mu[pq(t)]$$

or

$$c(t) = \mu[m(t-1) + f(t)]$$

with μ a constant in the steady state; and, with no idle balances,

$$m(t-1) + f(t) = \omega(t) + c(t).$$

It follows that, in equilibrium,

$$(1 - \mu)[pq(t)] = \omega(t)$$

that is

$$(1 - \mu)pbx_o(t)[G^{-(n+1)} + \ldots + G^{-(n+N)}] =$$
$$= w\{a^c x_o(t)[1 + G^{-1} + \ldots G^{-n}] +$$

$$a^u x_o(t)[1 + G^{-(n+1)} + \ldots + G^{-(n+N)}]\}$$

and hence, after manipulation,

$$(1 - \mu)pb = w(a^c G^{n^*} + a^u)$$

where

$$N = n + 1 = n^*$$

and $(a^c G^{n^*} + a^u)$ is the amount of labour required to obtain b units of final output in the steady state. Therefore the greater $(1 - \mu)$ the greater G, and hence g; that is, the greater the fraction of output 'taken out' μ, the smaller the steady growth rate of the economy, and vice versa. Thus the equilibrium growth rate depends on a preference parameter in the same way as in Harrod's model or in endogenous growth models.

This is due to the very character of the Neo-Austrian process of production. In this process labour and the resources required to make it work—physical output in the original Hicksian model, financial resources in the model we are dealing with—are strictly complementary. More labour can only be put to work if more resources are available to sustain it, and vice versa. No resource constraint arises, and hence no diminishing returns set in as the results of accumulation, if this complementarity relation is assured. However, given the time dimension and the sequential structure of the production process, this relation appears as a relation over time: what matters is intertemporal complementarity. This means, in particular, that more savings do not automatically lead to more growth—as would be the case if we could abstract from the intertemporal character of the complementarity relation, and as it actually happens in endogenous growth models. The structure of the model requires in fact that the supply of money must also be made to grow at the higher rate associated with a lower value of μ (higher savings) for complementarity to be assured over time and the new equilibrium steady path to be established.

Steady state, in any case, is a trivial solution. Let us look then for non-constant periodic solutions, such as for instance, business cycles or cyclical growth. It is immediately evident that this implies eliminating as much as possible the adjustment mechanisms which, as we shall see in particular in what follows, otherwise engender complex time paths of the economy: in such a way, however, as not also to eliminate the sequential structure of the model. This depends on assuming very specific behaviours of agents in an out-of-equilibrium context, that is, when a steady state has been broken up and a distortion of productive capacity occurs.

We assume in particular, in the first place, that firms systematically attempt to correct errors involving imbalances in the age structure of productive capacity, that is, to eliminate the distortion of productive capacity necessarily associated with any attempt to bring about a qualitative change. However, as already mentioned, the sequential structure of the model implies that changes can only take place at the junction of one period and the next, so that there is then necessarily a one-period lag in corrections—the minimum reaction period in the sequence sketched out. On the other hand endogenization of the money supply makes the correction possible. The money supply becomes a dependent variable and results from the decisions of firms making use of overdrafts.

Sticking for the moment to the one commodity–one input set-up, we assume that the rate of starts of new processes $u_o(t)$ is determined by firms in such a way as to compensate for the imbalances in the preceding period. So we have

$$u_o(t) = \tilde{u}_o(t) + \tilde{u}_o(t-1) - u_o(t-1)$$

where $\tilde{u}_o$ refers to the steady-state rate of starts.

The wage fund that allows firms to carry out the rate of starts thus determined is

$$\omega(t) = w[\mathbf{a}^c \mathbf{x}^c(t)' + \mathbf{a}^u \mathbf{x}^u(t)']$$

where the first element of $\mathbf{x}(t)$ is $u_0(t)$ as determined above.

This determines the money supply $f^S(t)$ that becomes endogenous and is given by

$$f^S(t) = \omega(t) + c(t) - m(t-1) - h^f(t-1) + h^f_d(t)$$

On the other hand, we also assume that firms systematically adjust their prices in order to clear the market for final output ($\kappa = 1$), but the wage rate is kept stable whatever the situation on the labour market ($\nu = 0$). The reason for this specific assumption is that the effects of a change in the wage rate are ambiguous. As a matter of fact, although an increase in the wage rate sustains the demand for final output, it also implies a stronger financial constraint, with the result that a bias appears to the detriment of production processes in the construction phase.

Finally, the 'take-out' is made to grow in accordance with the firms' money proceeds as in equation (42a).

We will now show that once a distortion of productive capacity occurs the economic process, as a result of the working of the adjustment mechanisms as modified by the above assumptions, tends to a sort of stationary attractor. This will cause regular fluctuations of the relevant variables generated by the first and only exogenous structural modification; successive shocks are not necessary for obtaining persistent cycles (Amendola, Froeschlé, and Gaffard 1996). On the other hand, the assumed behaviours keep imbalances constant over time.

Let us start from a steady state of the economy at zero growth rate and with full employment of the labour force, and consider an increase in the liquidity preference of the firms—for whatever reason—which finds expression in the appearance of positive desired idle balances $h_d^f(t)$. This is represented by the coefficient ϱ taking a value greater than zero, at which it was set in the original steady state, in equation (11) above.

This once-and-for-all change in the value of ϱ, given $c(t)$, implies a reduction in the wage fund $\omega(t)$ and, as a consequence, a reduction in the rate of starts of new processes which affects the balance between production processes in the phase of construction and in the phase of utilization and hence creates a first distortion in productive capacity in the same period. A fall in aggregate final demand, excess supply, and the involuntary accumulation of stocks of final output are the other consequences of the breaking up of the equilibrium sequence, since not only construction and utilization, but also investment and consumption and supply and demand are no longer harmonized over time.

One could suppose that the above-mentioned adjustments concerning prices and productive capacity prevent the economy from exhibiting fluctuations. This is not so. The numerical simulations carried out (the data are given in the Appendix) show the existence of very regular fluctuations which affect the rate of growth, the rate of starts of new processes, the balance between production processes in the construction phase and in the utilization phase, and the rate of change of the price of final output (Fig. 6.1). In fact, it is the regularity in the distortion of productive capacity (measured by the ratio of construction processes to utilization processes) that explains the regularity of the fluctuations in the growth rate. The very strong hypotheses made as to the behaviour of agents do not prevent fluctuations from occurring: they only make them regular. The initial perturbation comes back at a constant time interval. This is explained by the structure of the propagation mechanism (Fig. 6.2).

Out-of-Equilibrium Modelling

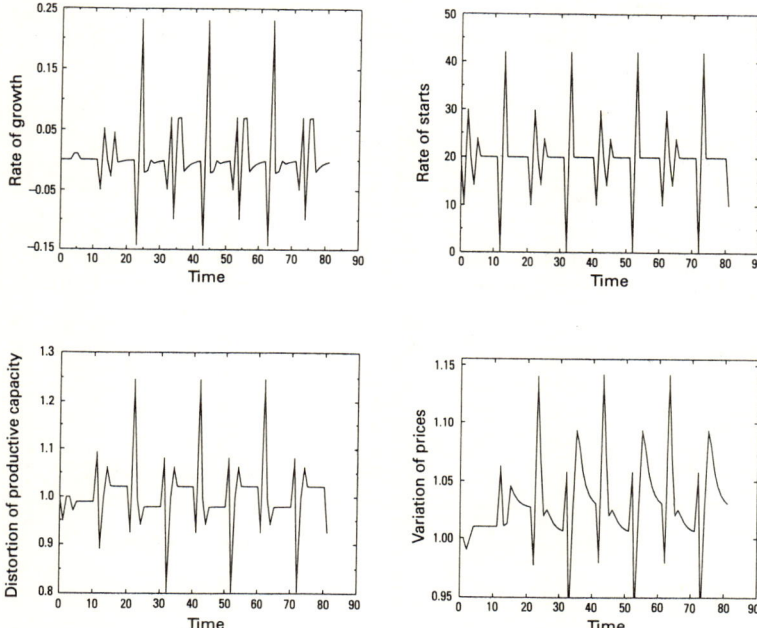

FIG 6.1

What really happens along the way? There are regular waves which reveal both persistent disequilibria (in the time structure of productive capacity) and persistent corrective mechanisms. As a matter of fact, provided that the firms do not change their short-term expectations and do not cut production processes as a consequence of the appearance of undesired stocks of final output, the first reduction of the rate of starts only has the effect of reducing the amount of sales after a number of periods which corresponds to the length of the construction phase and, therefore, to reduce the wage fund and finally the rate of starts once again.

Let us now assume instead that firms have 'rational expectations' in that they do not try to correct distortions of productive capacity after they have occurred, but maintain a constant investment behaviour aimed at preventing the distortions themselves from occurring—and likewise do not react to current market disequilibria (if any) which are considered as purely random phenomena. Consider the shock

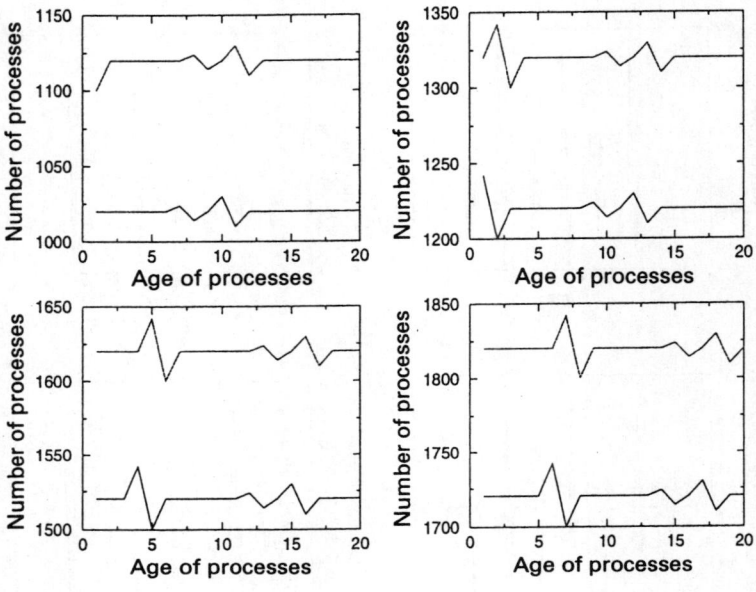

Fig 6.2

represented by the introduction of a superior technology characterized by lower labour costs, that is, such that

$$\hat{a}^c G^{n^*} + \hat{a}^u < a^c G^{n^*} + a^u$$

An initial fluctuation is immediately damped down and the economy converges to a new steady state corresponding to the superior technology and hence characterized by a higher level of productivity and full employment. This, we shall see in what follows, is the only case of a process of change that converges to a new equilibrium state completely determined by one of the 'fundamentals' of the economy: the properties of the new technology (Fig. 6.3). The initial fluctuation and the associated imbalances between supply and demand due to the sequential structure of the model do not persist, as in the case previously examined, because the hypothesis of rational expectations makes it possible to maintain the consistency over time of construction and utilization and hence hampers the problems of intertemporal complementarity of production that characterize Neo-Austrian models from appearing.

Out-of-Equilibrium Modelling

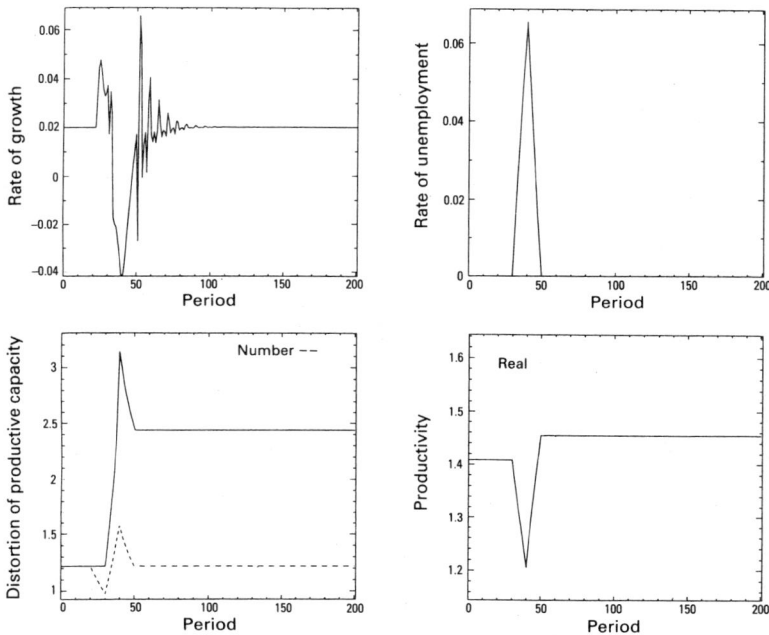

FIG 6.3

This is confirmed on the other hand by the fact that, if we introduce a behaviour based on adaptive expectations as regards the status of final demand, although maintaining the above-mentioned investment behaviour, the economy no longer converges to a full equilibrium but only to a pseudo-equilibrium characterized by permanent unemployment and a fall in productivity: the productivity paradox which will be illustrated more clearly in Section 7.5 below (Fig. 6.4).

6.5. COMPLEX DYNAMICS

The fully fledged working of the model, if we do not make the above restrictive assumptions as to the adjustment mechanisms and the control variables, engenders a complex dynamic which brings to light a crucial problem of the viability of the economy whenever a qualitative

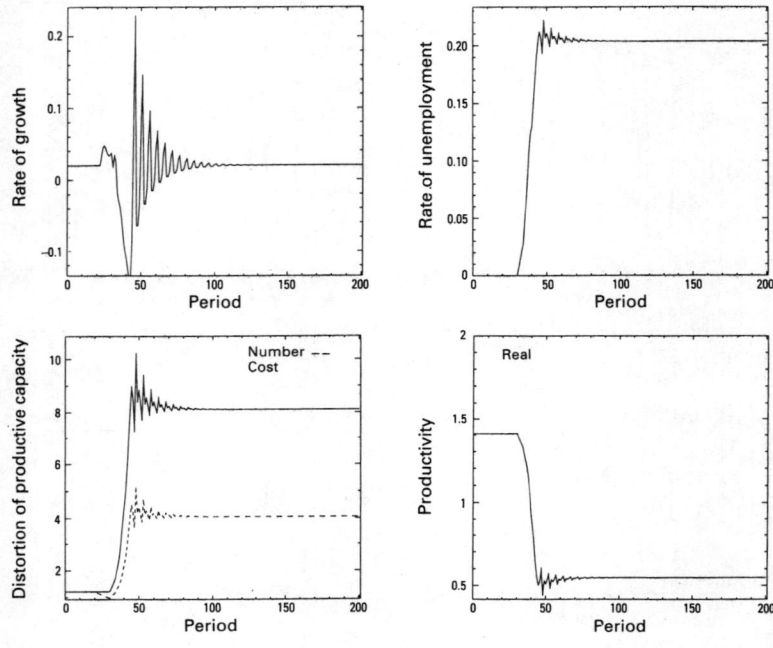

Fig 6.4

change is contemplated. This complex dynamic is mainly the result of the interaction of two lags: the construction lag in productive activity and a lag of transmission of information (see Section 4.8 above), which are the expression of problems of intertemporal complementarity and of co-ordination of economic activity in a sequential context.

The breaking up of a steady state always implies an abrupt change in the age structure of productive capacity. This is the case, as we have just seen, when at a given moment in time there is an increase in the idle balances desired and held by firms, as a consequence of a change in their long-term expectations. This is also the case, as we shall see in the following chapter, for all kind of shocks, real or monetary, which imply the breaking of the previously existing equilibrium sequence. As a result, in all cases there is no longer complete synchronization between construction and utilization, and hence also investment and consumption and supply and demand are no longer harmonized over time.

This distortion of productive capacity, once produced, has persistent effects. This is due to the interaction of the intertemporal complementarities of production and of the decision process, that is, to the fact that the working of price and wage reaction mechanisms tends itself to reinforce the distortion over time. When we try to eliminate the working of these mechanisms, as we have seen, we do not succeed in eliminating the effects of the distortion; we only obtain the specific case of periodic orbits analysed in the preceding section.

In the model the working of the market for final output is represented by two difference equations governing output and price changes. These equations determine to what extent resources will be devoted to the utilization of the existing productive capacity and to the construction of a new one, respectively. In this way they determine the age structure of productive capacity and its evolution over time.[9]

The wage mechanism has the same kind of influence. Wages—in the more general formulation of the model, not in the specific case analysed in the preceding section, where the wage rate is kept constant by assumption—are changing from one period to the next either in relation to labour market disequilibria (whose effects are more or less mediated) or as a result of some indexation rule. In any case there are two servo-mechanisms again, one regulating the wage rate, the other regulating the wage fund and the level of employment. These mechanisms contribute to allocating resources between the phase of utilization of productive capacity and the phase of its construction.

Consider for example the breaking of a full employment steady state, due to an increase in the liquidity preference of the firms, associated with the adoption of a new technology, which persists over time (Fig. 6.5). This implies the appearance of an excess supply of final output which, if external financial resources f and consumption by producers c are kept growing at the original steady rate, stimulates erratic fluctuations of the growth rate of output. These fluctuations are associated with increasing distortions of the structure of productive capacity, with a bias against the production processes in the phase of utilization. However, this is followed by a scrapping not

---

[9] As stressed by Leijonhufvud (1993), in this Marshallian kind of market 'this little system of *two coupled oscillators* may very easily generate complex dynamics' (ibid. p. 9).

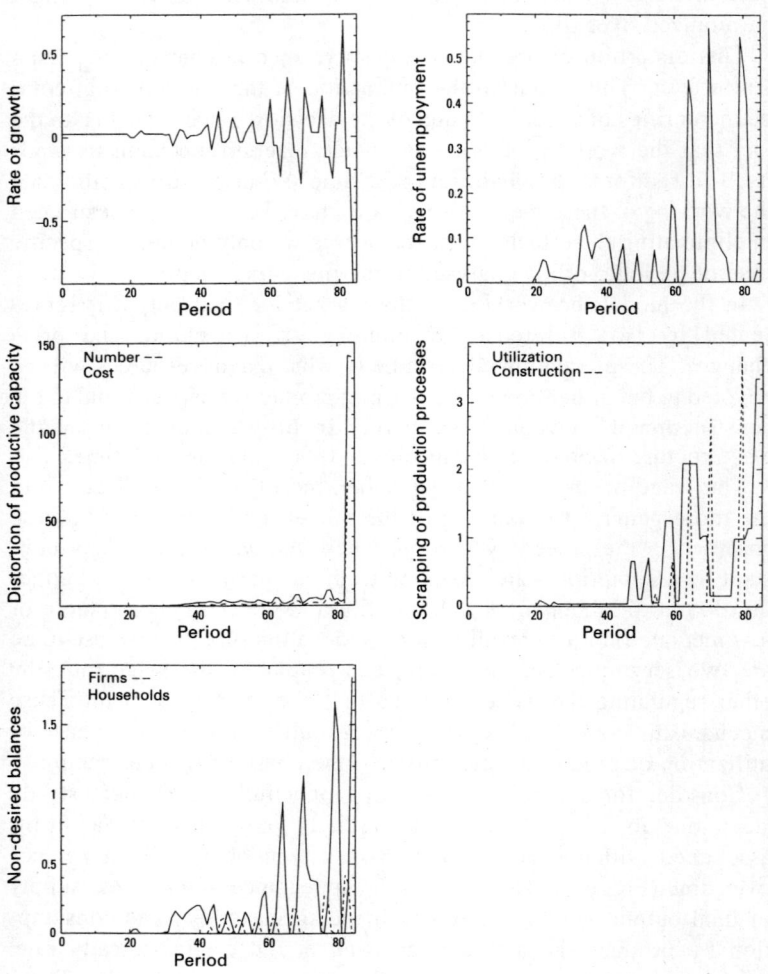

Fig 6.5

only of utilization processes but also, albeit later, of the extra construction processes which had been started with the resources freed up by the scrapping of utilization processes. Finally, important fluctuations in employment occur. However, due to the amplitude of the fluctuations of the growth rate of output, unemployment is fully re-absorbed and a human resource constraint appears in the phase of expansion: firms are then forced to accumulate idle balances, which helps to reverse the cycle.

In any case, as already stressed in Section 5.9 above, the time profile of the evolution of the economy depends both on initial conditions and the value of the parameters of the model, and on how expectations are actually formed and adjustments in productive capacity made (e.g. whether production processes are actually scrapped or left idle). Different conditions and values imply different results, in particular as regards the viability of the economy. For instance, the case considered in the last simulation presented is not viable (the economy collapses after 80 periods; collapse occurs when all the construction processes are scrapped[10]). Viability, in the first place, appears to depend on the functioning of markets (a co-ordination mechanism) as represented by the value of the reaction coefficients of the price of final output and the rate of wages. Simulations carried out over a maximum of 200 periods show (Fig 6.6) that—whatever the wage reaction coefficient—the higher the price reaction coefficient the more viable the economy is (the greater the number of periods over which the economy keeps functioning the more viable this is). The reason is that strong price variations do not allow the fluctuations in short-term expectations of producers to bring about excessively strong fluctuations in production (because the adjustments are made through price changes) and, as a consequence, excessively strong distortions in productive capacity with a bias against production processes in the phase of utilization. This, on the other hand, depends in turn on expectations and forms of adjustment in productive capacity already made. But in any case this shows that, as mentioned in Section 6.2 above, in processes of economic change there is a crucial interaction between the time dimension of productive activity and market mechanisms.

Even more important, as regards viability, are the values taken by the control variables $f(t)$ and $c(t)$ (another co-ordination mechanism). We have already seen how the endogenization of $f(t)$ helps to damp down fluctuations in the case of periodic orbits. If now we let both $f(t)$ and $c(t)$ change at the same rate at which the economy actually evolves step after step, we see that, after a period of turbulence, the

---

[10] The criterion according to which the economy is no longer viable when all the construction processes are scrapped will also be adopted in all the simulations carried out in Chapter 7 below.

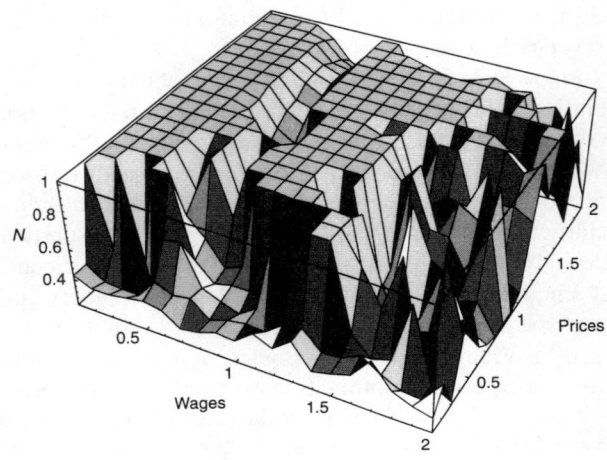

Fig 6.6.

economy itself tends towards a stable growth rate, accompanied by the disappearance of unemployment, as the result of an achieved stability of the structure of productive capacity (Fig. 6.7). The reason for this result will be made clear in the following chapter, where the problem of the management of the control variables of the model will be gone into in greater detail.

6.6. CANCELLING THE SEQUENCE

The model that we are dealing with is a model in discrete time. Its working and its results depend crucially on this feature. This might appear as a drawback in view of the belief that, from the analytical viewpoint, the qualitative results of a model should be invariant with respect to changes from discrete to continuous time, and vice versa.[11] But this is not so. What the proposed modelling in fact

---

[11] This is actually the case with the Neo-Austrian model proposed by Hicks, which was originally in continuous time (1970), but leads to the same conclusions (e.g. the 'machinery effect') once translated into discrete time (1973). However, this depends on the very restrictive assumptions as to the time profile of the production process.

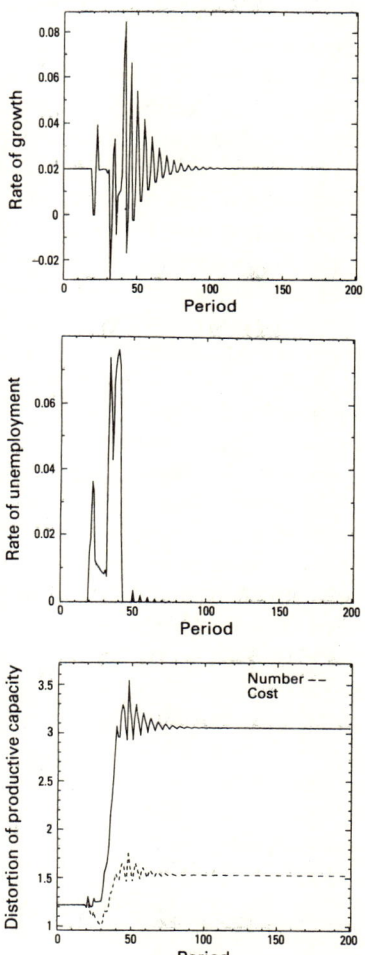

FIG 6.7

allows us to stress is that the essential features of an out-of-equilibrium process can only be captured by focusing on a sequential structure which brings to light certain lags and their interactions over time.[12] In particular, we recall, the complex dynamic of the model is mainly the result of the interaction of two lags: the construction lag in productive activity and a lag in the transmission of information (see Section 4.8 above). As a matter of fact, a certain 'inertia' in the decision process is essential for the original distortion of productive capacity associated with any attempt to carry out a qualitative change to bring about imbalances which feed each other by interacting over a sequence of periods, thus resulting in a threat to the viability of the change undertaken. This inertia is absent from Hicks's analysis, where equilibrium between supply and demand of final output is guaranteed at each and every moment of the sequence of periods through which a Traverse between techniques takes place;[13] but this, as already stressed in Section 5.6 above, is certainly an incongruity of the analysis itself, carried out in what is otherwise an out-of-equilibrium context.

Thus the conclusion as to whether the results of a model are invariant or less with respect to the time periodization of the model itself comes down to whether we are in fact sticking to an equilibrium approach or we are instead carrying out an out-of-equilibrium analysis. The latter evokes problems of intertemporal complementarity and co-ordination issues, which arise when decision processes are not perfectly harmonized over time. Lags in the decision process are necessary for the shocks which bring about complementarity and co-ordination problems not to be instantaneously re-absorbed, thus not allowing an out-of-equilibrium process to actually set in (see again Section 4.8 above). Discrete time periods, provided they have a sufficient length, make these lags stand out, and make them feed the interactions which trace the out-of-equilibrium path followed by the economy. Lags, and a certain inertia in the decision process, not only feed out-of-equilibrium processes, though; they can also contribute to making them viable, by diluting the effects of interventions aimed at re-establishing the consistency over time of productive activity which might otherwise result in too sudden and abrupt adjustments in the

---

[12] Which does not mean that lags are not consistent with continuous time models, but that, as we shall soon see, they can lead to the same results as in discrete time models only if their length is not such as to affect the adjustment mechanisms which maintain the economy within an equilibrium context.

[13] This equilibrium is the result of hypotheses which allow us to trace out the Traverse as a fully predetermined path, thus actually abstracting from a thorough decision process.

Out-of-Equilibrium Modelling

productive structure of the economy. We have already touched upon this point when discussing Harrod's model (see Section 5.5 above), but we shall go much deeper into it when we analyse specific out-of-equilibrium processes in the following chapter.

Out of equilibrium, then, discrete and continuous cases are not and cannot be equivalent. To show this let us consider the one commodity–one input version of our model, with a 'simple profile' of the production process. In steady state we have

$$\omega(t) = (1 - \mu)[m(t - 1) + f(t)]$$

If we assume that the phase of construction and the phase of utilization have the same length and call it n, from Section 6.4 above we have, after manipulation,

$$G^n = (1 - \mu)\frac{p(t)b}{w(t)a}$$

In discrete time the step Δt is given by

$$\Delta t = t_{i+1} - t_i = \frac{T}{N_{iter}}$$

where T is physical time, and N_{iter} is the total number of iterations considered (an integer multiple of the time $2n$ required for the construction and utilization of production processes). For a given value of N_{iter} we can analyse the effect of different kinds of discretization, that is, what happens for different values of Δt. These values are such that

$$\Delta t_k = \frac{T}{kN_{iter}}$$

where k takes successive integer values from 1 onwards. When Δt changes, some key parameters have to be 'normalized' if we want to represent the same system: the daily production b, or the growth rate g, are not the same as the corresponding weekly values. The chosen 'normalization' is such that

$$b_k = \frac{b_1}{k},$$

$$w_k a_k = \frac{w_1 a_1}{k}$$

This implies that $(1 - \mu)[m(t - 1) + f(t)]$ is constant for any Δt, so that

$$G^{kn}_{(k)} = (1 - \mu)\frac{bp(t)}{aw(t)} = G^n_{(1)}$$

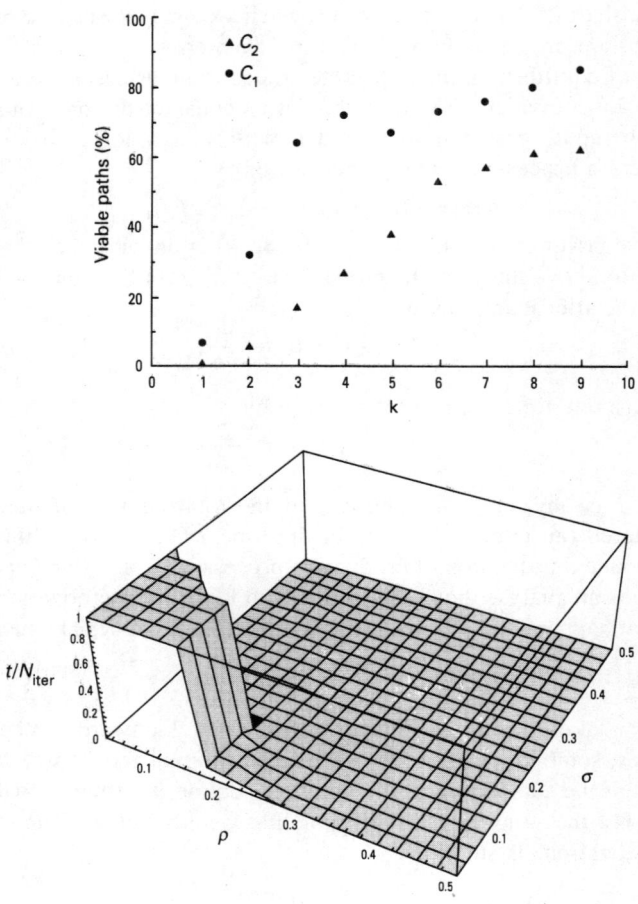

FIG 6.8

Consider now an economy disturbed by liquidity shocks (represented, in the model, by ϱ and/or σ taking positive or increasing values). These shocks disturb the economy for the same interval of real time $n_\varsigma(k) = k[n_\varsigma(1)]$. For each value of k from 1 onwards we compute a number Y = 20.20 of paths, each one corresponding to a particular value of ϱ and σ,

$$\varrho_k(\zeta) = \zeta \Delta \varrho_k, \zeta = 1, \ldots, 20$$
$$\sigma_k(\zeta) = \zeta \Delta \sigma_k, \zeta = 1, \ldots, 20$$

where $\Delta \varrho_k = \Delta \sigma_k = C/k$, with C constant. Once again the step size of the magnitude of the perturbation is reduced as the inverse of the duration of the perturbation itself.

For each path (and each simulation) corresponding to specific initial conditions we compute, if any, the time $t = \bar{t}$ at which the evolution path of the economy is interrupted, that is, the economy is no longer viable. If the simulations are run over a time T (which corresponds to a maximum number of periods) the economy is said to be viable for all paths for which $\bar{t} \geq T$. The distribution of $\bar{t}$ (means and variance) may be considered as a global indicator of viability of the economy.

In the particular case of liquidity shocks, the simulations performed show that the number of viable paths increases as the discreteness of the time representation becomes finer (Fig. 6.8).[14]

We see that the discretization opted for matters; discrete and continuous cases differ greatly. The results obtained depend on the step size. The greater the step size the stronger the inertia of the decision process. Beyond a certain size co-ordination issues are involved which raise the problem of viability.

We have highlighted, in the last three sections, the essential analytical features of the sequential model proposed and stressed their bearing on the dynamic behaviour of the model itself. We shall now use this model to analyse, in the next chapter, significant processes of qualitative change. This will make it possible not only to throw light on the basic aspects of the mechanism of growth but also, in Chapter 8, to put in the correct perspective some famous controversies in the history of economic thought.

---

[14] This result was obtained by Froeschlé and Lega (1995) by making use of the model presented in this chapter.

7
Processes of change

7.1. CHANGES IN TECHNOLOGY

Real, monetary, or expectational shocks may be at the origin of the out-of-equilibrium processes in which the attempts to bring about qualitative changes result. Some such processes portraying the most typical cases of economic change will be analysed in this chapter. In all cases simulations performed by making use of the model expounded in the preceding chapter will make it possible to trace out the out-of-equilibrium paths followed by the economy under different conditions. This will set the stage for investigating the viability of the different processes of economic change.

We shall start from a real shock, such as a change in technology. The simulations will bring to light the various effects of changes in technology—on wages, on prices, on employment—not dissociating them but taking into account the feedback mechanisms at work.[1]

Certainly the complexity of these mechanisms makes it extremely difficult to follow them closely and to interpret the results obtained. So the only way out is to consider a wide enough spectrum of cases, corresponding to different hypotheses as to the behaviour of agents and as to the values imputed to the reaction and adjustment coefficients of the model. The results will then be interpreted in the light of both the nature of the economic phenomena involved and economic theory, with specific reference to some significant relations established by the theory—like, for instance, the relation between the rate of inflation and the rate of unemployment, that between the rate of employment and the share of income going to wages, and so forth.

The main point of attention of economists who have dealt with the problem of the effects of changes in technology has always been the relation between technology and employment, beginning from Ricardo's 'machinery effect', according to which technical progress necessarily brings about unemployment in the short run. Our analysis will

---

[1] This is unlike in equilibrium models, where single relations are usually considered. This is particularly so with regard to employment, whether the focus is only on the functioning of the labour market or a more complex determination of employment is taken into account (Blanchard 1990; Layard, Nickell, and Jackman 1991).

show that the impact of changes in technology on employment cannot be reduced to technological factors only—whether a 'machinery effect', as revived for instance by Hicks's analysis (1970, 1973), or otherwise [2]—but reflects rather the complexity of the interaction between decisions (as to current production, investment, prices, wages, and so forth) and existing constraints in a sequential process.

Hicks's analysis, often mentioned in this book, relies on three specific assumptions, which are meant both to make the phenomenon involved stand out and to deal with it analytically. The hypothesis of a fixed real wage is associated with that of constant consumption out of profits (a constant 'take-out'), while the assumption of a perfectly elastic supply of labour at the prevailing wage rate makes it possible to dispense with the complications arising from the existence of a human resource constraint. These are clearly *ad hoc* assumptions.

In order to enrich the analysis without dispensing with the problem involved we shall now propose it again within the context of our sequential monetary economy, in the attempt to verify what degree of generality can be attributed to the phenomenon of technological unemployment. Less *ad hoc* assumptions will be made which, however, will not obscure the time articulation of economic activity (with the lags and errors involved) essential for the appearance of the 'machinery effect' at the analytical level[3]. At the same time this will make possible a better understanding of the phenomenon in question by allowing us to take into account not only the effects of the intertemporal complementarity of production but also those of a lack of co-ordination of the decision process over time. The complications due to the existence of a human constraint, excluded by assumption in Hicks's analysis, will also be taken into account.

---

[2] See e.g. Aghion and Howitt (1994), where the degree of unemployment shown to be associated with the equilibrium of the economy depends on the strength of the impact of changes in technology taking place in succession.

[3] As would instead be the case with the assumption of savings behaviour which, when confronted with the introduction of a new technique implying a greater construction cost (the case specifically put forward by Hicks as best representing Ricardo's viewpoint), would lead to a reallocation of consumption flows over time which made it possible to finance construction activity at the higher cost without distorting productive capacity; or of a real wage that would instantaneously adjust to changing market conditions. These assumptions would in fact dispense with the 'machinery effect': either by not allowing it to arise—due to an intertemporal optimization of consumption flows implying a full co-ordination of economic activity over time—or by instantaneously re-absorbing it through adequate wage changes. However, this would mean concealing a problem, not dealing with it in a more comprehensive way.

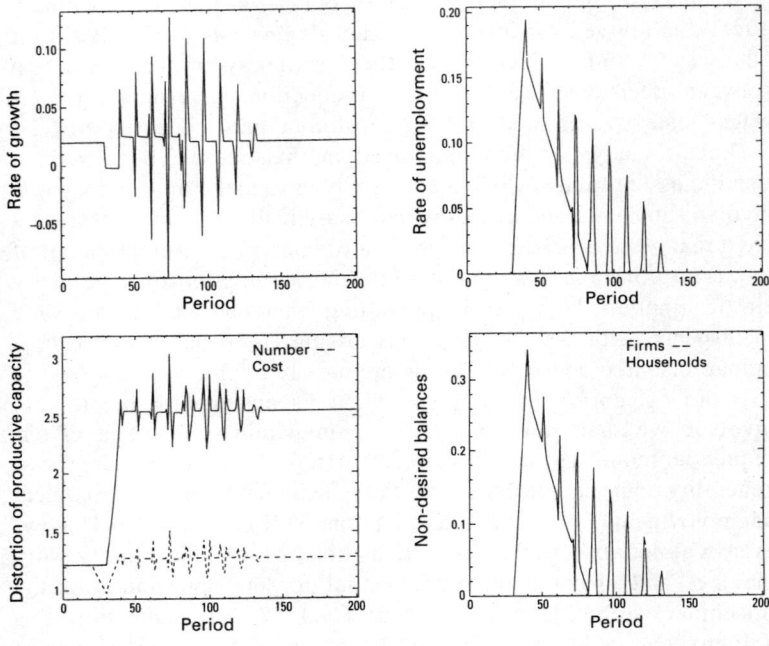

FIG 7.1a

We shall first consider the case of a single technological shock: the introduction of a new, more costly (in terms of labour) technique in the phase of construction but implying a more than proportional saving of labour in the phase of utilization (the same case of technical advance considered by Hicks), which takes place at a given moment in an economy with full employment at that moment.[4]

The simulations performed show that, with proportional savings[5], a

---

[4] In the simulations performed this happens after twenty periods during which both output and the labour force are assumed to grow at the same constant rate, say 2 per cent. However, although sticking to the hypothesis of a homogeneous final output, from now on we shall consider in the simulations a heterogeneous human resource made up of four types of labour characterized by different skills, with the corresponding wage rates.

[5] We have reinterpreted in this way, that is, by letting the 'take-out' grow at the same rate as output, the extreme Hicksian assumption of a constant consumption out of profits.

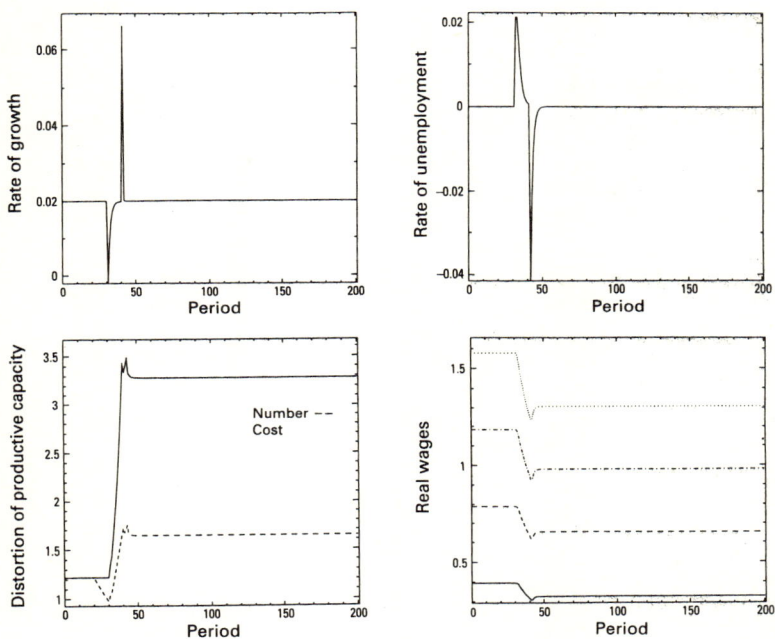

Fig 7.1b

'machinery effect', namely, a temporary fall in employment associated with a fall in final output, usually occurs after the end of the phase of construction (ten periods in the case considered) of the first round of the new productive capacity (that is, at the thirtieth period). This reflects the fall of investment in productive capacity which increasing construction costs imply with given resources.

With fixed prices and wages this happens whether labour supply is perfectly elastic or not (Fig. 7.1a).[6] The 'machinery effect' is repeated as the result of fluctuations of the growth rate of output which persist for quite a long time. Wage flexibility, if there is no human constraint, makes it possible to immediately re-absorb unemployment but cannot hamper it from appearing, as wages in the model do not adjust

---

[6] This is because in this case no human constraint arises along the way.

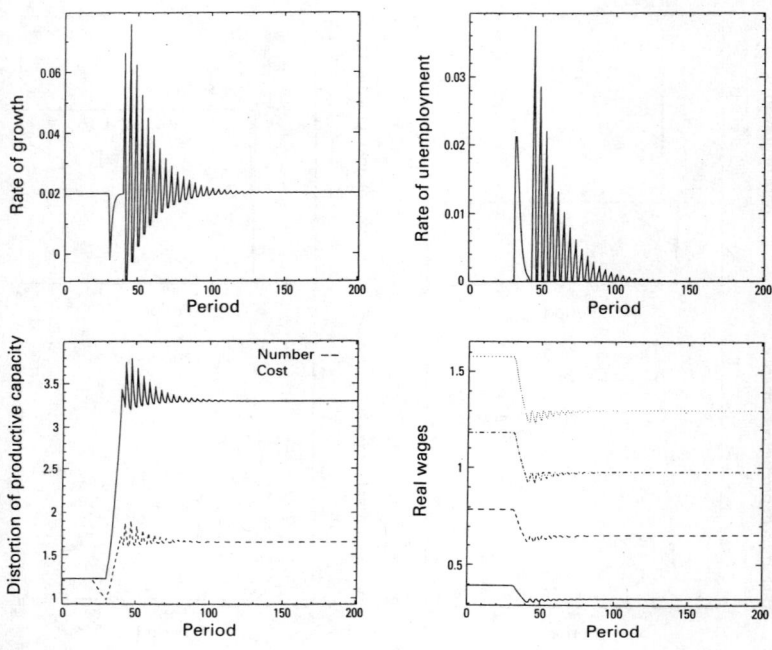

FIG 7.1c

instantaneously to the arising disequilibrium in the labour market, but only with a one-period lag (Fig. 7.1b). Co-ordination through price changes is effective but not instantaneous. This is due, of course, to the sequential character of the model, which reflects the sequential character of the decision process. In any case the out-of-equilibrium path followed by the economy is characterized by an increasing scrapping of production processes in the phase of utilization and by a falling ratio of these processes to construction processes, as the result of the fact that the activities of construction and utilization, and hence investment and consumption, are no longer harmonized over time.[7] If we introduce a human constraint the fluctuation of output induced by the technological shock persists for a while

---

[7] The distortion of productive capacity in the figures is measured exactly by the ratio of construction to utilization processes, in physical terms of cost.

and the 'machinery effect' is repeated while the economy keeps fluctuating (fig. 7.1c); it takes longer for unemployment to be reabsorbed, due to the interaction between the human constraint and the wage rate.

For the 'machinery effect' not to occur there should be no capital shortage, which appears to be the true reason for the fall in employment. Let us then accompany the adoption of the new more productive technique with a reduction in the 'take-out' (an increase in savings) so as to render it compatible with the higher growth rate made possible by the technical advance carried out, while letting the supply of money grow at the original steady rate. However, the attempt to adjust the productive structure of the economy to a different situation in one step represents a shock which is difficult to absorb, as will be shown in particular in Section 7.4 below. Thus we have considered a gradual increase in the amount of resources devoted to productive activity,

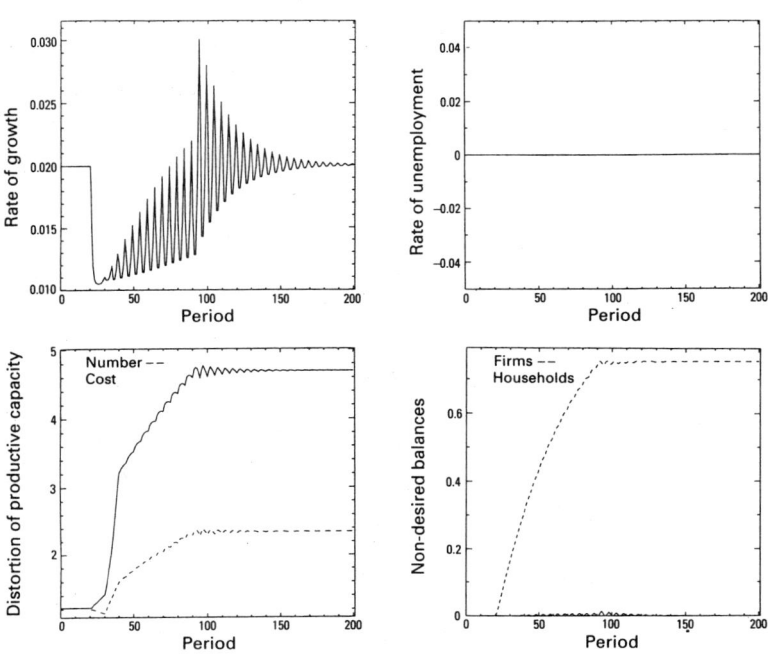

FIG 7.2a

176   *Out of Equilibrium*

namely, a gradual reduction in the fraction of output 'taken out' μ, so as to arrive at the new structure of productive capacity consistent with the higher growth rate through successive small changes in the rate of starts of production processes (see equation (42c) in Chapter 6).

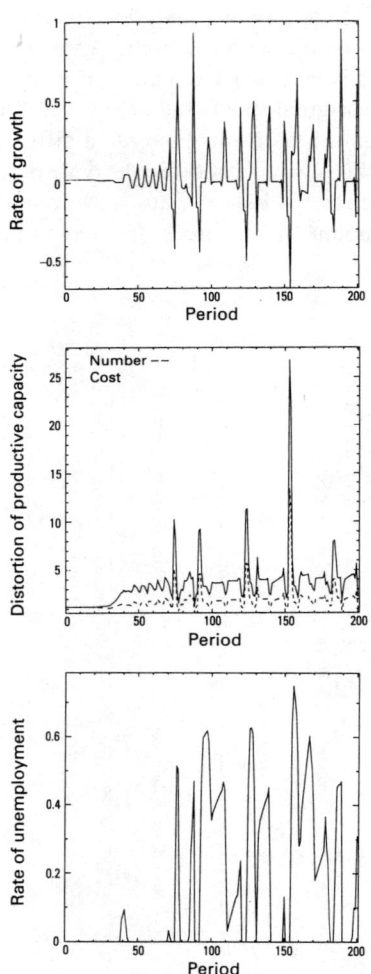

FIG 7.2*b*

Processes of Change

With a human constraint the 'machinery effect' actually disappears, provided that prices and wages are fixed and the time profile of the evolution of savings is such as not to stimulate fluctuations in the ratio of construction to utilization production processes (Fig. 7.2a). In this case the idle balances which pile up due to the human constraint can in fact be fully and immediately put back, which makes it possible to immediately re-absorb the potential unemployment associated with a shortage of capital. However, this is an extremely fragile result which a simple change in the time profile of savings may make vanish (see Fig. 7.2b, where the 'machinery effect' reappears). The fragility of the result is confirmed on the other hand by the fact that with flexible prices and wages we have again a 'machinery effect' which stimulates fluctuations in unemployment lasting for a certain time before this settles down (Fig. 7.2c). This is due to the fact that increases in wages

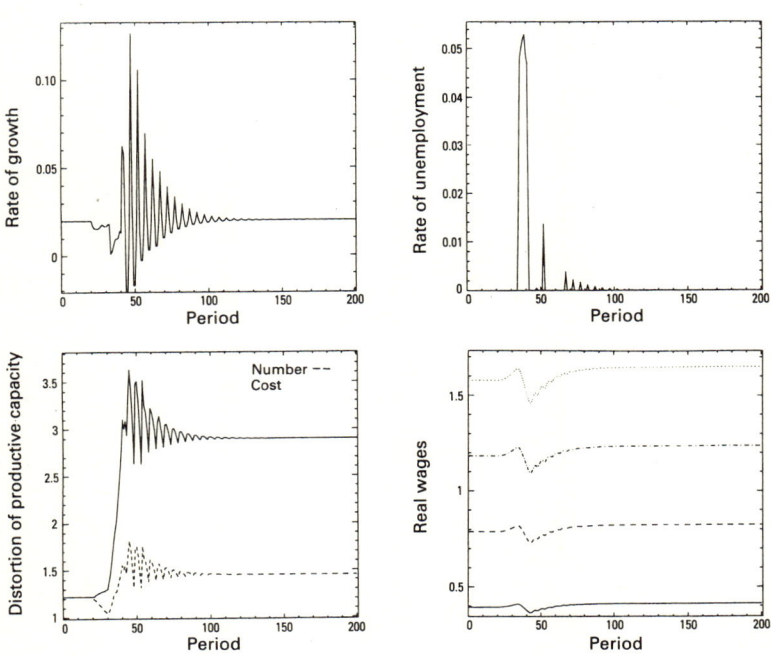

FIG 7.2c

178 *Out of Equilibrium*

reduce the amount of idle balances available for immediate re-employment in production processes, which implies a certain shortage of capital.

Finally, with constant real wages (flexible prices and fully indexed

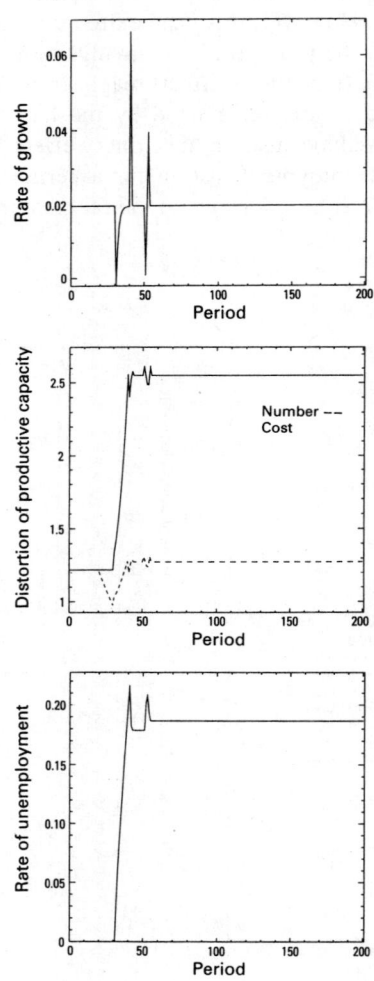

Fig 7.3*a*

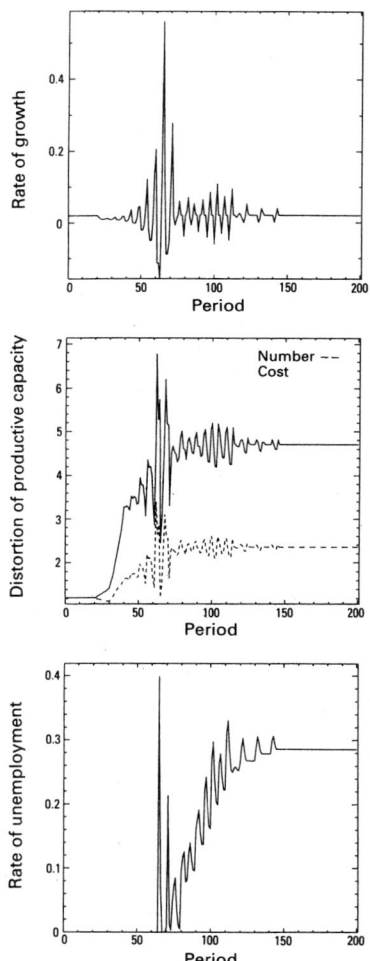

Fig 7.3b

wage rates), whatever the saving behaviour and whether a human constraint exists or not, we always have a 'machinery effect' and the resulting unemployment is never re-absorbed. The economy reaches a new equilibrium with a constant rate of unemployment (see Figs. 7.3a and 7.3b for proportional and gradually increasing savings, respectively, in the case of a human constraint).

The appearance of temporary unemployment as the result of a shortage of capital must therefore be considered as a normal consequence of technological shocks.

But what precisely do we mean by 'capital shortage'? Higher construction costs, if savings do not adjust, reduce the rate of starts of production processes below the level required to maintain full employment. The activity of the construction of productive capacity is insufficient. However, an increase in savings, as we have just seen, is not sufficient in itself. A human constraint may reduce the amount of savings actually channelled into production. On the other hand the shortage of capital is not only the effect of the original technological shock which distorts productive capacity but also the successive outcome of a lack of co-ordination of economic activity, as the crucial role played by price and wage adjustment mechanisms actually shows. It is, in other words, a result of the interaction of the intertemporal complementarity of production and that of the decision process.

We shall now consider a series of successive shocks (changes in technique of the same kind already considered) taking place at intervals such that the effects of the preceding shock have not been fully re-absorbed before the next one occurs. This will allow us to shift the focus away from the problem of convergence to a new regular state of the economy and towards short-and medium-run phenomena. We shall thus place ourselves in the perspective already stressed in Chapter 1 according to which, when we are dealing with a qualitative change, and in particular with innovation, what matters from the analytical viewpoint is the out-of-equilibrium process of which the change itself consists rather than its supposed point of arrival. And, on the other hand, we shall also be able to make this process less and less dependent on the initial conditions.

We shall confine our attention to the cases where a human constraint exists[8] and assume, in the first place, that the supply of money keeps growing at the original steady rate. With proportional savings and fixed prices and wages, repeated technological shocks bring about a sequence of 'machinery effects' and increasing levels of unemploy-

---

[8] A perfectly elastic labour supply does not change the results obtained very much.

Processes of Change

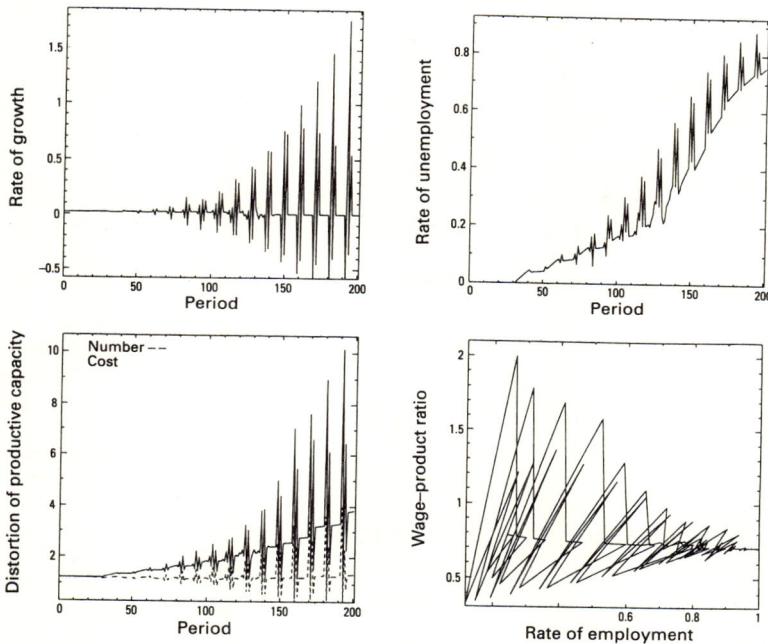

Fig 7.4a

ment associated with increasingly strong fluctuations of the rate of growth and of the distortion of productive capacity, as the result of a chronic and increasing shortage of capital (Fig 7.4a). Due to the absence of a market co-ordination mechanism through price changes, the share of wages rises to levels which cannot be sustained by the economy, and this is followed by sudden decreases in this share.[9] However, these overturns are always excessive and the previous situation is never re-established; this results in stronger and stronger fluctuations as unemployment reaches higher and higher levels. The economy is not viable. A kind of prey–predator interaction of the 'Lotka–Volterra' type concerning distributive shares appears as a

---

[9] This is the ratio of the resources paid as wages at the beginning of the period to the money proceeds of the same period. It can be greater than one when there is a strong excess supply, and this can be explained by the fact that in the model the resources advanced are paid out of the proceeds of the preceding period.

182   *Out of Equilibrium*

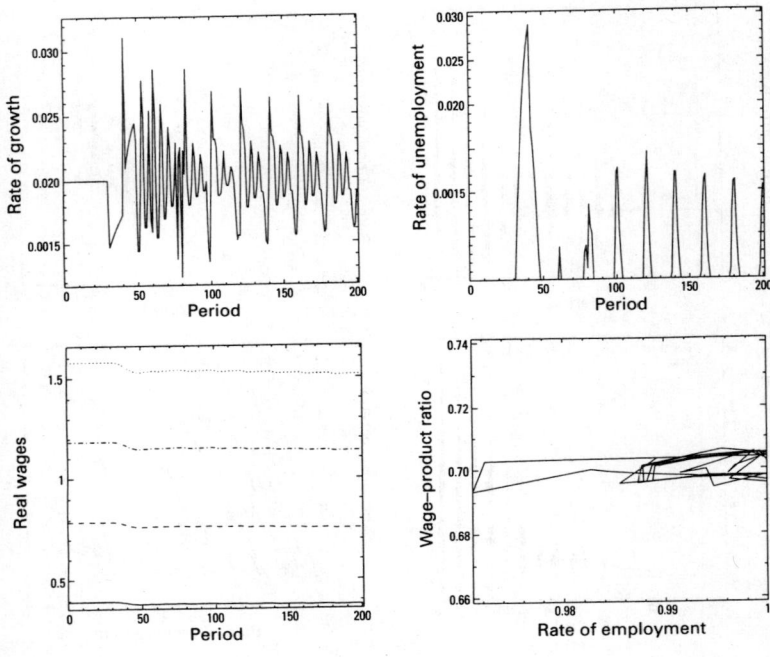

FIG 7.4b

corollary of the effects of technological shocks on employment in the absence of a market adjustment mechanism.[10]

If we introduce an element of co-ordination by letting prices *and* wages to change in response to market disequilibria the economy is somewhat stabilized. The fluctuations of output and of the share of wages are no longer explosive (price adjustments prevent a prey–predator interaction), and a recurrent 'machinery effect' no longer implies increasing levels of unemployment. This is associated with a limited decrease in real wages. The phase diagram shows a phenomenon of stagflation typical of an economy characterized by supply shocks (Fig 7.4b).

When failure of savings to adjust results in a shortage of capital,

---

[10] Flexible prices do not change things if wages are fully indexed.

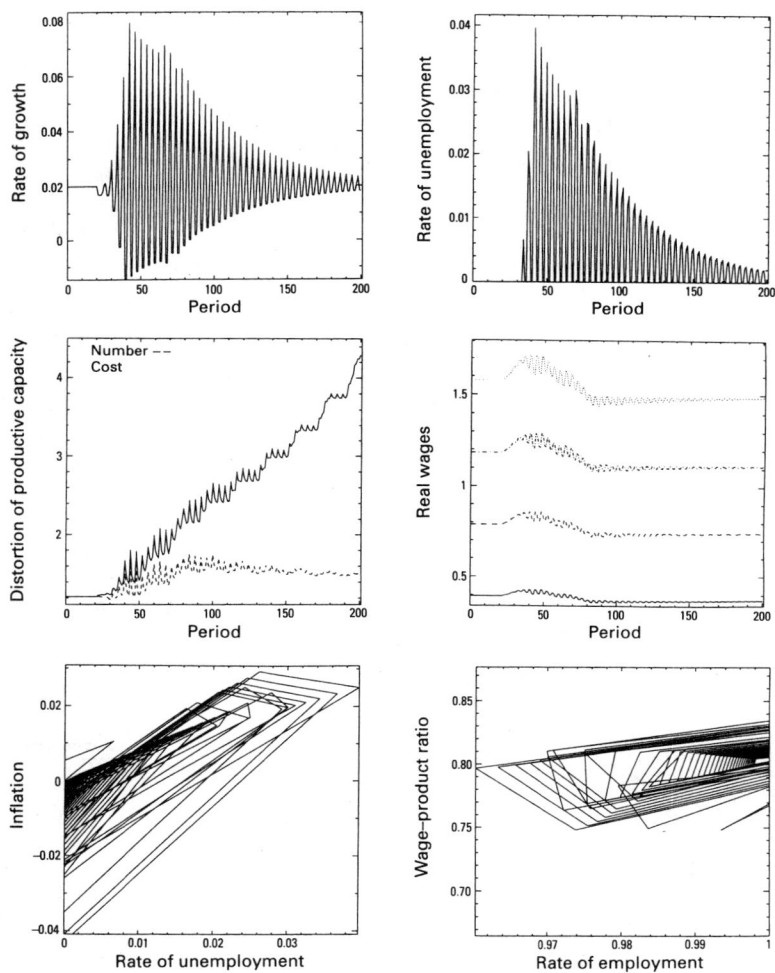

FIG 7.5a

no attempt at co-ordination avoids the appearance of a ' machinery effect', and a certain degree of price flexibility is required for the economy to be viable.

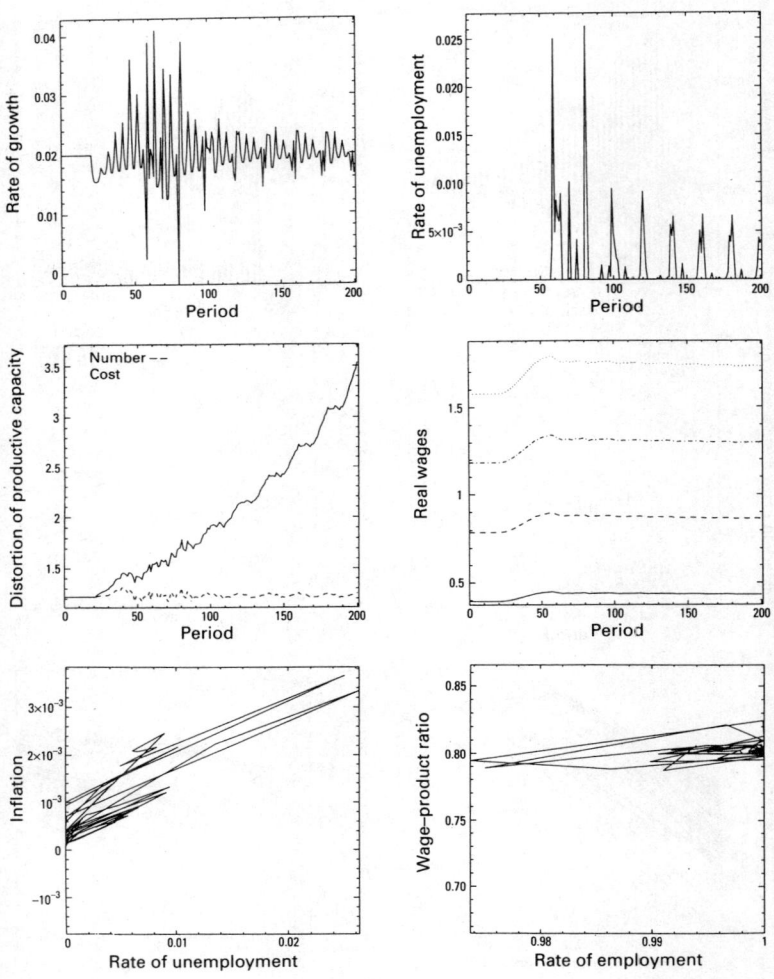

FIG 7.5b

Let us then try to remove the shortage of capital by increasing savings, and, as in the case of a unique change in technology, let us do it gradually so as to avoid inflicting excessive shocks on the economy. With flexible prices and wages we still get a 'machinery effect':

output and employment keep fluctuating, although the fluctuations damp down as time goes by (Fig. 7.5a). This result depends on the values actually taken by the reaction coefficients of prices and wages. If the value of these coefficients is reduced from 0.5 to 0.1 employment is almost fully re-absorbed and we not only obtain an increase in real wages but also a smaller fluctuation of the wage share (Fig. 7.5b).

A gradual increase in savings, provided this is associated with a moderate flexibility of prices and wages, renders an economy subject to repeated technological shocks viable and allows unemployment to be re-absorbed.

Finally if we consider a monetary policy aimed at maintaining stable prices—by letting the rate of change of money supply in

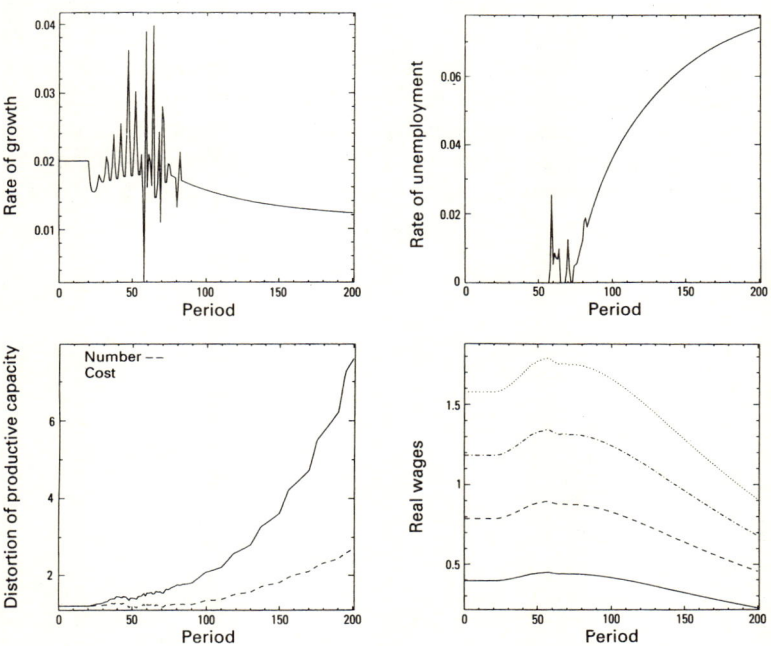

Fig 7.6a

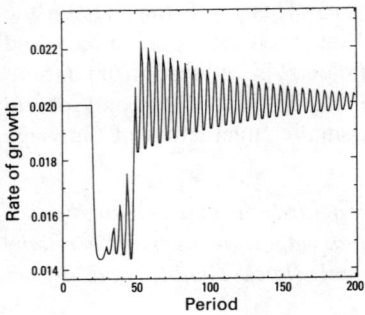 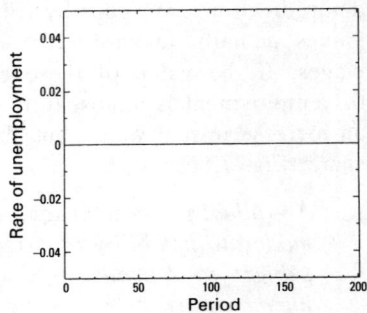

Fig 7.6b

each period be inversely related to the change in the rate of inflation in the preceding period (see equation 41c in Chapter 6)—the above results are reversed. Flexible prices and wages bring about an asymptotic increase in unemployment, a fall in the growth rate of output and in real wage rates, and a strong scrapping of utilization processes (Fig. 7.6a). With constant real wages, however, full employment may be maintained, but only with a very low price reaction coefficient (see Figs. 7.6b and 7.6c, with reaction coefficients of 0.05 and 0.5 respectively). This suggests that *the use of a restrictive*

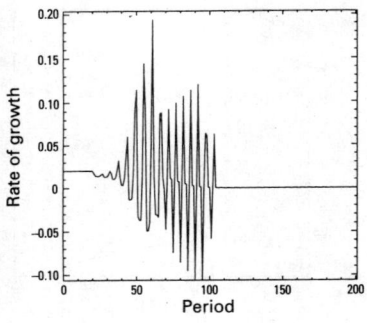 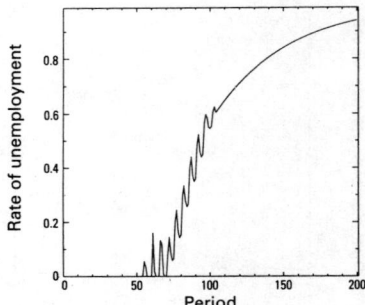

Fig 7.6c

monetary policy is not appropriate when prices and wages are flexible, as it hinders the construction of production processes, while, by checking prices, it reduces the increase in wages when these are fully indexed, and thus favours investment. *Restrictive policies may not go well along with free-market mechanisms*, as mainstream policy-makers seem to believe (see Section 8.5 below for the important empirical implications of this result).

We should stress at the end of this section that our analysis of the relations between technology and employment focuses on the interaction between short-term and long-term phenomena (as a thorough dynamic analysis actually should: see Chapter 5). Its long-term aspect, which concerns the structure of productive capacity, is rendered by the 'machinery effect', while the short-term aspect, which has to do with the degree of utilization of this capacity, has an essential Keynesian character. This is clearly visible in the contemporaneous consideration of the two aspects of wage changes, one affecting costs and the other final demand. The dynamics of wages therefore has a crucial role in the analysis. In conclusion what happens to employment in an economy subject to technological shocks depends not only on the specific character of changes in technology but also on the co-ordination of economic activity as made possible by the interaction of all variables involved, that is, the supply of money, saving behaviour, and prices and wages.

7.2. CHANGES IN SKILLS

In the preceding section we have considered a technological shock—or a series of such shocks—represented by the adoption of a technique characterized by different labour coefficients with respect to the technique currently in use. However, we have considered changes in labour coefficients (increases during the phase of construction and more than proportional decreases during that of utilization) which are the same for all types of labour involved in the production process. We shall now consider instead technological shocks characterized by changes in labour coefficients which imply a modification of the structure of the demand for labour so as to make it no longer consistent with the existing structure of supply, and hence the appearance of a human resource constraint as the immediate result of the shocks themselves.[11] Furthermore, we shall associate the adoption of a new technique with a learning process resulting in a (more or less complete) adaptation of the structure of labour supply to the prevailing structure of labour demand (see equation 21 in Chapter 6). This process is not only the source of greater productivity but also the means of re-absorbing the disequilibrium on the labour market, and that on the market for final output associated with it, resulting from the original technological shock. We shall thus move from the problem of a change of the technique in use to the analysis of a process of innovation leading to new and different productive options. As a matter of fact a change of technique consisting of a change in the structure of the human resource employed actually comes down to the appearance of a different final commodity.

The distinctive aspect of a shock like the one considered is a labour mismatch which implies the co-existence of unemployment and unfilled vacancies.

In the case of a once-and-for-all shock, with proportional savings and a rate of learning slowly increasing over time (from 0.2 to 1.0 that is, a degree of adaptation which initially concerns only one-fifth of the existing labour force but goes up so as to bring about after a while a labour supply whose structure is fully adapted to that of demand) the fluctuations of the growth rate of output stimulated by the change in technology gradually damp down (the economy actually goes back to the original steady growth rate), and unemployment and unfilled vacancies are fully re-absorbed. An increasing scrapping of production processes in the phase of utilization and a bias towards construction processes characterizes the distortion of productive capacity whose fluctuations, however, also gradually disappear. Real wages decrease but there is no change in the skill-dispersion of wage rates (Fig. 7.7).

The unemployment gradually taken care of by the learning process originally arises from the mismatch between demand and supply of skills resulting from the technological shock. This determines, in turn, a reduction in the demand for final output and unemployment of a Keynesian type. Furthermore, a shortage of capital (the supply of money is kept growing at the original steady rate and this

---

[11] In particular, given a heterogeneous human resource made up of four types of labour characterized by different (increasing) skills, we have considered technological shocks that come down to small, different increases in the demand for the two types of labour with the higher skills and corresponding decreases in the demand for the other two types.

Processes of Change

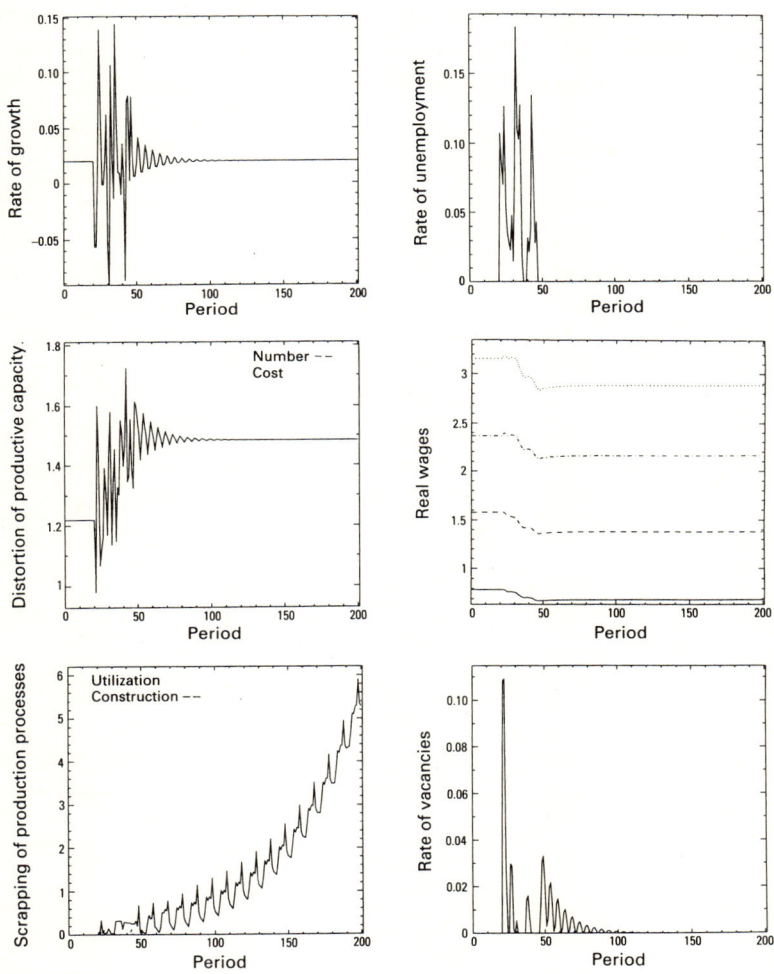

FIG 7.7

acts here as a brake on investment in productive capacity) determines a 'machinery effect', that is, unemployment of a Ricardian type.

With a constant rate of learning (0.9 in the case considered, that is, a constant over time although with a very high partial degree of adaptation) the fluctuations of the economy eventually damp down but unemployment reaches a certain level and is never re-absorbed, while the disparity among real wage rates referring to different skills

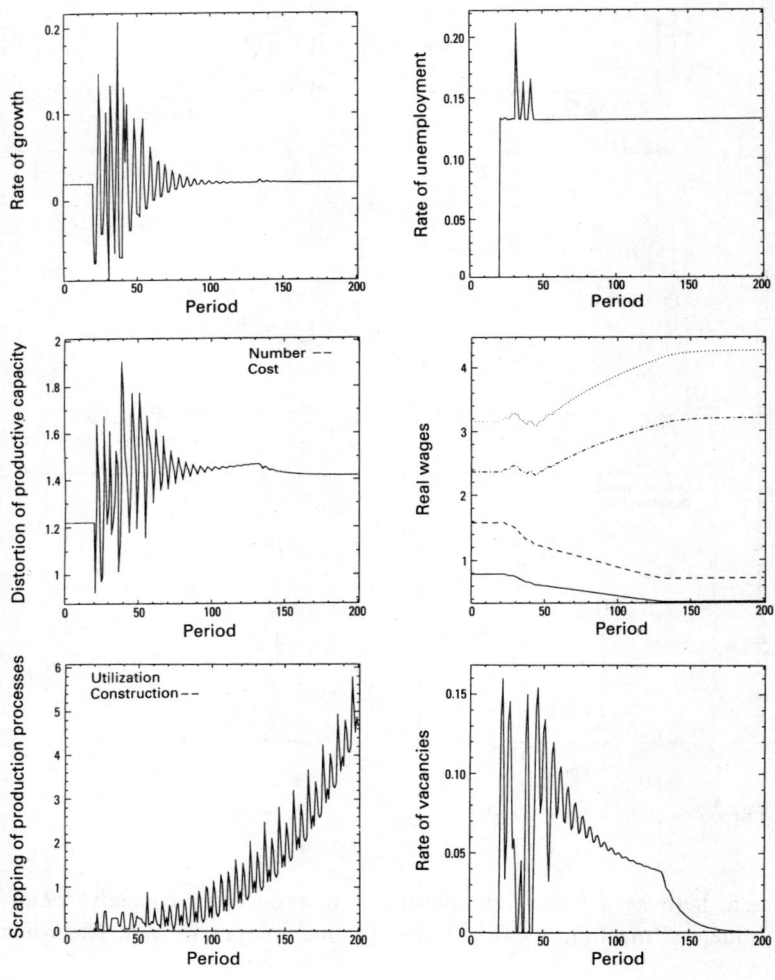

FIG 7.8

becomes more and more pronounced and the increase in the real wages of higher-skilled workers reduces the supply of jobs and eliminates vacancies (Fig. 7.8).

Wage differentiation appears as a surrogate for learning

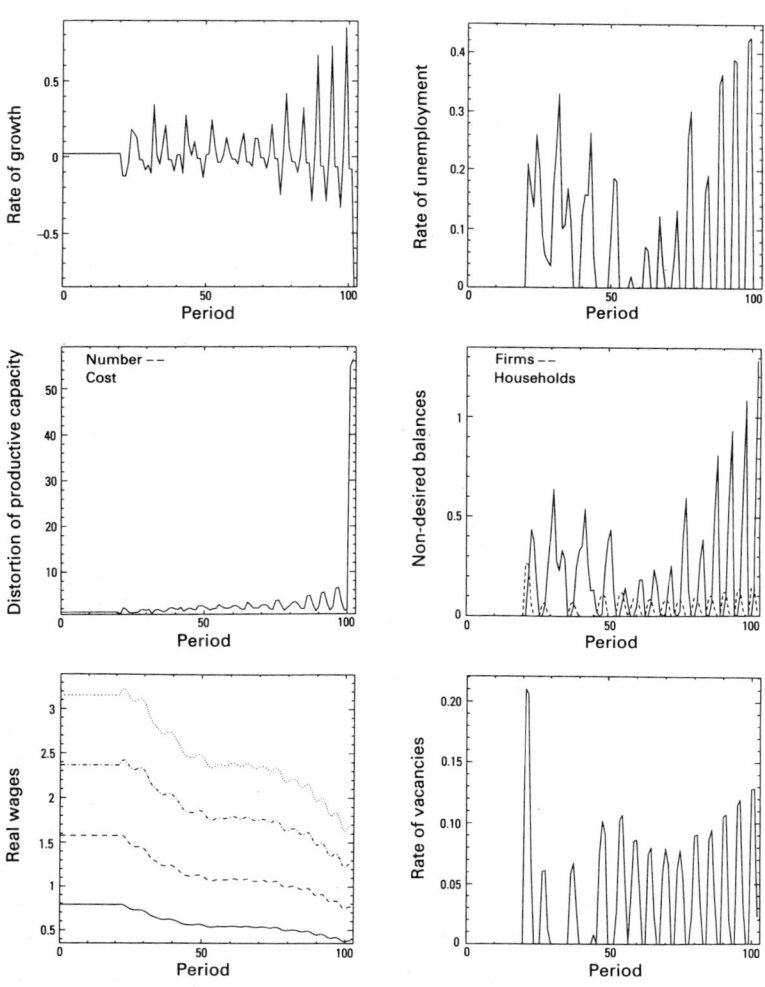

FIG 7.9a

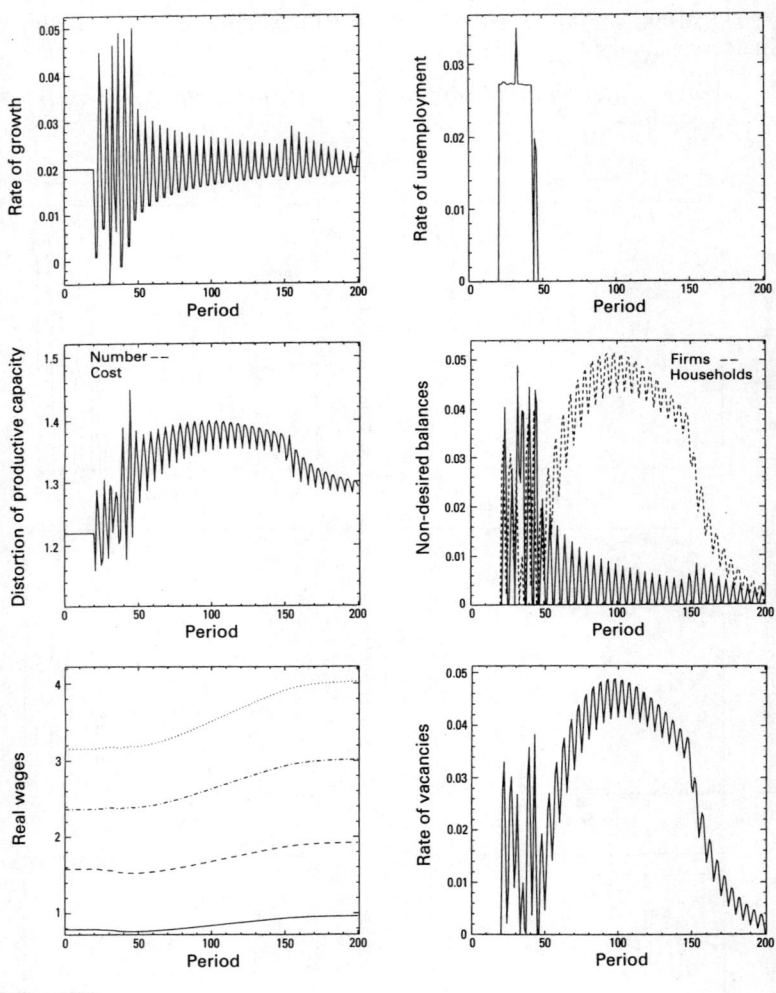

FIG 7.9b

(although not a perfect one) in determining the adjustment of the economy to a technological shock.

If we now accompany an increasing rate of learning with increasing savings the fluctuations become explosive and the economy is no longer

Processes of Change

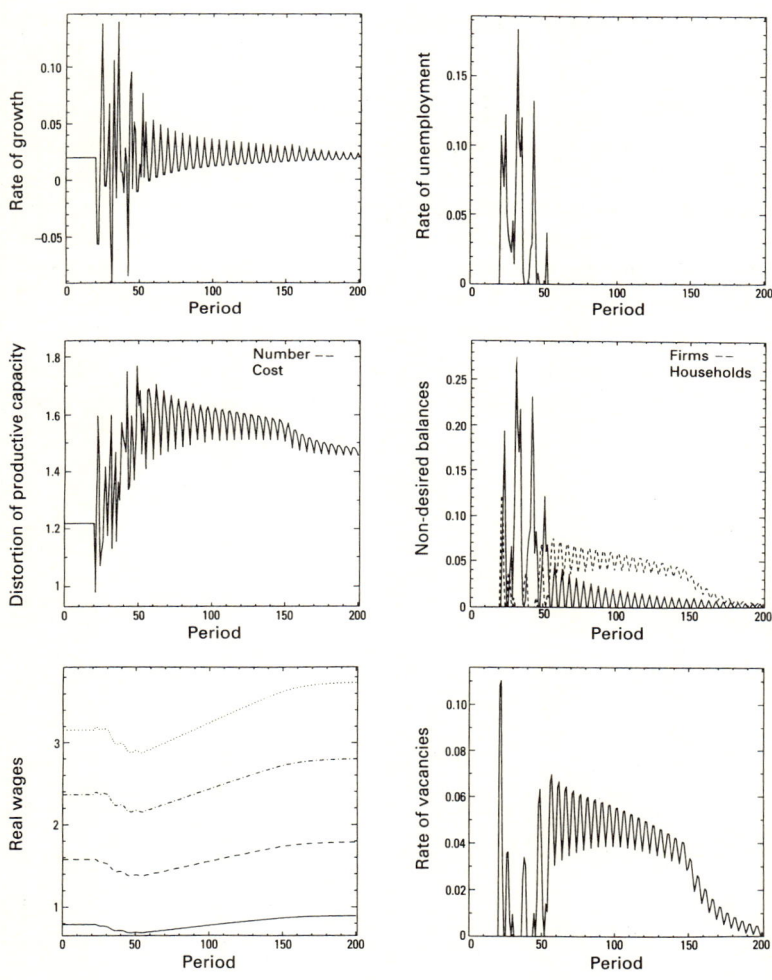

Fig 7.9c

viable (Fig. 7.9a); unless the initial rate of learning is very high (e.g. 0.98), in which case the fluctuations tend to disappear, unemployment is re-absorbed, and real wage rates go up (Fig. 7.9b). This confirms that the mismatch between demand and supply of labour is a crucial factor in determining the evolution of the economy. Higher savings and the attempt to carry out more intense productive activity result in a stronger human constraint: as a consequence significant idle balances are involuntarily accumulated by firms, which affects the demand for final output in a negative way. The interaction of the human and the financial constraint brings about a succession of supply and demand shocks, which result in turn in excessive distortions of productive capacity. The same obtains if firms do not scrap production processes in the phase of utilization as the answer to a contraction of final demand but react by simply reducing the degree of utilization of existing productive capacity. This is so because here the supply shock prevails over the demand shock induced by the labour mismatch (Fig. 7.9c).

Learning (accumulation of human capital) must be consistent with the accumulation of physical capital (saving) for the com-

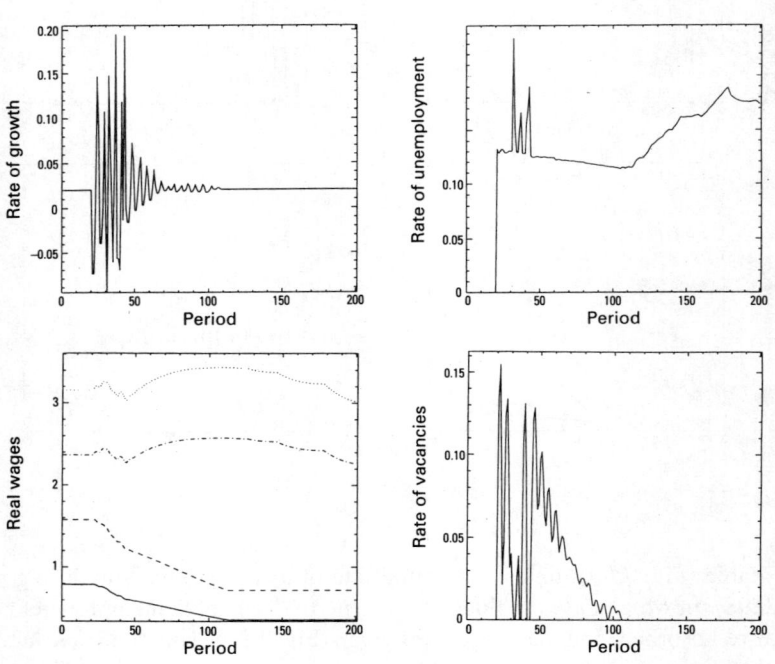

FIG 7.10a

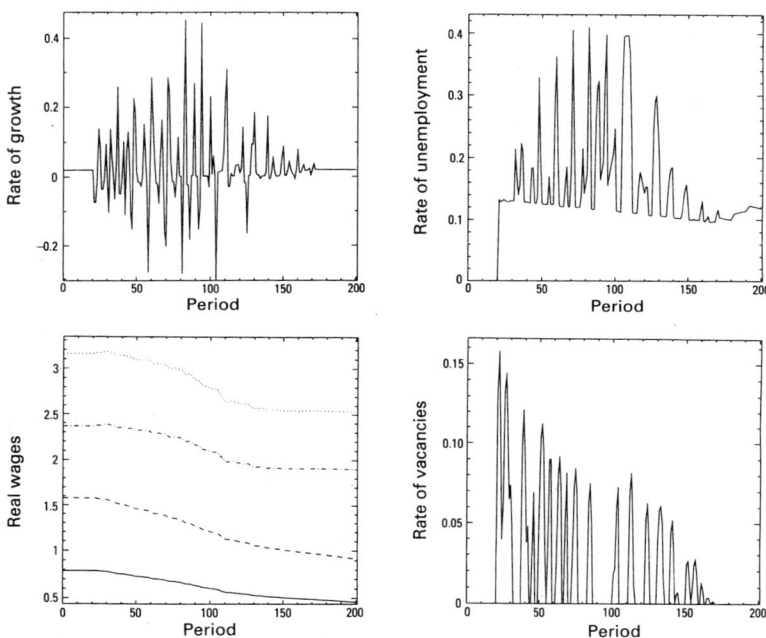

FIG 7.10b

plementarity of resources to be re-established and the evolution of the economy to be viable.

The consideration of a series of successive technological shocks essentially confirms the results obtained in the case of a unique shock (the main determinant of the evolution of the economy is always the mismatch between demand and supply of labour: a mismatch which, due to the repeated shocks, the learning process cannot fully re-absorb), but also adds interesting insights to the analysis.

With proportional savings and a constant rate of learning, higher price and wage reaction coefficients favour the adjustment of the economy, at the cost, however, of a greater wage dispersion (compare Fig. 7.10a and 7.10b characterized by values of the reaction coefficients of 0.05 and 0.01, respectively). Downward wage rigidity results instead

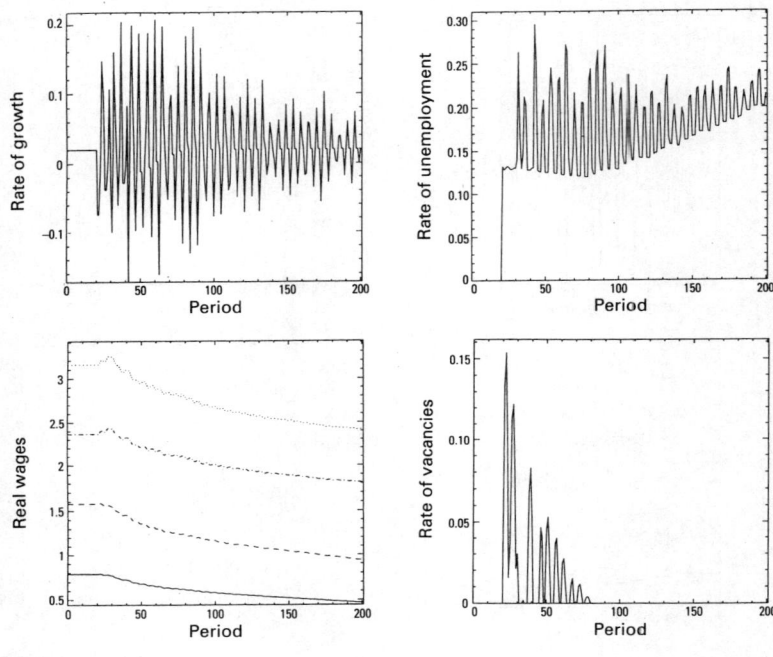

Fig 7.10c

in wider fluctuations, increasing unemployment, and a decrease of real wages not associated with a greater dispersion (Fig. 7.10c). Consideration of increasing savings does not essentially change things.

> *Different ways of functioning of the labour market—different wage regimes—essentially affect the evolution of the economy.*

Finally, a monetary policy aimed at keeping the general price level stable reduces the amplitude of the fluctuations of the growth rate of output but at the cost of strongly increasing unemployment and a fall of both money and real wages. An initial supply shock brings about an insufficient level of final demand as the result of a restrictive monetary policy which checks investment (Fig. 7.11).

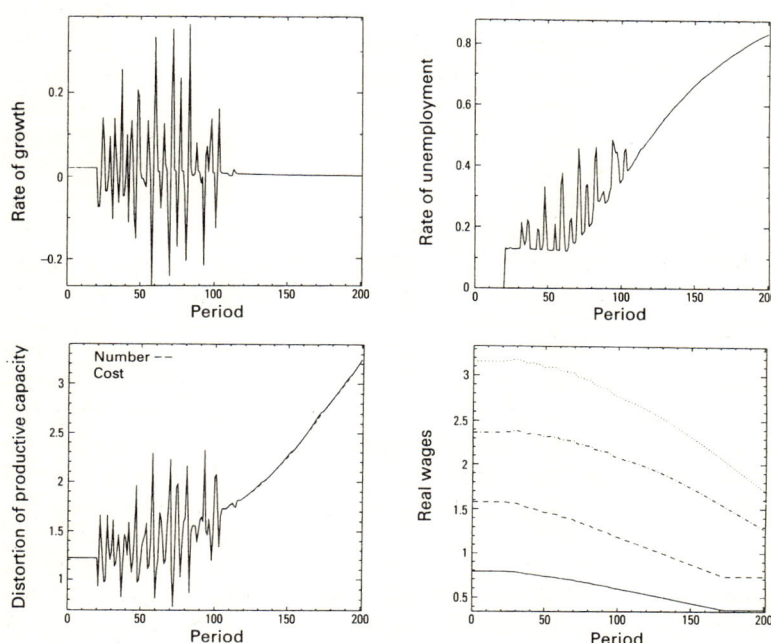

Fig 7.11

7.3 CREDIT CREATION

The creation of money—or the withdrawal of money from hoards, which amounts to the same thing as regards its effect on the evolution of the economy—is what a monetary shock consists of. This is rendered in the model by an increase in the value of the control variable $f(t)$.[12] In any case—whether the increase in the supply of money comes from an autonomous decision by bankers or in response to an increase in the producers' demand for money—we assume that supply and demand are always kept in balance.

The difficulties encountered by a process fuelled by the creation

---

[12] When a withdrawal of money from hoards is contemplated this could be rendered by a fall in the value of $\varrho(t)$, that is, by a reduced liquidity preference. However, in the simulations performed in this section we shall confine our attention to changes in $f(t)$.

of additional money have always been present for economists, together with the more or less explicit perception of this having to do with the time structure of productive activity. In particular, as is well known, Hayek (1931), following along the line originally traced by Wicksell, has stressed the disruptive effects of net credit creation. The reason, which our analysis allows us to see more clearly now, is that the creation of money interferes with the co-ordination of consumption and investment over time—although what we mean by this is not exactly what Hayek had in mind, as we shall see in particular in Section 8.2 below. The additional purchasing power, which in our model accrues to firms,[13] is used to start a greater number of production processes. This results in a distortion of productive capacity with a bias in favour of construction activity and in the appearance, sooner or later, of an imbalance between supply and demand of final output. A complex dynamic then sets in as the result of the working of price and output adjustment mechanisms, and this ends up being a threat to the viability of the economy.

A distortion of productive capacity certainly occurs when the growth rate of f is raised all at once, that is, when additional financial resources make a sudden and abrupt increase in the rate of start of production processes possible. The point is vividly summed up by Robertson (1940), who, referring to 'the monetary fuel of expansion', writes that

to Pessimist A the processes by which [economic expansion] is being fuelled—the withdrawal of money from hoards, the creation of money by the banks—are sufficient evidence that it can come to no good. For his eyes these are very things which constitute unneutrality in the behaviour of money, bringing on to the markets for goods a one-sided stream of demand. True the output of goods is expanding; but it is expanding lopsidedly, with capital goods in alarming prominence (ibid. p. 145).[14]

The simulations performed confirm this insight; in particular

---

[13] This is the same as in Hayek's analysis, where the expansion of credit, associated with a divergence between the natural and the market rates of interest, takes place through loans granted to firms which produce intermediate goods.

[14] 'Unneutrality' of money, according to Robertson, consists in introducing 'an incidental element of distortion or disturbance'(ibid. p. 142). This definition of unneutrality comes surprisingly close to our focusing on the distortion of productive capacity to bring into light the essential role of money in the analysis of out-of-equilibrium processes of change (see Section 2.1 above).

they confirm Hayek's conclusion as to the disruptive effects of the process set forth by a monetary shock, and the co-existence of inflation and unemployment.

Following Hayek, full employment has been assumed at the out-

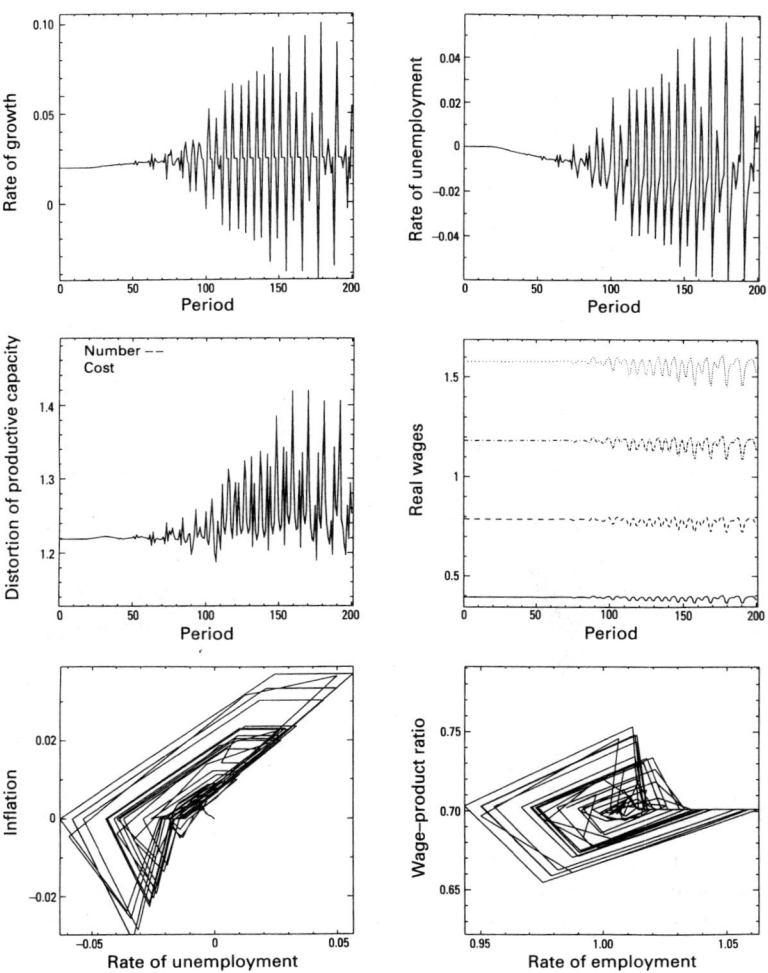

FIG 7.12a

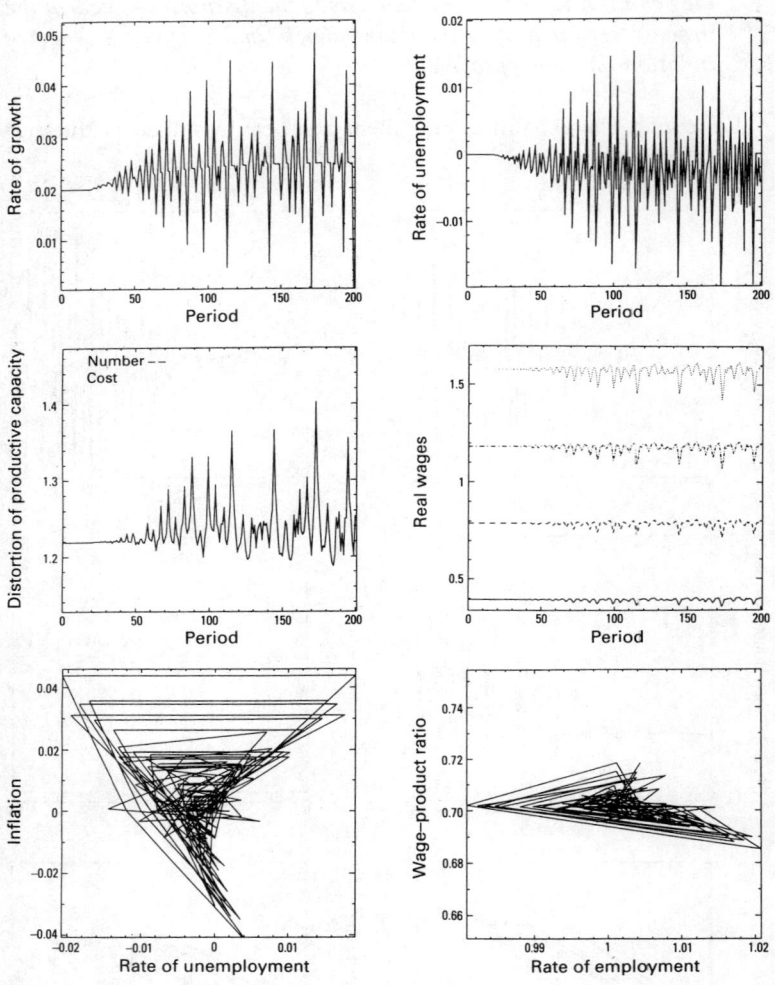

FIG 7.12*b*

set. Without a human resource constraint and with flexible prices and wages,[15] after a short lapse of time the increase in the supply of money brings about strong fluctuations in the growth rate of output,

---

[15] The case with fixed prices and wages is not relevant when dealing with credit creation

inflation, and unemployment, associated with a succession of excesses of demand and excesses of supply of final output. Real wage rates also start fluctuating after a certain number of periods. Stagflation (an inverted Phillips curve) is evident. The process set forth is in the nature of a chaotic process as the phase diagrams hint at (Fig. 7.12a).

Much depends on the sensibility of prices and wages to market disequilibria. Higher reaction coefficients (from a value of 0.5 for both price and wages in Fig. 7.12a to a value of 1.8 in Fig. 7.12b) are associated in fact with weaker fluctuations in the growth rate of output, of unemployment, and of the share of wages (Fig. 7.12b).

With a human resource constraint the additional money pumped

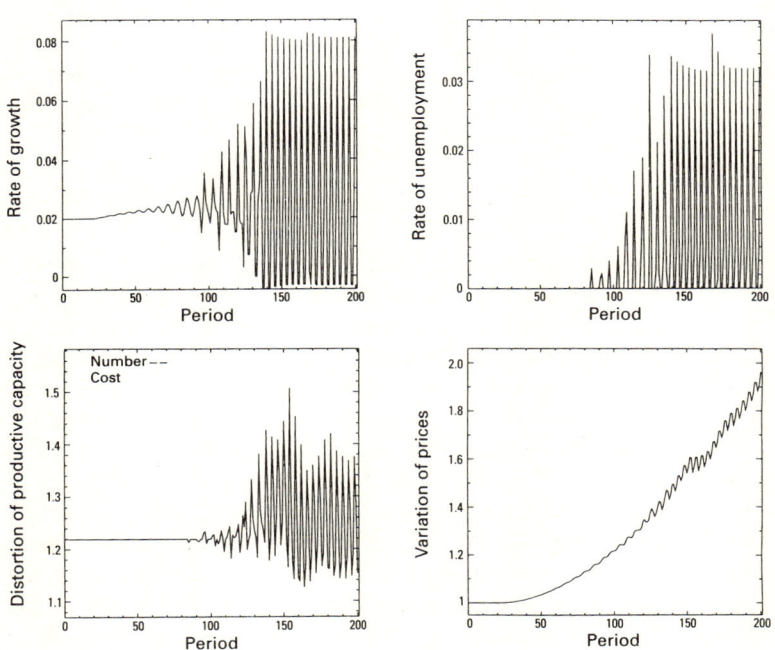

FIG 7.13a

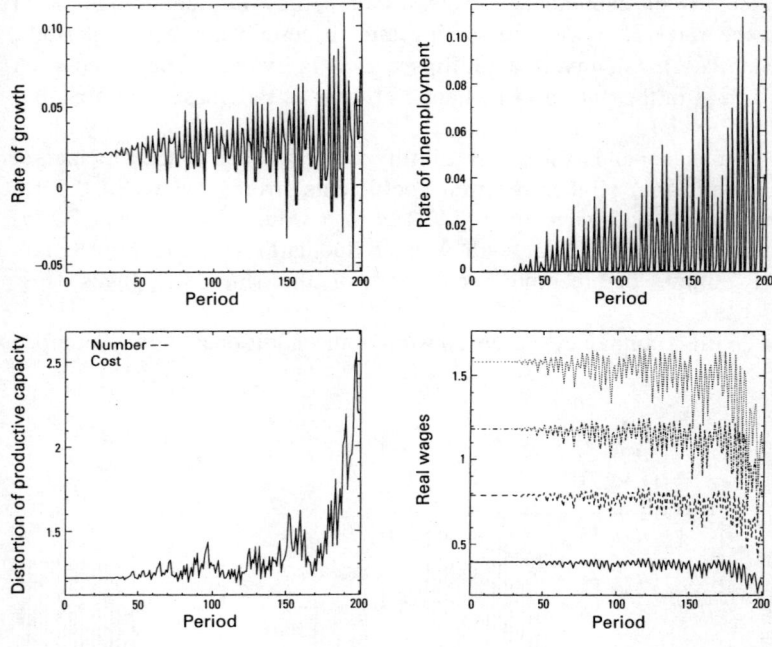

FIG 7.13b

into the economy cannot go towards increasing construction activity and therefore adds to the idle balances of firms. These are not desired balances. They are therefore immediately put back on the market and, given the existing limits to the supply of labour, go to increase wage rates and final demand. This results in part in an increase of the price of final output and in part in an increase of the idle balances of households. The increase in prices, in turn, implies a further transfer of idle balances to producers, and so forth. Thus we once again have fluctuations in the growth rate of output and in unemployment (Fig. 7.13a). Higher reaction coefficients for prices and wages bring about stronger fluctuations of real wage rates and of the distortion of productive capacity (see Fig. 7.13b, where the value of the reaction coefficients, with respect to the case considered in Fig. 7.13a, is increased from 0.5 to 1.8).

Processes of Change

There may be cases—which depend on the specific values taken by price and wage reaction coefficients—where the economy tends asymptotically to a higher growth rate in a monotonic way. However, this acceleration is purely nominal, as confirmed by the constancy of

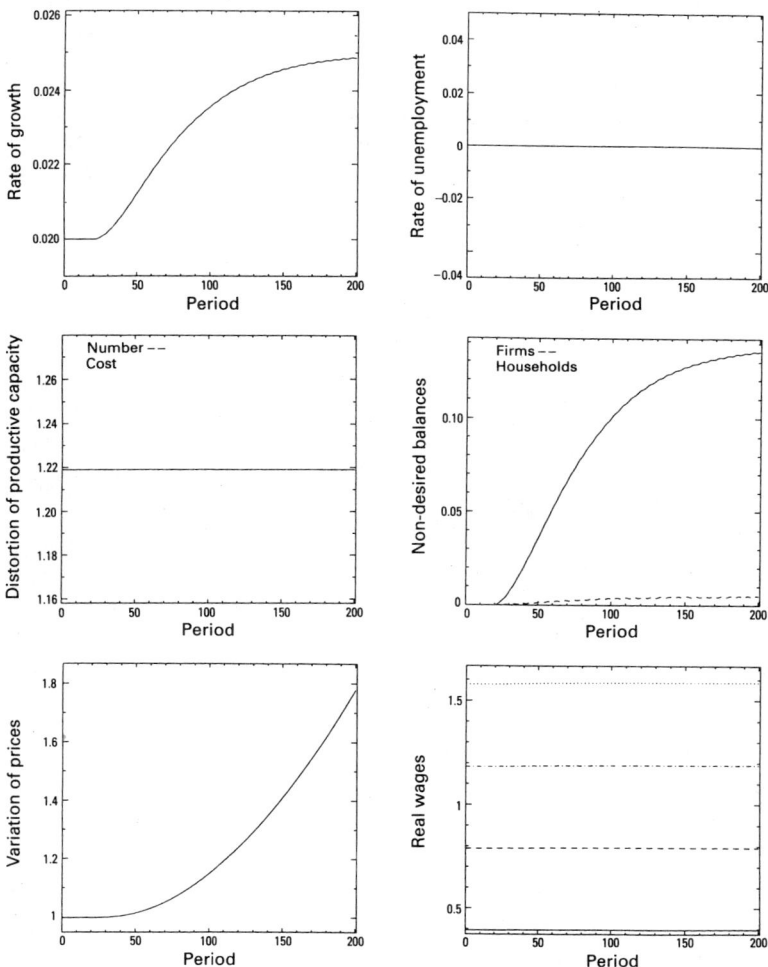

Fig 7.14

real wage rates, and the pseudo-equilibrium state to which the economy converges is characterized by an increasing accumulation of idle balances by households (Fig. 7.14). The reason is that, along Hayekian lines, the constancy of real wages implies the absence of distortion of productive capacity.

> *The crucial role of the dynamic of wages in out-of-equilibrium processes, already stressed when considering technological shocks, is thus confirmed by the analysis of monetary shocks.*

In particular, when the fluctuations of real wage rates become too strong (e.g. as the result of high values of price and wages reaction coefficients) a problem of viability arises. At the opposite extreme

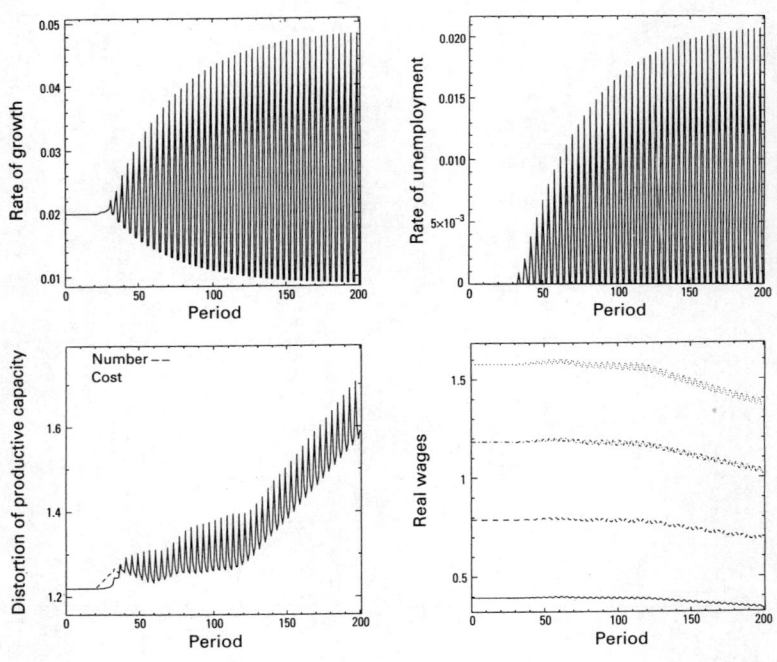

Fig 7.15a

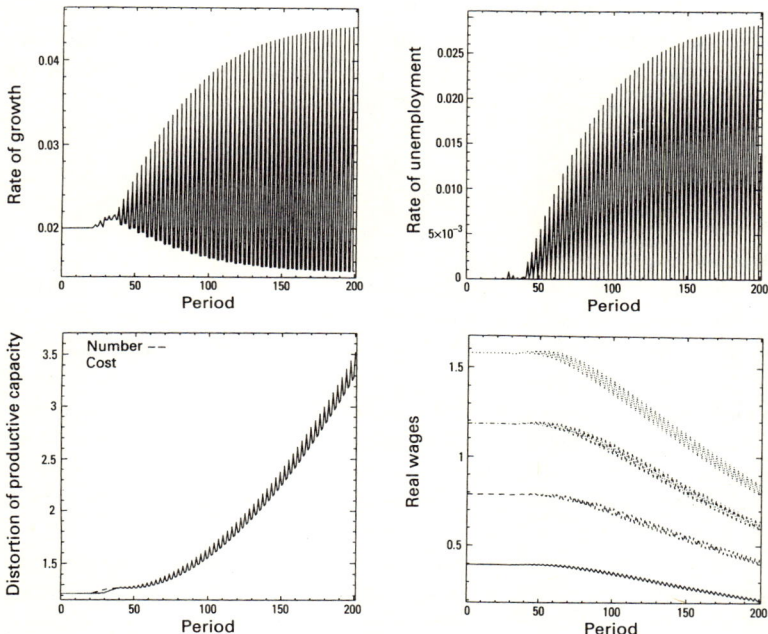

FIG 7.15b

constant real wage rates are associated with a monotonic convergence to a new pseudo-equilibrium state of the economy.

> This shows that what actually matters are not the absolute values of prices and wage rates but the changes in nominal wage rates in relation to those of the price of output, which reflect the changes in the structure of productive capacity.[16]

Things do not essentially change if the original net credit creation is not arbitrary but occurs in response to a technological shock. Consider a change in technology of a neutral character[17] which makes a greater

---

[16] The importance of the relation between the changes of relative prices and the structure of productive capacity has also been stressed by Heymann and Leijonhufvud (1994), although within a different analytical context.

growth rate of the economy possible, and raises the supply of money to this higher rate (e.g. from 0.0200 to 0.0246). The simulations performed show that the fluctuations observed are the stronger the higher the price and wage reaction coefficients (Fig. 7.15a with lower coefficients and 7.15b with higher ones).

7.4. CHANGES IN EXPECTATIONS

We shall now take into account a shock determined by a change in expectations. This is a problem already examined both by Keynes and Harrod, according to whom the fact that entrepreneurs become more pessimistic is translated into an increase in their liquidity preference and a corresponding decrease in the resources devoted to investment. In the same mood we shall consider an increase in the value of $\varrho(t)$ in our model,[18] as the expression of a change in their long-run expectations, and study the out-of-equilibrium processes stimulated by this shock under alternative hypotheses as to the other relevant variables.

The analysis of the effects of a change in expectations carried out along Keynesian lines is a short-term equilibrium analysis. The values of all relevant variables are determined simultaneously on the basis of a given informational context. The effect of a change in expectations is worked out by comparing the equilibrium states of the economy under different expectational contexts, before and after the change. The co-ordination failures that the analysis brings into light are equilibrium phenomena. That is, they lead to the definition of 'sub-optimal' equilibria, due mainly to price rigidities of institutional origin or reflecting rational behaviour under asymmetric information or the agents' ignorance that market conditions have changed.

However, when the information is incomplete 'the temporal order of decisions is of analytical significance' (Leijonhufvud 1983, p. 67). Things occur at different moments, and co-ordination must be

---

[17] That is, such as to affect the phase of construction and the phase of utilization of productive capacity in the same way. In particular, in the simulations performed, the labour coefficient has been lowered from 8 to 7.8 for all types of labour in all the periods of the production process.

[18] That is, an increase in the amount of financial resources put aside and held as voluntary idle balances by firms.

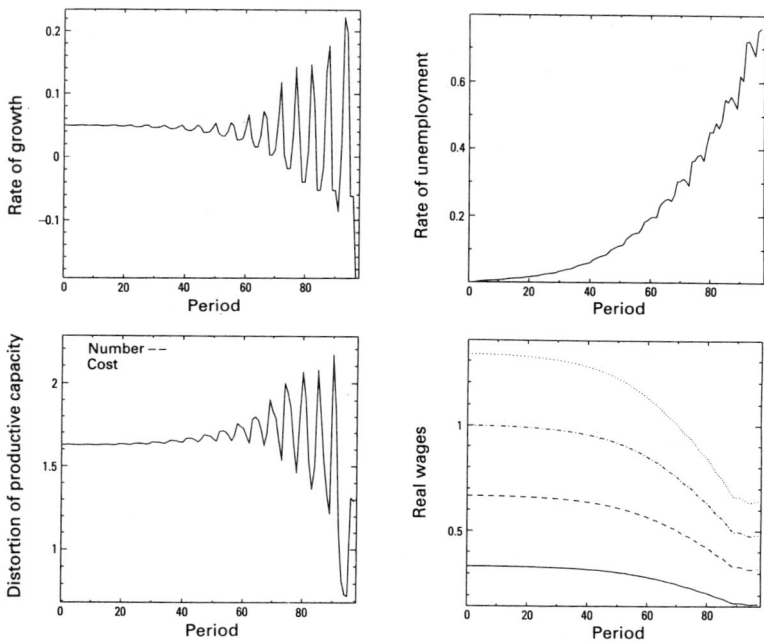

FIG 7.16a

exerted over time. In this context price and wage rigidity conditions set once-and-for-all are not relevant; rather we have a situation where adjustments to oncoming disequilibria, although more or less rapid, cannot be instantaneous. The acquisition of information through successive adjustments becomes crucial, and once again the interaction over time of constraints and decisions (the 'constraints-decisions-constraints' sequence) determines the evolution of the economy out of equilibrium.

The simulations help to trace out the evolution path. A greater liquidity preference immediately reduces the wage fund and hence final demand, which implies the appearance of an excess supply of final output. This affects in turn the short-run expectations of producers and leads to a reduction in the degree of utilization of existing productive capacity. This is a source of instability. When, to remain

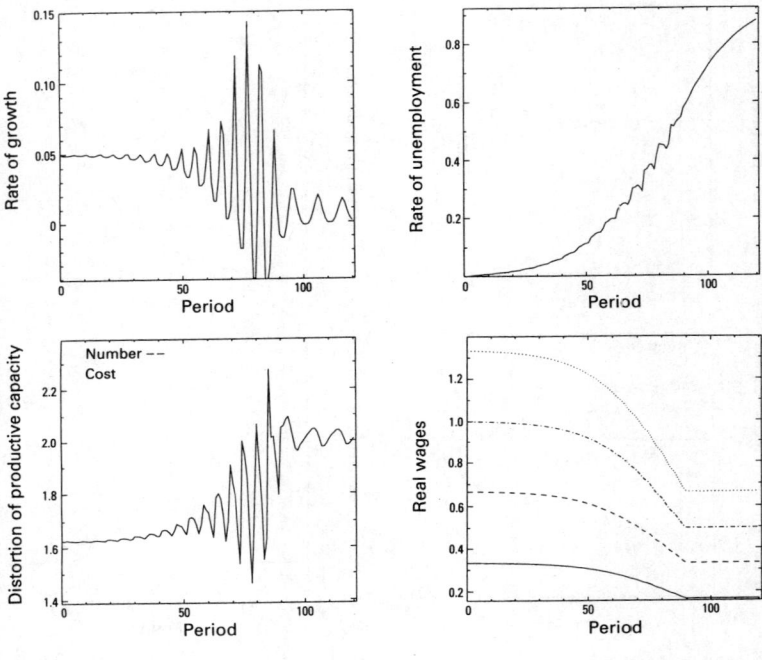

FIG 7.16b

with Harrod, investments are affected by the current performance of the economy, the reduction in the utilization of productive capacity also brings about a reduction in the activity of construction.[19]

If the 'take-out' keeps growing at the original rate, and prices and wages are flexible, the economy becomes strongly unstable and eventually not viable (Fig. 7.16a). This depends mainly on the excessive growth of the fraction of output 'taken out' (excessive growth of μ). A ceiling on the value of μ does not prevent the fluctuations of the economy from becoming explosive, unless we also put a floor under the fall in wage rates, which otherwise would continue indefinitely (Fig. 7.16b). Indexation of wages does not assure stability either (Fig. 7.16c). Stable real wages sustain final demand, although it outpaces

---

[19] In Harrod's terminology the existing stock of capital exceeds the desired level.

productive capacity resulting in an accumulation of idle balances on the part of households.

If we link the growth rate of the 'take-out' with the current growth rate of the economy things do not change. The economy quickly reaches a state where wage rates are at the floor level and unemployment explodes. This is due to the cumulative reduction of final demand as the result of a fall in the 'take-out' geared to the current growth rate (Fig. 7.17a). If we introduce instead a non-linear determination of price and wages (the reaction coefficients are equal to zero when excess demands are negative) we reduce the amplitude of the fluctuations, which are no longer explosive, and contain the increase in unemployment (Fig. 7.17b). This proves that downward rigidity is what really matters.

The problem evoked by the simulations is the Harrodian instabil-

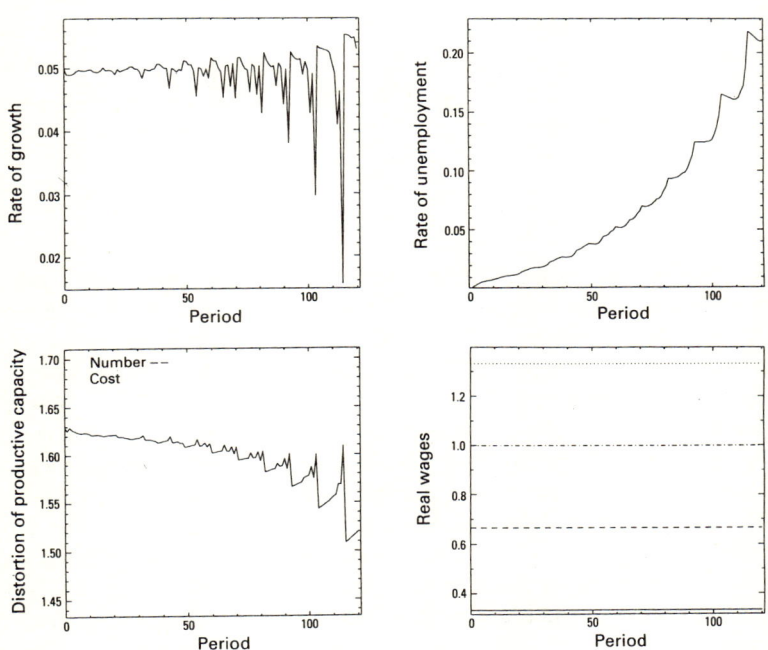

FIG 7.16c

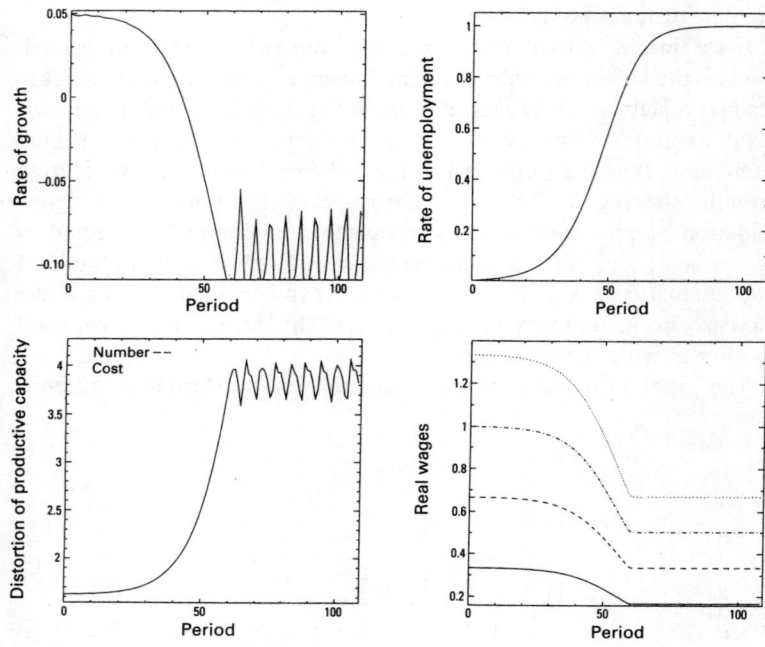

Fig 7.17a

ity, that is, the vicious circle whereby a fall in investment feeds itself in a cumulative way. According to Howitt 'the standard resolution to this problem is to say that if entrepreneurial expectations do not respond appropriately, then sooner or later wages will have to fall, and the problem will go away.'(1994, p. 770). We have shown that this is not so. Falling wages do not stop instability or hamper unemployment from growing. *The viability of the economy, when there is an increase in the liquidity preference, calls for sustained final demand.* This, however, must preserve a balanced structure of productive capacity, which is the reason why sustained final demand resulting from an increase in the rate of 'take-out' would not do. The right kind of intervention is *to couple it with a downward price rigidity, or with an indexation of wages*, which affects both the construction and the utilization of productive capacity, and not

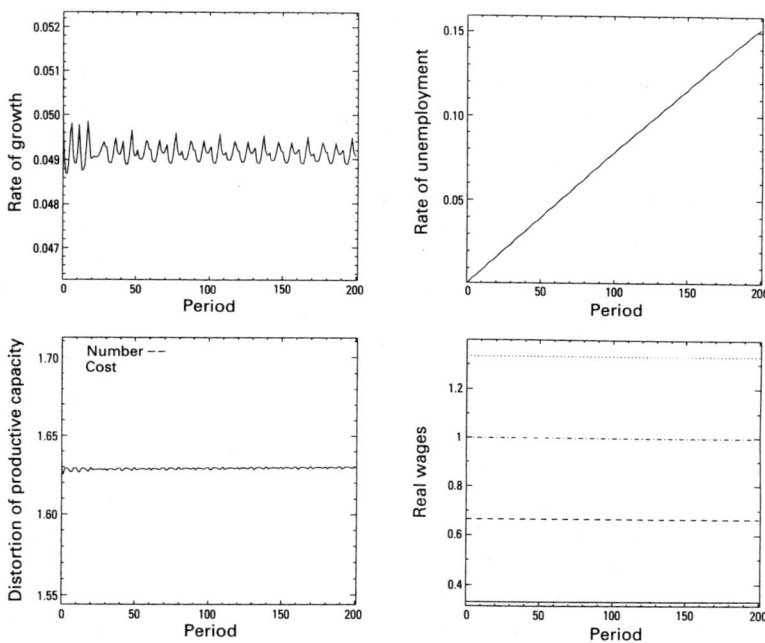

Fig 7.17b

only the latter, as is the case when we only increase the 'take-out' (Fig. 7.17b).

7.5. LIMITS TO GROWTH

We can now sum up the results obtained and put them in a comprehensive framework taking into account the various interactions at work. The analyses developed in the preceding sections in fact provide essential elements for a better understanding of the mechanism of growth (which is at the heart of all qualitative changes) and hence of the effective determinants of and limits to growth. A speeding up of the growth rate of the economy—sought for whatever reason—allows to make all this clear.

Different productive structures are required to sustain different growth rates; a higher growth rate in fact needs a different balance (at each given moment and over time) between production processes in the phase of construction and processes in the phase of utilization with respect to a lower growth rate. However—as we have seen for the qualitative changes considered in the preceding sections, and as we shall see better in what follows—a 'new' productive structure does not immediately come about after a modification of it is contemplated; the economy must actually go through the phase of construction of a different productive capacity before this happens. This implies that 'acceleration,' that is, the process by which we pass from a certain growth rate, characterized by a given productive structure, to a higher growth rate characterized by a different one, is the dynamic problem involved here, not comparison between the productive structures associated with different growth rates.[20] Standard growth theory—an equilibrium theory—is suited to deal with the latter problem; it is therefore hardly likely to bring to light the obstacles actually encountered during the process of acceleration of growth. This can only be the object of an out-of-equilibrium analysis.

The first point to stress as regards the problem of speeding up growth is that additional financial resources are required by the productive system to finance a higher growth rate, with respect to the resources needed to finance the previous lower growth rate (see Sections 1.5 and 2.8 above). This can come from an internal shift of resources: in our model, a shift from consumption out of profits to the financing of production processes (a reduction of c—not only in absolute terms, but as a fraction of total available resources, and hence a lower value of μ —and a corresponding increase of the wage fund ω). Or it can come from an increase in the inflow of external financial resources (an increase of f).[21] In both cases the balance between production processes in the phase of construction and production processes in the phase of utilization is affected, and there is a distortion of productive capacity which, due to the existing adjustment and reaction mechanisms, stimulates an out of equili-

---

[20] The same can be said for 'catching up', the problem of the convergence or divergence of productivity levels between countries (see Abramovitz 1986; Baumol 1986).

[21] We recall that c and f are the two main control variables considered in our model.

brium process which the economy must go through for the attempted transition to be accomplished. Two strictly related problems then arise: the conditions required for this out-of-equilibrium process to be viable and those required for the speeding up of the growth rate to actually be realized. The solution to these problems, as we shall see, depends on adequate external interventions concerning not only financial resources but all the productive resources involved, and on the functioning of the co-ordination mechanism represented by price and wage determination regimes.

Let us first consider the case of an internal shift of resources. This we assume to take place at the twentieth period of the evolution path of the economy followed by our simulations, an economy originally growing at the steady rate g_0, say 0.02, associated with a value μ_0 of the fraction of output 'taken out', but willing to increase its growth rate to g_1, say 0.025. We have seen in Section 6.4 that in equilibrium the rate of growth is inversely related to the value of μ; that is $g_1 > g_0$ implies $\mu_1 < \mu_0$. However, this is true in a comparative dynamics sense, that is, when complementarity relations along the equilibrium paths considered are assured by definition (in particular, the growth rate of the human resource at the required rate is assured). We are interested instead, as already mentioned, in acceleration, a process of which the allocation of resources is just the preliminary step and whose first effect is the breaking up of the above-mentioned complementarity relations. Whether the attempted transition to a higher growth rate will actually be accomplished, and under what conditions, will then depend on what actually happens along the way, from the date at which there is a reduction of μ, and hence a stepping out from the original steady-growth path followed by the economy, onwards: this will be the object of our investigation.

Consider in the first place a once-and-for-all reduction of μ (from 0.3 to 0.28) such that $c(t)$ and the wage fund acquire exactly the (lower and higher, respectively) values compatible with the higher growth rate sought. With an initial human constraint[22] and with flexible prices and wages this reduction in the value of μ does not bring about the required acceleration of growth but just a short fluctuation of output and its price. The ratio of construction processes to utilization processes increases as the result of an increasing

---

[22] Labour supply is not infinitely elastic. In the simulations performed it is made to depend on the rate of change of wage rates (see eqn. 17 in Chapter 6).

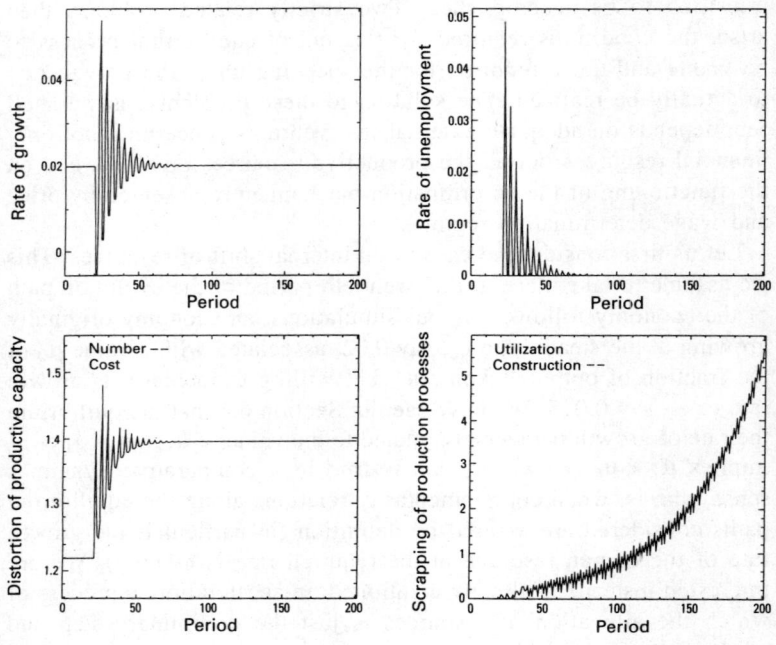

FIG 7.18a

scrapping of the latter. This, together with transitory unemployment, is the result of a temporary fall in final demand: as a matter of fact, due to the existing human constraint, the resources freed by the reduction of consumption out of profits cannot go to increase the wage fund but pile up as involuntary idle balances of firms (Fig. 7.18a).

A stronger decrease in the value of μ, greater than that required to reduce the 'take-out' at the level compatible with the higher growth rate, is not successful either in obtaining an acceleration of growth. If this reduction goes beyond a certain limit the fluctuations and the distortion of productive capacity become so strong as to render the economy no longer viable (see the case portrayed in Fig. 7.18b, where the economy collapses after a little bit more than hundred periods as the result of a reduction in the value of μ from 0.5 to 0.01).

Thus an increase in savings, whatever its size, is not likely in itself to bring about an acceleration of growth. We have already mentioned, when discussing the comparative dynamics of the model, that the structure of the model itself implies that a higher growth rate must be associated not only with higher savings but also with a higher growth rate of money supply for the required complementarity relation between productive resources to be assured in the sequential context considered. However, if we now let the supply of money grow at the higher rate sought, we observe strong and persistent fluctuations in the rate of growth and in the rate of unemployment as the result of an increasing distortion of

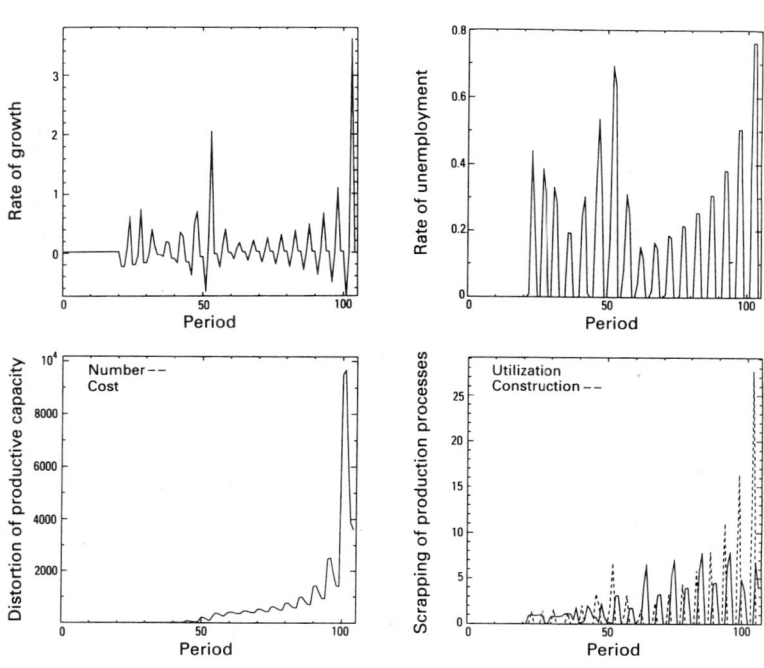

FIG 7.18b

productive capacity, a higher and higher price level and falling real wages (Fig. 7.19a). These are the typical results of an excessive credit expansion as already examined in Section 7.2. Lower values

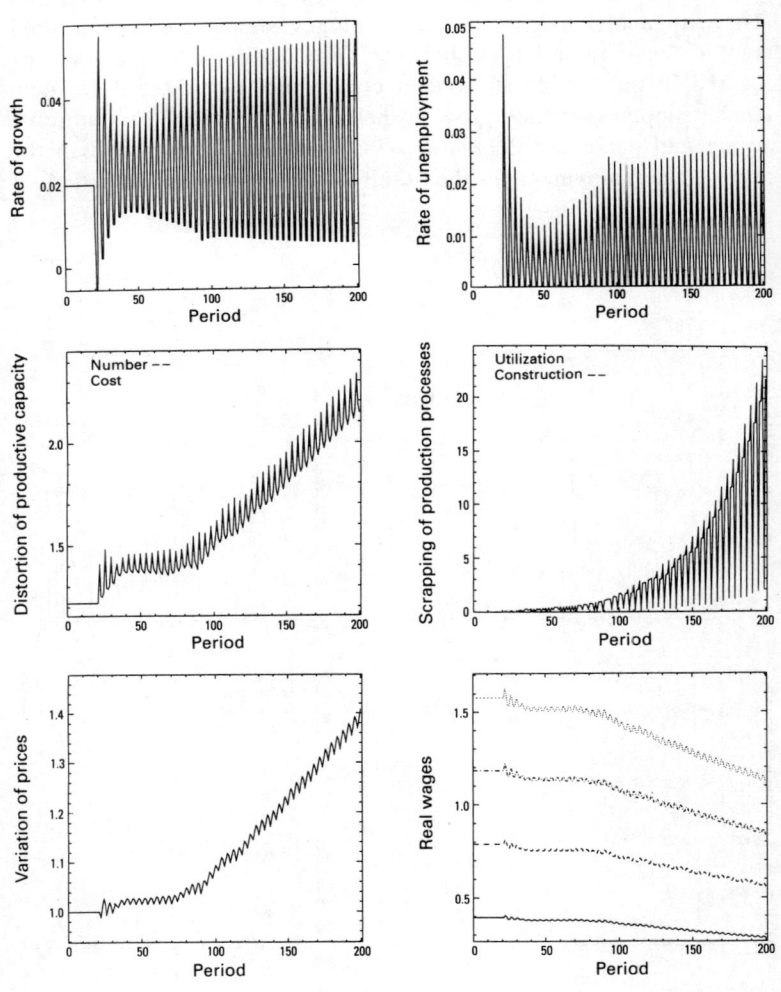

FIG 7.19a

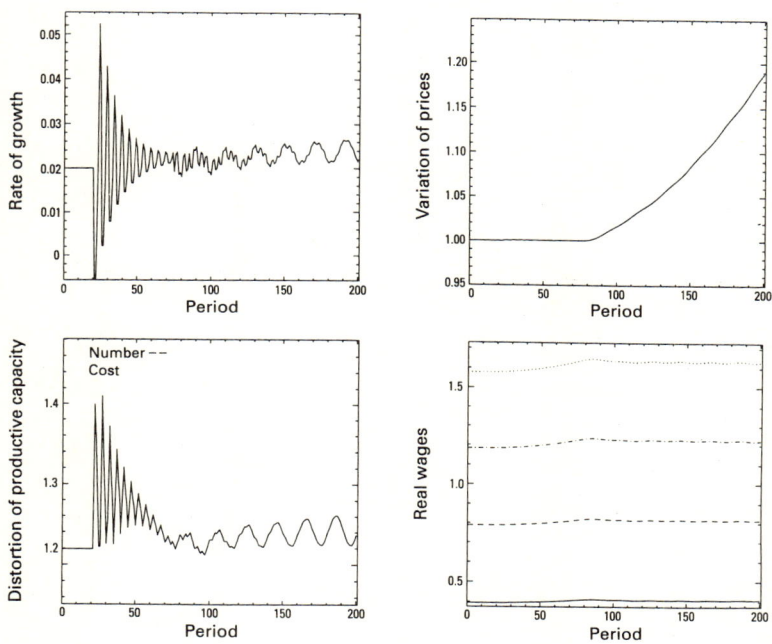

FIG 7.19b

of price and wages reaction coefficients (0.01 instead of 0.5) reduce the amplitude of fluctuations and the strength of inflation, thus restoring viability to the economy; but still no acceleration of growth is obtained (Fig. 7.19b).

The reason for these results is that the attempt to speed up growth has the immediate effect of breaking the complementarity over time between productive resources prevailing in the original steady state. A rigid labour supply does not allow us to re-establish this complementarity at the higher level required by the greater financial resources made available by greater savings and/or a higher growth rate of money supply. The stronger and the more abrupt the increase in savings and/or in the money supply the quicker the appearance of a human constraint which

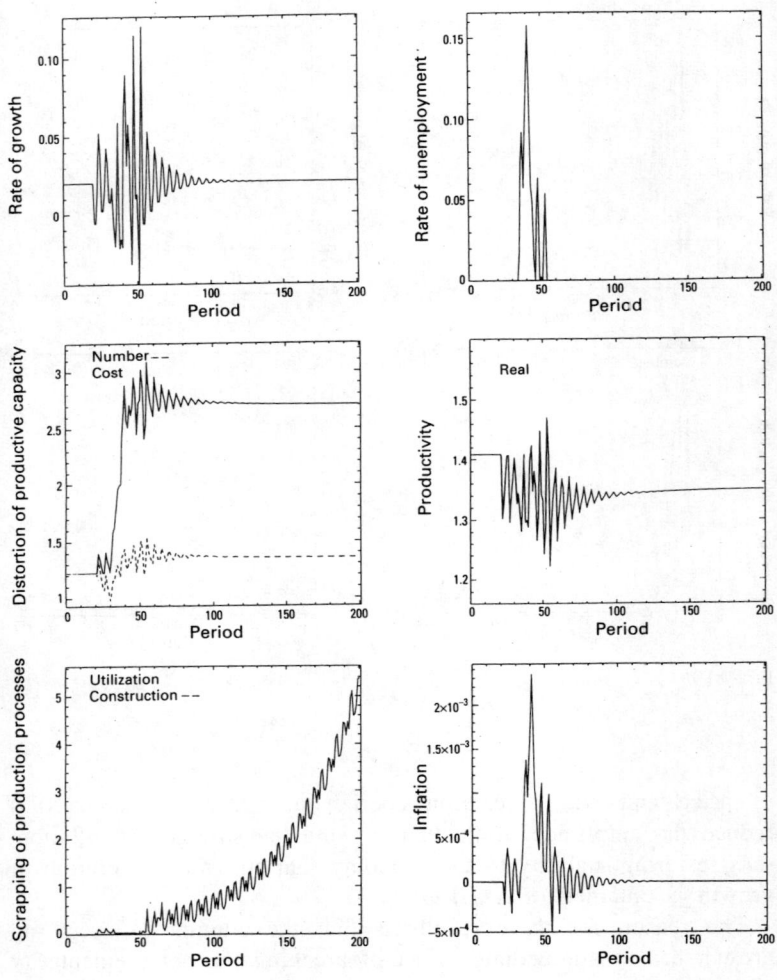

Fig 7.20

affects the rate of starts of new production processes in such a way as to bring about wider and wider fluctuations in the distortion of productive capacity and to eventually cast doubts on the

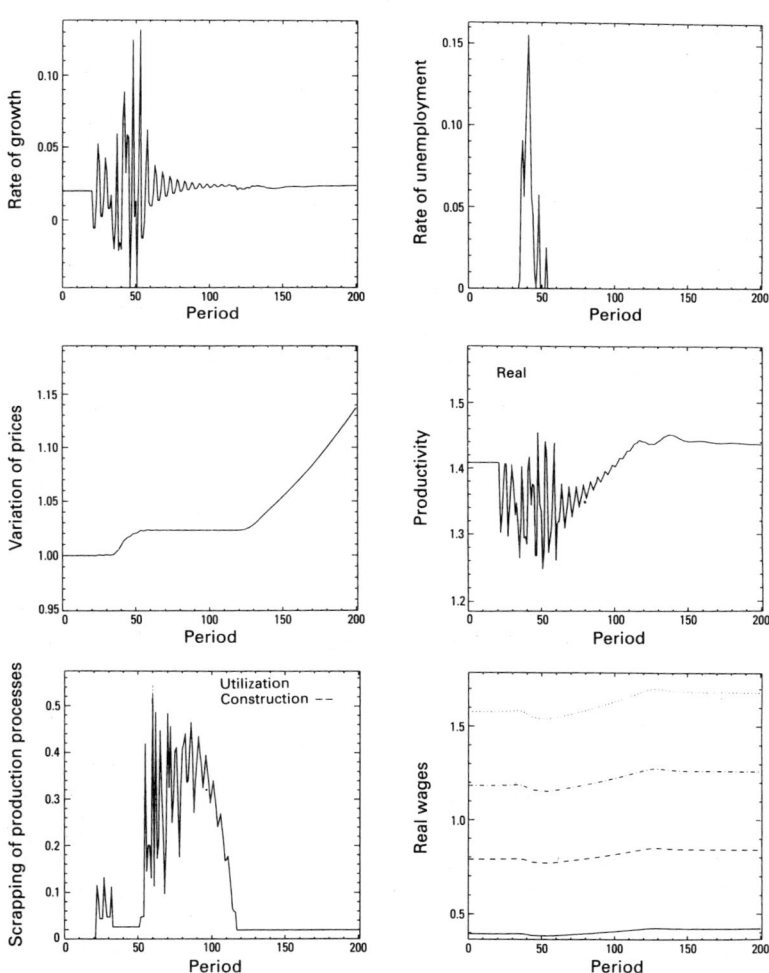

FIG 7.21a

very viability of the process of change undertaken.[23] The only way out, failing the possibility to relax the emerging human constraint by

---

[23] We have seen in the preceding sections that, whatever the nature of the original shock, the greater and the more sudden the attempted adjustment of productive capacity the less likely it is that the economy is able to carry it out.

adjusting labour supply in physical terms, is an increase in the efficiency of the human resource.[24]

Let us then associate an increase in financial resources with a change in technology of the kind already examined in Section 7.1, that is, such as to bring about an overall increase in the efficiency of labour notwithstanding an increase in its cost during the phase of construction. If the financial resources made available for speeding up growth only come from a reduction of the fraction of output 'taken out' (again, from 0.3 to 0.28) we observe a fluctuation of the growth rate of output and of the rate of unemployment associated with an increasing scrapping of utilization processes that is almost immediately re-absorbed; but still no acceleration in growth. Furthermore there is a fall in the level of productivity: in other words the potential benefits of the superior technique adopted are not actually appropriated by the economy (Fig. 7.20).

If, besides a reduction in the value of μ to the level compatible with the higher growth rate made possible by the advance in technology, we consider an increase in the supply of money (an increase in the value of f) such as also to bring external financial resources to the level required by this growth rate, a small acceleration of growth, accompanied by the re-absorption of unemployment and an end to the scrapping of production processes, obtains; provided, however, the value of price and wages reaction coefficients is sufficiently low (e.g. 0.01 as in Fig. 7.21a). At the same time there is a once-and-for-all increase in productivity: re-establishing a certain complementarity of productive resources makes it possible to reap the benefits of the new technology at the economy level. But more is required (in particular, an increase in the 'growth rates' of both labour supply and productivity) to effectively obtain the acceleration of growth sought; the small increase in the growth rate registered is in fact purely nominal (it is just equal to the increase in prices, as shown in Fig. 7.21a).

The possibility of actually taking advantage of technological advances, and the effects of this on the growth rate of the economy,

---

[24] Thus, although the behaviour of our model resembles that of endogenous growth models in a comparative dynamics sense, out of equilibrium it faces the same complementarity problems as Solow's model, which has to rely on exogenous labour-augmenting technical progress to avoid reaching a a state with a zero growth rate in output per head. In Solow's model a higher saving rate does not bring about a higher growth rate but results in an increase in the capital–labour ratio. In a Neo-Austrian type model this results in an increase in the ratio of construction processes to utilization processes.

thus depend on being able to re-establish the required complementarity relations between productive resources. And, besides that, on the existing adjustment mechanisms. As a matter of fact, with higher values of price and wage reaction coefficients, the fluctuations of output, of the distortion of productive capacity, and of the rate of

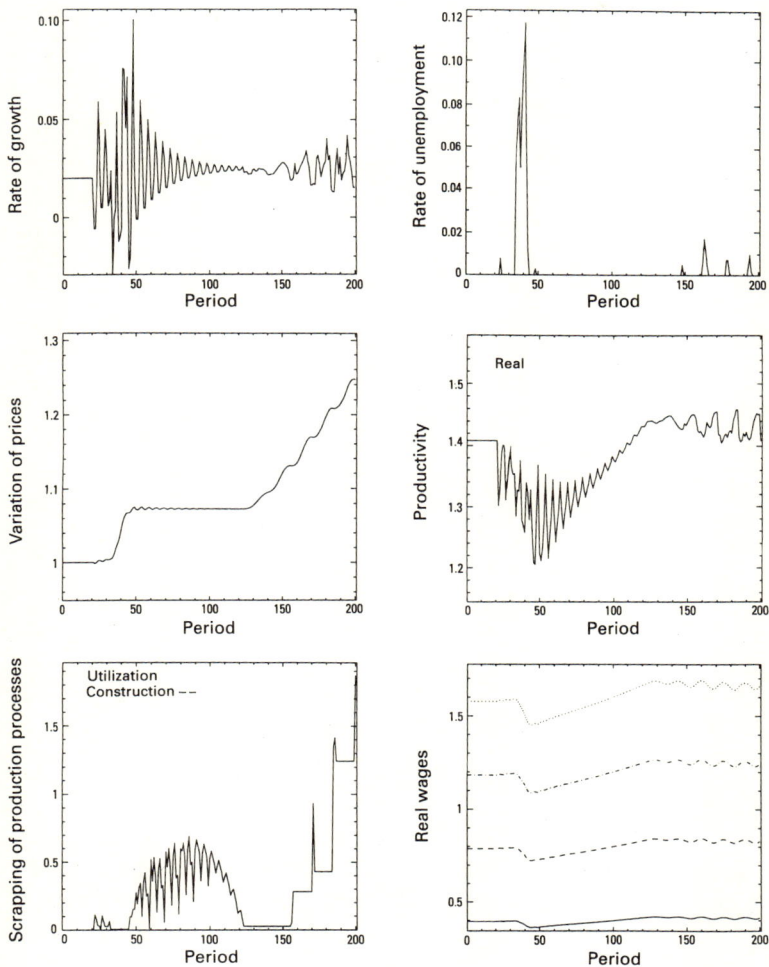

FIG 7.21*b*

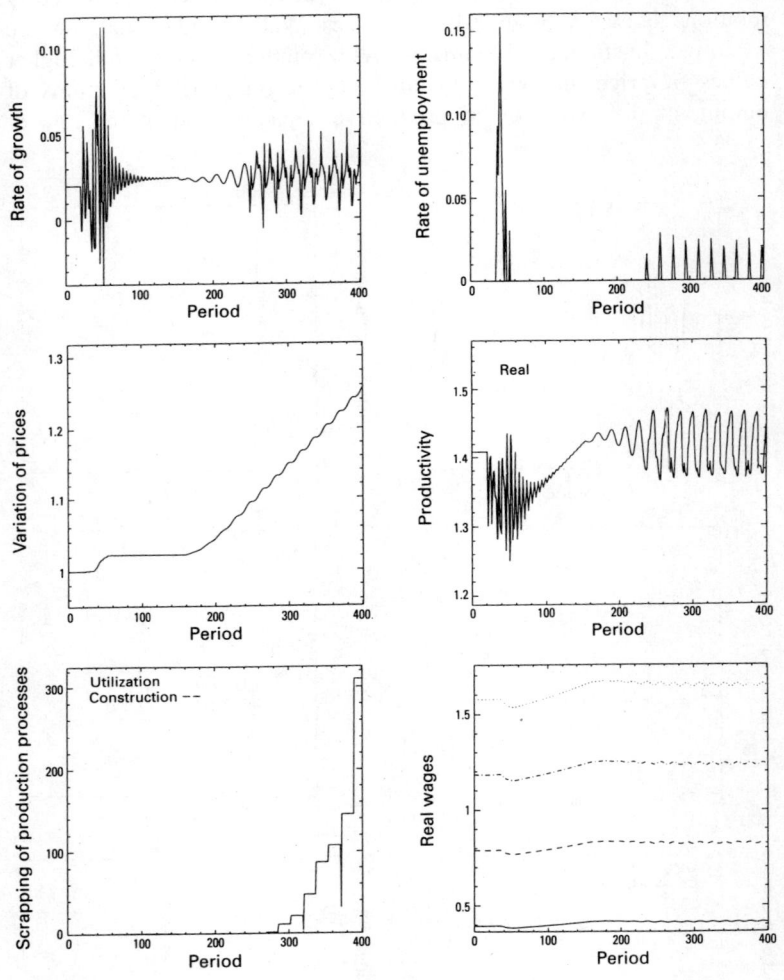

FIG 7.22

unemployment are not re-absorbed; there is no convergence to a semi-regular state of the economy (Fig. 7.21b).[25] A similar role is played by

---

[25] We obtain the same qualitative results as in Figs. 7.21a and 7.21b if production processes are not scrapped but are retired from production and kept aside at a cost.

the reaction coefficient of the supply of labour to changes in wage rates. An increase in the value of this coefficient no longer allows convergence (Fig. 7.22).

Thus for the economy to converge to a new steady growth, after productive resources have been adjusted, the co-ordination mechanism represented by price and wages changes must be characterized by a certain inertia or stickiness.

This can be the result of the fact that economic agents do not want (or cannot) exploit their short-term market power and let long-term considerations prevail. Or it can be the result of adequate interventions of intermediaries like merchants, trade unions, and so forth.

The cases just considered illustrate the productivity paradox, that is,

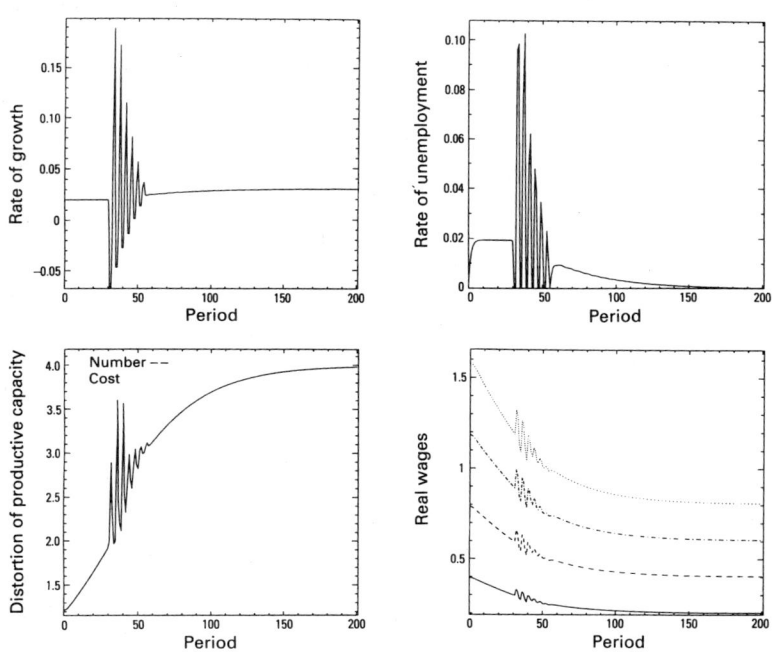

FIG 7.23a

a fall in productivity notwithstanding the introduction of a more productive technique. This appears as an essentially macroeconomic phenomenon which depends on the divorce between the productivity of the technique, which can only be verified in an economy in the steady state associated with this technique, and the effective productivity of the economy out of equilibrium. This divorce has nothing to do with the specific character of the technique concerned; it depends on the co-ordination failures arising in a context where there are problems of intertemporal complementarity of production.

The hypothesis of initial full employment and of a rigid labour supply has been made in order to bring clearly into light the effects of the breaking of the complementarity over time between productive resources which is the immediate result of the attempt to speed up the growth rate of the economy. What happens if we assume instead that

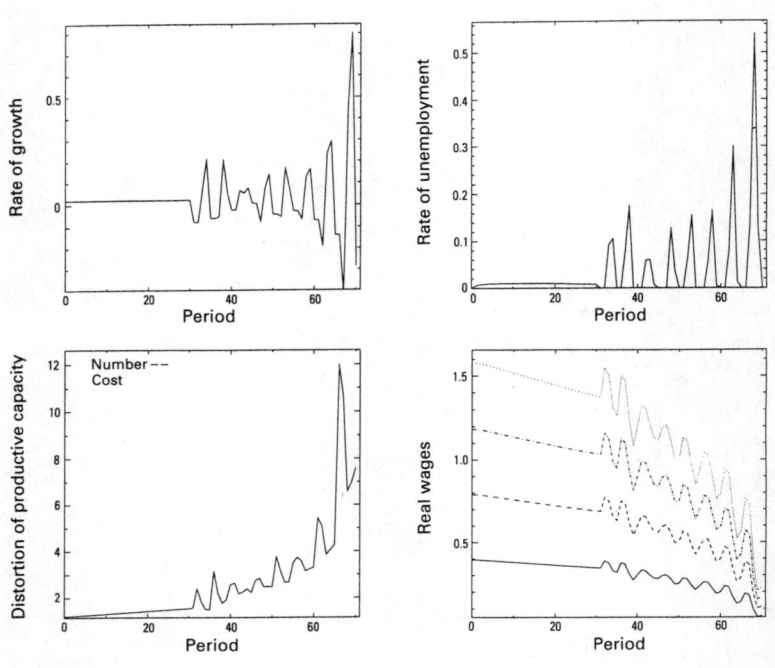

FIG 7.23b

there is initial unemployment and that the acceleration of growth is sought for precisely to re-absorb the unemployment resulting from a growth rate which does not keep pace with the dynamics of demography?

Let us consider first a big enough difference between the growth rate of population and that of output (0.03 and 0.02, respectively) which persists for a time long enough (say, the first 30 periods of the evolution path of the economy followed by our simulations) to bring about a significant amount of unemployment. With increasing savings and a high value of price and wage reaction coefficients (0.5) there is actually an acceleration of the growth rate and a re-absorption of unemployment associated with a decrease of both money and real wage rates (Fig. 7.23a).

With a smaller difference between the growth rates of labour and

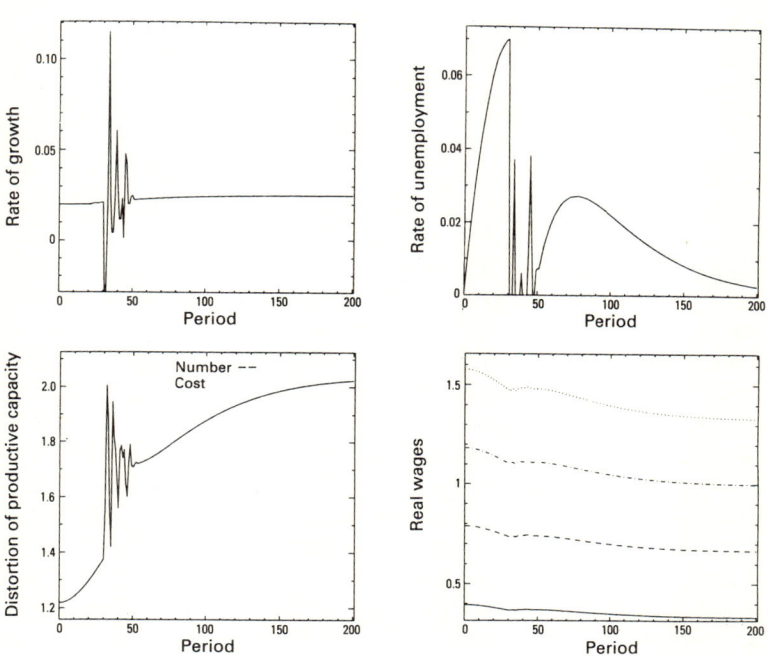

FIG 7.23c

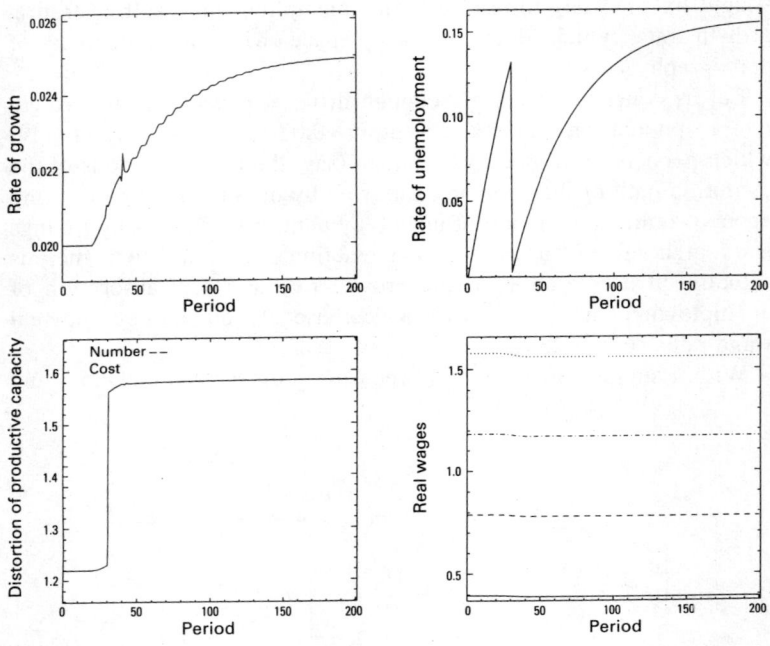

Fig 7.23d

output over a shorter time (0.025 and 0.020, respectively, over 20 periods) and high reaction coefficients (0.5 again), an increase in savings in the attempt to speed up growth renders the economy no longer viable. The existing amount of unemployment is no longer sufficient to re-establish the complementarity of productive resources, the human constraint periodically checks the construction of production processes with the result of excessive fluctuations in the distortion of productive capacity (Fig. 7.23b). Downward wage rigidity restores viability; there is an acceleration of growth but at the cost of unemployment rising asymptotically to a given level (Fig. 7.23c). Lower values of price and wage reaction coefficients (e.g. 0,05) restore viability too, and, furthermore, also allow unemployment to be re-absorbed (Fig. 7.23d). Finally with a high value of the reaction coefficients (0.5 again) but with proportional savings,

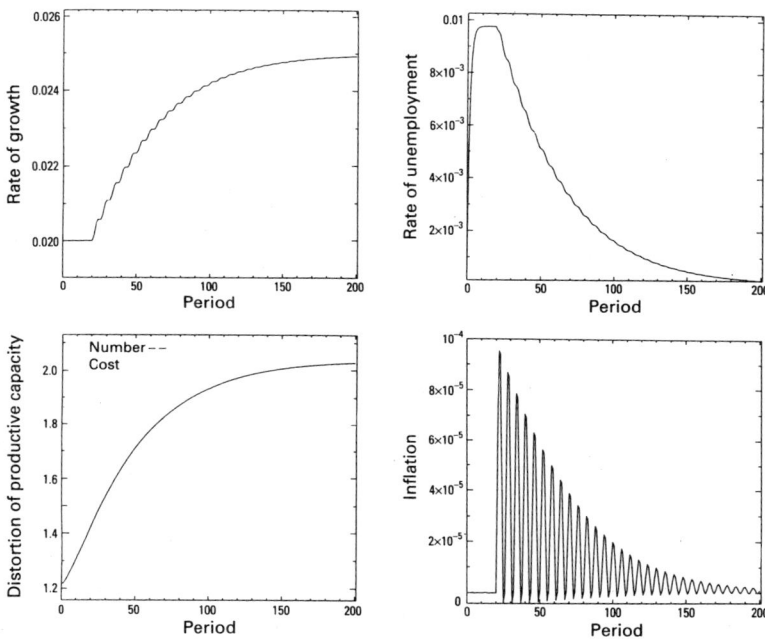

Fig 7.24

there is an acceleration of growth, unemployment tends asymptotically to zero, and inflationary tensions are gradually re-absorbed (Fig. 7.24).

Another way to obtain an acceleration of growth as the result of increased savings is to have an external demand which at each given moment makes it possible to absorb the excess of final output over internal demand (if any). However, this is so only if the additional proceeds made possible by external demand and paid out as wages to keep productive capacity in line with total final demand are kept as desired idle balances by households (Fig. 7.25a as opposed to Fig. 7.25b, where this assumption does not hold). On the other hand higher price and wage reaction coefficients (0.5 instead of 0.005 as in Fig. 7.25a) bring about strong fluctuations which do not allow an acceleration of growth (Fig. 7.25c).

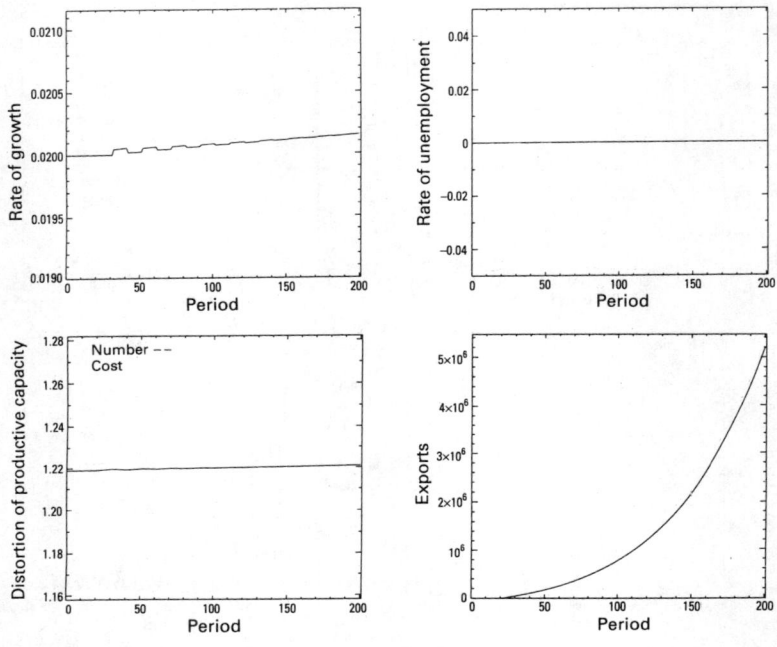

Fig 7.25a

In conclusion, the viability of the structural change undertaken, as well as the effective speeding up of growth, depends in the first place on being able to re-establish the complementarity of productive (physical and financial) resources which is essential for the consistency over time of capacity creation and capacity utilization. This stresses the relation between investment and consumption, in this dynamic process, as one of intertemporal complementarity rather than of substitution. Intertemporal coherence of production does not depend only on availability of productive resources, though; it also needs intertemporal coherence of decisions. The limits to growth, then, are not specifically supply constraints or demand constraints. Thus removing the scarcity of a particular resource at a given moment of time is not enough: we need the 'constraints–decisions–constraints' mechanism which is the back-

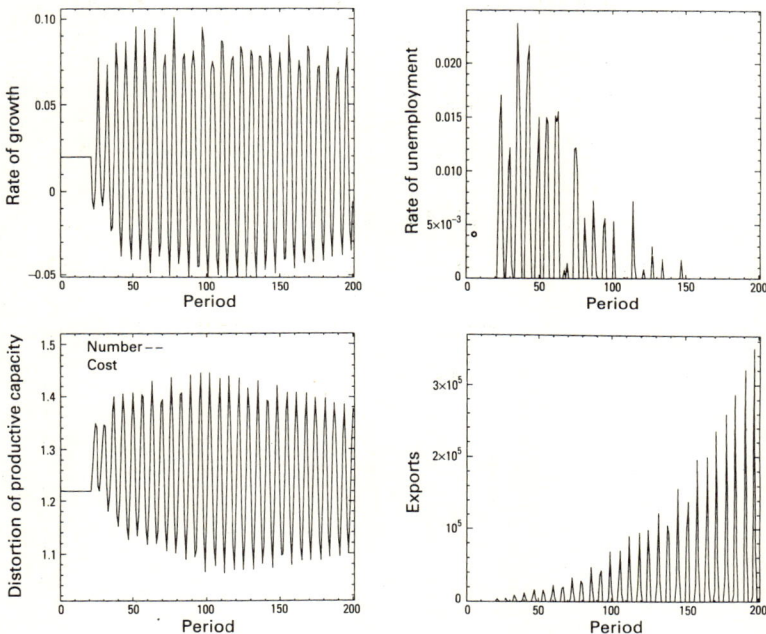

Fig 7.25b

bone of an out-of-equilibrium process to work in such a way as to re-establish the coherence between the time profile of financial flows and the sequential articulation of productive activity which also implies the consistency over time of capacity creation and capacity utilization.

This, as we have seen, in any case requires 'external' interventions aimed at co-ordinating productive activity distorted by the attempt to bring about a structural modification. These interventions concern on the one hand productive resources, and the working of market mechanisms as represented by price and wage determination regimes on the other. Now, it is quite clear that only an extremely sophisticated and actually quite difficult 'fine tuning' makes possible the right intervention, of the exact amount needed, and just at the very moment when it is actually required. We can more reasonably assume that, in particular when a change involving a structural modification is under-

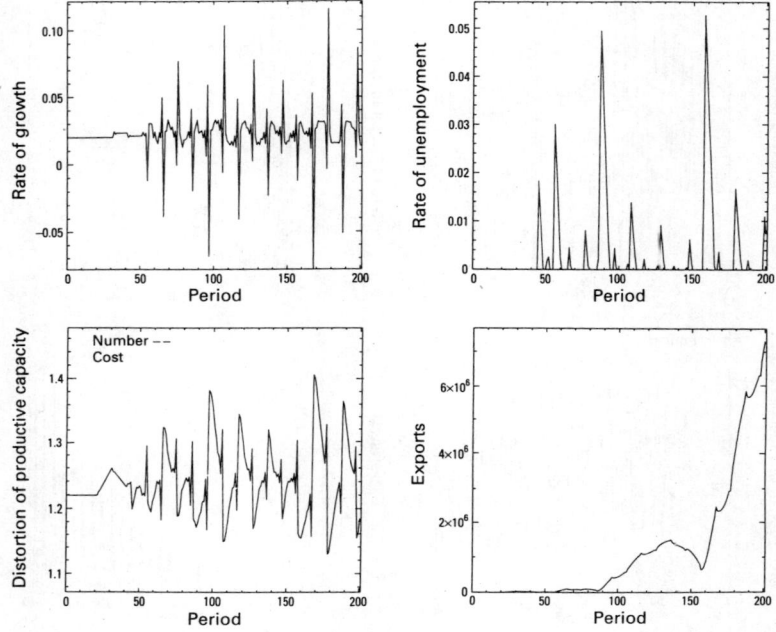

Fig 7.25c

taken, incomplete information is likely to bring about interventions which rather widen the gaps with respect to what is required. We have seen, in particular, how an excessive decrease in the 'take-out' or excessive variations in the demand for labour in the presence of a rigid supply result in fluctuations in the structure of productive capacity which are a threat to the viability of the economy; and the same can be said for sudden increases in the supply of money. The real problems, it is worth stressing again, are then problems of co-ordination over time.

This calls for a change of perspective for economic policy, no longer focused on adjusting the 'fundamentals' of the economy, as it is in the dominant approach, but aimed at smoothing out the working of the growth mechanism. We shall see in the next chapter that this implies the choice of a policy mix that can be at times just the opposite of what standard theory advocates.

8
Rethinking the Basic Issues

8.1. CONSUMPTION, INVESTMENT, AND SAVING

The numerical experiments performed in the preceding chapter have an essentially heuristic character. They have to be valued for the light they shed on basic issues of economic theory rather than for the specific results obtained.

In his last paper, published *post mortem* in *The Economic Journal*, Hicks (1990) deals with a fundamental issue for dynamic analysis: the nature and definition of economic activities and, behind this, the time structure of production. The insights provided by this paper strictly complement the analysis developed in the preceding chapter in helping to put into the right perspective the crucial theoretical aspects of the relation between consumption, investment, and saving in a dynamic context.

Hicks's paper is essentially a critical revisitation of Smith and Keynes in an attempt at the unification of macroeconomics. The focus is on the time articulation of economic activity. This facilitates a discussion of the shortcomings of the analyses of both authors, but also shows that these analyses are in a way complementary: each of them lacks exactly what the other has, so that, together, they make up the basis for a coherent system of thought.

Hicks moves from the consideration that Smith 'like Keynes, is working with analysis of the behaviour of an economy during a period . . . a period which has a past and a future, which are not to be assumed to be just like itself carrying on in a static manner' (ibid. p. 532). This viewpoint depends on the fact that Smith was interested in growth—in the course of which specialization comes into existence—rather than in the comparison between the wealth of different nations, like his predecessors. The argument has a bearing on the Smithian definition of 'productive' and 'unproductive' labour, and from this, on the interpretation of the role of investment and consumption.

The main point stressed by Hicks is that if Smith had considered a period of finite length characterized by an initial and a final stock (of capital)—and not, as he actually seems to do, a time divided into periods of infinitesimal duration—he would have naturally defined productive labour as that devoted to increase, in the period considered, the stock of capital, and hence unproductive labour that employed during the period, the product of which was consumed within the period. Then the 'unproductive consumption' and 'production' of Smith would obviously have been transformed into the 'consumption' and 'investment' of Keynes.

But something more, Hicks argues, would also have come out within the structure of Smithian economics: the possibility of hoarding, that is, the possibility of using the initial stock neither for production nor for unproductive consumption (that is, for an unproductive use different from consumption). Then parsimony, as opposed to industry, could not be reckoned to be the immediate and automatic cause of an increase of capital, as stressed instead by Smith; nor the only source, as there would be the possibility of drawing on reserves.

The conclusion is that in this light to consider consumption as flatly opposed to investment—which comes from basing the distinction between 'productive' and 'unproductive' on the nature of the activity carried out (with the focus on producer goods industries as opposed to consumer goods industries: the same idea behind the distinction between basic and non-basic goods)—is not correct. The problem is more complex: Keynes's analysis of the multiplier, stressing the role of consumption in helping to bring about output and employment, is instructive in this sense.

However, a more accurate consideration of the time articulation of production reveals not only the shortcomings of Smith's analysis—that is, opposing consumption to investment—but also the shortcomings of Keynes's analysis. These, according to Hicks, are just the opposite, that is, the consideration of consumption and investment on a par, as perfectly interchangeable components of demand, which is only possible if we overlook the time dimension of these magnitudes. This is a theme that Hicks had already developed, with reference to the multiplier, in *The Crisis in Keynesian Economics* (1974). If production takes place over a period of finite length, labour must be applied at the beginning of it while the product will be obtained only at the end of it. Thus for the multiplier to actually work, and for the results in terms of output and employment to be obtained, there must be savings or real reserves (with constant real wages) to maintain employment while production is going on. And, according to Hicks, this is where Smith comes to the rescue: his statement about parsimony, qualified by the possibility of hoarding, and hence of drawing on reserves, complements the analysis perfectly.

Failing this possibility, the only way to make things work is to transmute the capital that was embodied in the late stages of old processes into capital embodied in the early stages of new processes; that is, a disruption of other economic activities which 'is bound to be a strain' (ibid. p. 535). This is where Hicks stops, that is, at the threshold of a proper out-of-equilibrium analysis. And this is where we have taken over, showing by means of the analysis developed in the preceding chapter what the above strain actually is, how it results in out-of-equilibrium processes, and what the evolution paths of the economies undergoing these processes are likely to be.[1]

In particular, we have seen that the evolution of an economy undergoing a process of qualitative change depends mainly on the relation between consumption and investment. This relation appears as one of intertemporal complementarity rather than of substitution, though, as it must be when the different nature of these magnitudes comes to light in a thorough dynamic context and they are more adequately looked at as construction and utilization of processes of production that take place over a sequence of periods. The viability of an out-of-equilibrium process of change, as we have also seen, depends directly on the possibility of re-establishing the consistency over time of capacity creation and capacity utilization.

The complementarity of Smith's and Keynes's views on investment and consumption, stressed by Hicks in the above-mentioned paper, has thus not only been confirmed but also given a more precise definition by the analysis carried out in the preceding chapter.

On the other hand our analysis also helps to clarify the difference between Smith's and Malthus's viewpoints as regards the role of necessary consumption (and its relation to unproductive consumption) in the process of growth, thus bringing to light essential structural

---

[1] This is the way in which we have 'continued with continuation—into the future' (ibid. p. 538), a task to which Hicks himself calls others at the end of his paper. We recall that, in Hicks's own words (1982, p. 223) 'continuation theory', that is the theory dealing with the linking up of successive periods in a sequence, is, together with the single period theory, one of the two moments that make up dynamic analysis interpreted as sequence analysis.

aspects of this process and at the same time clarifying the relation between saving and investment in the same process.

Smith's analysis of the process of accumulation—a process that, by means of a particular use of the comparative statics method, can be sketched out as taking place through a sequence of periods (see Hicks 1965, Chapter 4)—relies on the equality between *ex ante* savings (taken as determined in each period from last period's output) and investment. Thus equilibrium is actually kept along the sequence of periods over which accumulation occurs, although this does not necessarily imply a regularly progressive economy, and the matching of supply and demand is ensured whatever the relation between necessary consumption (investment) and unproductive consumption. So different proportions of these two types of consumption (different saving rates) will only imply different equilibrium growth paths.

Malthus (1820) held the different view that a matching of supply and demand is not necessarily ensured when there is 'a change' in the relation between necessary and unproductive consumption and that 'a process of investment is likely to generate a level of productive employment that cannot sustain itself unless there is a source of additional effective demand *external* to the production system' (Baranzini and Scazzieri 1990, p. 286; emphasis added). In other words, the rate of growth cannot be increased by simply increasing the rate of savings; supply and demand must co-evolve so as to dynamically interact as required for an acceleration of growth to be brought about.

We maintain that this surprisingly modern conclusion, perfectly in line with the analysis developed in the preceding chapter, depends mainly on Malthus moving from a comparative statics analytical framework to one 'emphasising changes through historical time, and hence disequilibrium' (von Tunzelmann 1991, p. 289), with the focus, in particular, on demand and supply interactions over time. Within an equilibrium context—as with Smith—changes take place smoothly and supply and demand grow in accordance so that, whatever their structure, they always match. Out of equilibrium this is no longer the case. Malthus clearly saw that an increase in necessary consumption could actually take the economy out of equilibrium: measures would then be required to bring about additional demand so as to fill the gap with supply thus opened up. Putting Smith's and Malthus's contributions in different dynamic perspectives allows us to not only account for their different viewpoints, but also to stress more generally that some kind of external intervention appears as an essential element of the out-of-equilibrium process of change involved in a structural modification (Amendola, Froeschlé, and Gaffard 1993). The need for final demand to keep pace dynamically with productive capacity, and how this necessarily requires an external intervention, is exactly what the simulations performed in particular in Section 7.5 above have drawn attention to (see Fig. 7.25).

In conclusion, lack of co-ordination over time between investment and consumption (construction and utilization), on the one hand, and between investment and saving on the other is what characterizes an economy out of equilibrium. This is a well-known conclusion, but we interpret it here in a different way from normal, as is explained in the following section.

8.2. STRUCTURE AND CYCLES

The analysis developed in Chapters 6 and 7 has shown that fluctuations of the main magnitudes of the economy are the distinctive aspect of the out-of-equilibrium processes started off by the attempt to carry out qualitative economic changes, and that this depends mainly on the distortions of productive capacity brought about by these changes. However, for the time structure of production to become an essential element of the analysis of business cycles—we ought better say, as we shall see in a moment, of cyclical growth—problems of co-ordination of the decision process must interact with the co-ordination over time of the production process.

This is certainly not the case with real business cycles (Long and Plosser 1983; Plosser 1989), which are viewed as the outcome of the response to shocks in technology, tastes, and so forth, given by individual agents acting to maximize over time their utility subject to production possibilities and resource constraints. The shocks, whether of a real or of a monetary character, only push the agents to modify their choices between consumption and saving, between income and leisure, which represents optimal behaviour on their part. This does not put the economy out of equilibrium, though: markets always clear and the structure of production is not perturbed.[2] In this context, where the

---

[2] This is true also when a 'time to build' technology is assumed. As a matter of fact 'provided the firm can freely buy and sell capital goods at any stage of production or building, no new issues are introduced by the assumption of a time to build technology' (Blanchard and Fisher 1989, p. 297).

intertemporal optimizing behaviour of agents makes it possible to reabsorb the time dimension of production in its sequential impact, fluctuations appear as an equilibrium phenomenon.

We propose an altogether different interpretation. In our view fluctuations are the typical expression of a growth process. As a matter of fact they are the result of the interaction of the short and the long term, that is, the result of the way the functioning of markets 'out of equilibrium' interacts with the distortions over time of productive capacity associated with economic change involving structural modifications.

There are Hicksian and Hayekian reminiscences behind this interpretation. What Hicks has contributed to our analysis has already been stressed many times. As to Hayek, we have already mentioned (see Section 7.3 above) how our analysis of the effects of a credit expansion recalls in many ways the analysis developed by Hayek in *Prices and Production* (1931), and how this depends mainly on the common interest in the time structure of the production process. However, there are significant differences between the two analyses. To discuss them makes it possible to throw light on the issue of the origin and character of the business cycle and of its relation with the process of growth.

Hayek stresses the monetary origin of the cycle in a theory which tries to reconcile the equilibrium method with a consideration of the essential character of the time dimension of production. For Hayek any net creation of credit in a full employment economy is a potential source of disturbance, and it actually brings about a business cycle. The expansion and the following slump result from successive (and opposite) movements of the relative prices of consumption goods and producer goods which determine distortions in the structure of productive capacity. The injection of bank credit considered, which places the newly created purchasing power in the hands of investors, causes in the first place a rise in the money prices of capital goods (including wages) which, however, does not lead to a corresponding increase in the prices of consumption goods.[3]

More round about methods of production are thus set in motion, using resources bid away from consumers, but no mechanism that might lead to a

---

[3] This is so, according to Hayek, because of a lag in the spending of wages. Hicks considers this consumption lag quite implausible, but adds that Hayek's story can be made consistent by substituting a wage lag, that is 'a lag of money wages behind the balance of supply and demand in the market for labour' (Hicks 1967, p. 209).

corresponding tendency on the part of consumers voluntarily to defer their consumption plans is allowed to intrude. In due course, therefore, consumption demand materializes before the new investments have borne fruits, and hence before the goods necessary to meet that demand are available. (Laidler 1994, p. 11).

Consideration of the time dimension of production is behind this lag in the supply of consumption goods, which pushes up their prices, reversing the balance of relative prices. The excess demand for consumption goods and the existence of a stock of partially completed investment projects which must be abandoned because of a shortage of savings bring about the crisis.

There is a horizontal sectoral view of the economy which implies relations between sectors expressed by relative prices behind this approach. It is an equilibrium approach that confines the analysis to a consideration of how monetary factors distort the intertemporal relative price and thus disrupt the co-ordination of saving and investment. Two equilibrium positions, characterized by different price structures which reflect the existence of two different lags, are actually compared. In the first higher real wages—due to the fact that an increase in wage rates is not immediately followed by their spending and hence by a corresponding increase in the price of final output—are associated with more roundabout methods of production. In the second, a production lag brings about an excess demand for final output, a higher price, and hence lower real wages.

It is the wrong proportion of the production of producers goods and that of consumers goods that brings about the cycle: a wrong proportion which results from inappropriate changes in relative prices which are the expression of lags in market adjustments, that is, of problems of co-ordination. Thus the time dimension of production only matters if considered in relation to the time dimension of market processes. However the co-ordination problem, within the intertemporal equilibrium framework adopted, actually comes down to a wrong intertemporal allocation of resources.

Within this context, although the importance of the time dimension of production is clearly perceived, the deeper implications of the distortion of productive capacity brought about by monetary factors cannot be dealt with. An adequate analysis of the interaction between monetary factors and changes in the structure of productive capacity puts at the centre of the stage the co-ordination problems which arise 'out of equilibrium'. And this implies in the first place abandoning the pure logic of essentially timeless choice which characterizes intertemporal equilibrium to focus on how agents react sequentially to market disequilibria.[4]

This calls for a theory of market adjustments *in time*, a theory to which Hicks has made an important contribution with his fix-price method (see Section 4.8 above). In particular, reference to this method has made it possible for us to model the functioning of markets out of equilibrium by introducing the lag of transmission of information stressed by Richardson which, by interacting with the construction lag—through which are perceived in turn the effects of the intertemporal complementarity of production—allows us to sketch out the evolution path of the economy out of equilibrium. Due to this interaction any shock which implies a distortion of productive capacity triggers a process fed by the reaction and the adjustment mechanisms at work in the economy and characterized, in general, by strong and erratic fluctuations.

Business cycles appear, then, as the expression of the way qualitative change (growth, technical change, changes in tastes) takes place; and this, we repeat, is due to the distortion of productive capacity associated with change, whatever its origin, in a context where problems of co-ordination of economic activity arise. This puts the accent on the mechanism whereby business fluctuations come about rather than on their specific source. In this perspective the discussion on the nature of the original shock which has affected the economy, whether a real or a monetary one, loses salience, in the same way as does the discussion on the exogenous or endogenous character of business cycles.

Our analysis, on the other hand, throws light on what is required for an economy subject to fluctuations to remain viable out of equilibrium. For this purpose a co-ordination of the decision process must be taken into account together with that of the production process. Thus, for instance, we have seen that when the intertemporal constraints on production are very strong to start with, or become so along the way (as usually happens with an innovation process), a certain stickiness of price and wage adjustment mechanisms may be

---

[4] Which, after all, is what Hayek himself suggests in his 'Economics and Knowledge' (1937), i.e., that what really matters is how the agents acquire the information by interacting over time rather than the 'fundamentals' of the economy.

Rethinking the Basic Issues

required for the fluctuations not to become explosive (see Section 7.5 above). The same stickiness is required when changes in expectations render producers more pessimistic (Section 7.4). We have also seen that the fluctuations in real wages associated with changes in the structure of productive capacity, rather than the absolute values of prices and nominal wages, represent the real threat to viability (Section 7.3). However, these are just examples, referring to specific cases, of what is needed, out of equilibrium, to keep the 'constraints–decisions–constraints' sequence right. As a matter of fact no general rule can be formulated. Different institutional set-ups and different kinds of interventions may be consistent with the viability target in different cases.

8.3. UNEMPLOYMENT

Intolerable levels of unemployment, as we have seen, are the main threat to the viability of out-of-equilibrium processes of change. Dominant theory, in its standard or in more modern versions (see e.g. Layard, Nickell, and Jackman 1991; Bean, 1994), postulates a monotonic inverse relation between employment and the (real) wage rate, and hence advocates wage flexibility to make the re-absorption of unemployment resulting from whatever shock possible. This depends on focusing on the 'cost' aspect of wages, a viewpoint that neoclassical theory has in common with the classical wage fund theory which, although through a different mechanism, also establishes an inverse relation between employment and the wage rate. Along the same lines the 'neoclassical synthesis', wrongly considered as a true interpretation of Keynes's view on the argument, explains unemployment in terms of wage rigidity; while in so-called 'new-Keynesian' models the high level of wages which determines unemployment is no longer the result of rigidities but the outcome of optimizing procedures carried out in contexts characterized by imperfect competition. A main aspect of imperfect competition is in fact imperfect, asymmetric information which leads to the fixing of excessively high wages (efficiency wages, wages resulting from contracts through wage unions, and so forth).

In all cases the stage set for the analysis is a macroeconomic equilibrium model where the main variables (including the price and quantity of labour) are determined simultaneously given the prevailing institutional and information context. The resulting unemployment is an equilibrium unemployment, in the same way as credit rationing is an equilibrium phenomenon. On the other hand the focus is on the mechanism of determination of employment as if it where a mechanism of its own, with the real wage rate as the crucial variable. Institutional factors determining the way wages are actually set then come to the fore and become the main focus of policy interventions[5]. A corollary of this approach is that we can distinguish between equilibrium unemployment, due to structural factors concerning the labour market, and the excesses of actual unemployment over its equilibrium level, which reflect aggregate demand (Bean, Layard, and Nickell, 1986; Solow, 1986).

Keynes himself focused instead on the 'demand' aspect of wages, which led him to consider a more complex determination of employment than the simple inverse relation with the real wage rate. Changes in money wages[6] can have an effect on the aggregate level of production, and hence on employment, only to the extent that they affect aggregate demand. The propensity to consume, the marginal efficiency of capital, and the rate of interest are all called in to explain how, and when, this happens.

In a Keynesian perspective both Leijonhufvud (1968) and Hahn and Solow (1995) stress the role of the interest rate in the determination of unemployment when its level is such as to imply a failure of intertemporal co-ordination in the allocation of financial resources. In this case, according to Hahn and Solow, 'making real wages stickier improves the stability of the . . . economy'. As a matter of fact 'it does what Keynes saw that it might do: protect the economy against dysfunctional fluctuations in the real rate of interest' (pp. 56–7). And they conclude 'Certainly it is far from clear that the curve for employment lies with falling money wages' (p. 137). These conclusions are reached by the authors by simply introducing the consideration of adjustment lags in an otherwise standard equilibrium analytical framework; that is, by not confining the attention to a long-run equilibrium where all adjustments have already been realized.

---

[5] The model by Aghion and Howitt (1994) is no exception. Although looking at employment from the perspective of growth, it assigns a crucial role to the mechanism through which different types of labour are remunerated and hence ends up by actually determining employment on the basis of the functioning of the labour market only.

[6] As is well known Keynes reasons in terms of nominal wages as he believes that labour has no means of determining its real wage.

Rethinking the Basic Issues 241

The focus of the analysis is thus enlarged, but this still remains essentially an equilibrium analysis, characterized by a simultaneous determination of all variables involved.

Out of equilibrium, instead, we have a sequential determination of prices and quantities (see Section 3.2 above), which reflects the evolution of the economy resulting from the interaction over time of a production process with complementarity problems and a decision process with co-ordination problems. At the heart of this evolution there is the capital accumulation through which all processes of qualitative change take place. In a model with a more realistic time structure than the overlapping generation one considered by Hahn and Solow, where durable capital is assumed away, the effects of wage changes on the activities of construction and utilization of productive capacity, and on the strengthening and relaxing of the constraints to them, must be taken into account, which implies focusing on both the cost and the demand aspect of wages. But this is just part of the story: real and monetary factors, besides wage changes, contribute to the effective articulation over time of the above-mentioned determination process. This is thus the result of feedback mechanisms which depend on how the economy actually evolves and that can therefore change along the way. In this context real wages and employment both become endogenous variables. In particular, employment appears as the result of a sequence of disequilibria which concern both financial and human resources and result from lack of co-ordination between the wage adjustment mechanism, the saving behaviour, and monetary policy.[7]

The analysis carried out along these lines in Chapter 7 confirms in the first place the doubts about the existence of an inverse relation between unemployment and real wage rates. As a matter of fact, in the case of a technological shock characterized by an increase in the labour input in the phase of construction of productive capacity, real wages may be required to go up or down, or even to be unchanged, in order to eliminate unemployment resulting from the 'machinery effect', depending on the prevailing saving behaviour.[8]

---

[7] However, without a theory focusing on the time dimension of production we would not be able to follow the sequence of disequilibria actually sketched ou by the conditions determining the process of capital accumulation, and we would necessarily fall back on an explanation of unemployment based only on the working of the labour market.

[8] A saving behaviour which, on the other hand, must be considered together with the supply of money.

Thus with proportional savings we need a reduction in real wages to re-absorb unemployment (see Figs. 7.1b and 7.4b in Chapter 7) while with gradually increasing savings the re-absorption of unemployment is associated with increasing real wages (see Figs. 7.2c and 7.5b). The optimal policy with increasing savings would indeed be fixed wages, as this would allow the idle balances unvoluntarily piled up to be fully channelled to the financing of production processes (see Fig. 7.2a).

With a monetary shock, on the other hand, we can have an extreme case where a tendency to a fall in real wages is associated with an increase in unemployment (see Fig. 7.15). Just the opposite of what standard theory maintains, but something that would be found in Keynes's theory. He argued in fact that a reduction in wages would redistribute income in favour of income recipients with a lower marginal propensity to consume, with the result of a reduction of aggregate demand and the ensuing negative effect on production and employment (Keynes 1936, p. 262).

Co-ordination problems arise out of equilibrium, in the wake of the complementarity problems brought about by the distortions of productive capacity associated with qualitative economic changes. Wage regimes, together with monetary regimes and so forth, are a way to determine the interaction required for co-ordination to be assured. The effects of any particular regime, however, depend on how the interaction actually takes place. Consider wage indexation. With technological shocks indexation leads to an equilibrium with permanent unemployment, whatever the saving behaviour (see Fig. 7.3). This is so in all supply shocks, as in these cases wage indexation checks investment in the construction processes. With expectational shocks, on the contrary, indexation allows for a reduction in the amplitude of the fluctuations of the economy and thus contains unemployment (see Fig. 7.17). It all depends on how wage behaviour interacts with the dynamics of the other variables which, together, determine step by step the effective evolution of the economy. Unemployment is the result of this evolution; we can only deal with it by affecting this evolution.

Two main implications for economic policy stand out. Once-and-for-all structural measures concerning the labour market affect only one of a number of elements involved. These elements, on the other hand, interact sequentially in a process and need different interventions according to how the sequence of disequilibria are linked step by step and hence the process itself actually evolves.

8.4. FLEXIBILITY AND VIABILITY

Harrod's main contribution to dynamic analysis is his emphasis on the interaction between the short and the long run and the appearance of coordination problems that this implies.

The growth theory developed since then has led instead to a dissociation of the short and the long runs. All the attention has been concentrated on the long-run equilibrium position of the economy and the short run, confined to the transition to this position, has gradually shifted out of sight. This transition, in fact, does not appear as a process in the usual sense, as the equilibrium behaviours considered in the analysis imply that the economy adjusts immediately to the requirements of the long-run equilibrium sought. A stability analysis then prevails, where stability is the postulate of instantaneous adjustment of the values of all relevant parameters to changes in the value of one or more of them. This, of course, hampers the appearance of co-ordination problems.

Perfectly flexible prices, which allow the immediate re-establishment of demand–supply equilibria, are a way of obtaining instantaneous adjustments. Another way is changes in the distribution of income, as in neo-Keynesian models. But the two ways are actually two faces of the same problem. As Hahn clearly puts it, with reference to the case when a deepening of capital is required to absorb surplus saving because of a warranted rate of growth exceeding the natural rate: 'to induce the deepening in the one good economy, the interest rate must be falling and real wages rising. The former could be attributed to an excess of saving over investment that is instantly corrected by the fall in the interest rate' (1990, p. 24).

In all cases true disequilibria are assumed away as co-ordination problems cannot arise. Within this context price flexibility is a good thing, as it is interpreted as the possibility of always having the 'right' price associated with whatever equilibrium relation exists between the 'fundamentals' of the economy.

This approach implies, on the other hand, that there are no limits to growth other than those represented by the 'fundamentals' themselves. Thus in a backward economy characterized by the existence of labour reserves which can be shifted from agriculture to industry (Kaldor 1966) or from a sector with a low rate of learning to one with a high rate of learning (Lucas 1993) an increase in the saving rate is a sufficient condition for a higher growth rate. Once the resources required are available no co-ordination problem prevents the economy from making full use of them.

In this analysis, as already mentioned, the short run is only apparently taken into account. No transition process is actually dealt with, as adjustments are always instantaneously realised. But, as Solow himself has recently stressed: 'the short run disequilibrium properties of growth paths are just as important as their asymptotic properties' (Solow 1990, p. 223), while 'equilibrium growth theory can only discuss the characteristics of equilibrium paths, not the disequilibrium dynamics surrounding them' (ibid. p. 222).

We need an out-of-equilibrium approach to deal properly with adjustment processes, characterized by sequences of disequilibria where the short run matters in itself as the results depend on what happens on the way. Out of equilibrium there is room for co-ordination problems, and the way we deal with them determines the evolution path actually followed by the economy. The essential problem then is to render this evolution viable, and flexibility still plays an important role in this. A different flexibility from the standard price and wage flexibility stressed in equilibrium models, though. As a matter of fact, as we have shown in the preceding section, wage flexibility does not necessarily imply a re-absorption of unemployment but, by bringing about wage fluctuations, may become a factor of instability. Weak flexibility may help co-ordination, while strong flexibility may result in fluctuations so pronounced as to be a threat to the viability of the economy.

According to Hicks (1985), flexibility consists in rendering the existing constraints less binding by making the complementarity relations between resources less strict. This can be obtained, for instance, by accumulating or decumulating stocks of final goods or by different degrees of utilization of a given productive capacity. Prices—which out of equilibrium are not necessarily the right prices—must not necessarily be flexible for adjustments (in the case considered by Hicks, the Traverse to a new technique) to be realized. 'If unsuitable prices are adopted, and adhered to for long, unsuitable techniques will be adopted. The problem of getting into equilibrium will be further complicated' (ibid. p. 143).

The analysis carried out with our model allows a deeper understanding of flexibility, with reference to the viability problem which is the main issue involved out of equilibrium. We have seen that the viability of out-of-equilibrium processes depends essentially on the inertia of adjustments and on the avoidance of strong or abrupt reactions to shocks. Flexibility must then be valued in relation to these requirements, which, once again, may not coincide with price and/or wage flexibility in the standard sense. There may be cases in fact—significant ones have been shown by our analysis—where price (wage) variations must be kept within certain limits for smoothing out sequential adjustments so as to also reduce the fluctuations of the economy and keep it within a viability corridor.

Thus wage reaction coefficients must not be too strong for the acceleration of growth to be obtained as the result of a gradual decrease in the take-out when external demand always allows the clearing of the market for final output (see Fig. 7.25 in Section 7.5 above). In the same way, when an increase in the supply of money is associated with a technological shock of whatever kind the fluctuations of the economy are ever stronger, with evident threats to viability from the higher price and wage reaction coefficients (see Figs. 7.21 and 7.23 Section 7.5 above). In this case if we let labour supply vary in relation to changes in wages, fluctuations are damped down if the reaction coefficients of labour to wages are positive but not too strong. In fact we need to relax the human constraint, but gradually and not too abruptly. On the other hand, with demand-determined investment behaviour à la Harrod, instability can only be avoided by a complete downward rigidity of prices and wages (see Fig. 7.17*b* in Section 7.4 above).

Viability depends on being able to reduce the imbalances between supply and demand on all markets. Flexibility, in the sense of the size and speed of adjustment as expressed by price and wage reaction coefficients, may be a good or a bad thing depending on whether it contributes to reducing or to widening these imbalances and hence the fluctuations of the economy.

8.5. ECONOMIC POLICY

Reference to intertemporal equilibrium is a bias common to all modern approaches to economic policy. In particular, two main positions stand out. On the one hand New Classical economists maintain that the economy can only suffer random and weak perturbations provided it is guided by simple and efficient rules and institutions. There is no place then for discretionary interventions, nor would these be effective due to the expectations of private agents who have a perfect knowledge of the functioning of the economy. Simple rules derived from the behaviour of the economy at equilibrium—like price flexibility, a monetary policy aimed at keeping the general price level stable, and so forth—is all that is required.

On the other hand New Keynesian economists, although still focusing on intertemporal equilibrium, stress that the evolution actually experienced by the economy in order to realize it may be characterized by excessive fluctuations. Discretionary interventions are then required and these must concern the structural parameters of the economy, as if it were possible to modify immediately the behaviour of individual agents and pass instantaneously from one equilibrium to the other.

The whole line of thought developed in this book clearly points beyond these approaches by shifting the focus from intertemporal equilibrium to an out-of-equilibrium context where the articulation over time of constraints and decisions is what actually matters. In this different light economic policy, although reduced to simple rules, cannot be 'neutral', while policy interventions, rather than affecting structural parameters, must be conceived as keeping the evolution of the economy within a viability corridor.

Leaving aside the steady state, which does not involve qualitative change, we have seen in Chapter 6 how we can get simple analytical solutions to our model which assure viability even when a structural change is contemplated. This is the case of periodic orbits considered in Section 6.4, or the case dealt with in Section 6.6 where the periodization is pushed to the point of cancelling the lags which characterize the sequential process through which change takes place.

However, the assumptions that in these cases render the evolution of the economy viable have very little if any economic meaning[9] and, besides, are such as to conceal the essential aspects of the out-of-equilibrium processes of change brought to light in Part I of this book.

More generally the result of the attempt to bring about a qualitative change, is a complex dynamic which is most likely to end up being a threat to the viability of the economy. We then have a substantial problem, not a formal one, that is, *whether (and how) an economy*

---

[9] In the same way, it should be stressed, as the assumptions about the values of the relevant parameters are introduced in endogenous growth models to assure the strict complementarity relations required by the models themselves (see Section 5.4 above).

Rethinking the Basic Issues 247

undergoing an out-of-equilibrium process of change can be viable if we abstract from extreme hypotheses. The answer given by the analysis developed in the preceding chapter is that this is only possible if external interventions are contemplated, which is exactly the opposite of merely formal solutions that always come down to endogenizing something.

This opens a space, and an essential one, for economic policy. As a matter of fact, whatever the nature of the original shock, in the absence of 'full information' and given the existing irreversibilities, the economy necessarily undergoes fluctuations which are the result of co-ordination failures and of problems of intertemporal complementarity. Following Robertson's original intuition, the aim of economic policy, and in particular of monetary policy, is to reduce the amplitude of the fluctuations of the economy so as to be able to keep its evolution within a stability corridor (see Sections 1.7 and 2.4 above).

Out-of-equilibrium processes are processes over time. This sets the 'discretionary interventions versus fixed rules' debate in economic policy in a particular perspective. Thus, on the one hand, it must be stressed that a policy of 'fine tuning' is not possible within the context considered, as it requires the authorities not only to possess complete information but to possess it at the right moment. This is the same reason why an intertemporal optimizing strategy on the part of individual agents must also be ruled out.

On the other hand the analysis carried out has shown that *ex ante* rules which focus on a single objective to be pursued by means of a given instrument (e.g. a monetary policy aimed at keeping the price level stable) would not do either. The model behind this policy approach assumes that the economy is intrinsically stable and can reach its long-run equilibrium spontaneously: and this equilibrium is defined independently of short-term adjustments. In other words the model abstracts from the 'interdependence of disequilibria over time'. Thus we can have more growth, or an advance in technology, without having to suffer more inflation. The conclusion is that a rigorous monetary policy aimed at keeping the price level stable favours growth rather than checking it. Our simulations have shown instead that this kind of policy may bring about cumulative imbalances. We then have a conflict between price stability and viability, if not growth. What actually happens, out of equilibrium, is the result of the interactions over time between all the relevant variables of the economy, including the existing constraints and the control variables which are made endogenous to the ongoing processes. Policy interventions must therefore concern all factors involved; to focus only on price stability, or on a systematic sustaining of final demand, actually means abstracting from the essential interactions just mentioned.[10]

Different interventions concerning real, monetary, and financial factors are then required, and they must be consistent with each other in view of restoring the coherence over time of the 'constraints–decisions–constraints' sequence, that is disturbed by the original shock. These interventions are 'discretionary' in the sense that they depend on the particular context dealt with and hence may differ from case to case. We have seen that, in the case of a technological shock, a restrictive monetary policy may be effective when wages are more or less fully indexed but is not consistent with flexible prices and wages (see Section 7.1 above), and that in the case of an expectational shock (bringing about an increase in the liquidity preference of firms), downward wage rigidity is required for the economy not to fall into a cumulative depression (see Section 7.3).

However, these interventions may have the opposite effect of increasing the amplitude of the fluctuations of the economy, if they are abrupt and/or too strong.[11] The graduality required for interventions, not to add further shocks to the original one, reflects the need for a certain inertia in adjustment processes characterized by incomplete information due to lags in its transmission.

This sort of anti-turnpike conjecture (see Section 5.4 above) is an answer to Lucas's critique to most existing macroeconometric models, according to which it is not possible to ignore the links between government action and private sector behavioural decisions via the expectations of private agents (Lucas 1976). Our conjecture implies

---

[10] This is put vividly by Hicks as it concerns monetary policy. 'Suppose . . . that there is a change in preferences (or in some other external data). The course which has hitherto been pursued (and to which the economy, and its monetary policy, is more or less adjusted) is then found to be intolerable, or untenable. Course has thus to be changed, and let us suppose that the change of direction is to be made by monetary policy. From the point of view of the old equilibrium, any change in monetary policy is disequilibrating; but it is required that a way should be found from that disequilibrium to a new equilibrium. Can that be done by monetary policy alone? It does not, in these terms, look very likely' (1977, p. 72).

[11] In particular, we have seen this to be the case when the interventions take the form of a decrease in the 'take-out' or of an increase in the supply of money, in order to avoid the appearance of a capital shortage, or of a sustaining of final demand for this to keep pace with productive capacity (see Section 7.5 above).

Rethinking the Basic Issues

that economic policy, by affecting the behaviour of individual agents, does act on the 'constraints–decisions–constraints' sequence and hence changes the evolution path of the economy. This does not lead us to deny the relevance of policy interventions, though; out of equilibrium there is no way for economic policy to be neutral. As a matter of fact the very notion of neutrality implies considering an equilibrium state of the economy which may or may not be affected by an external action. Out of equilibrium governments, central authorities, and the like contribute to determining the evolution of the economy as any other economic agent; there is no given configuration of the economy to use as a benchmark for interventions. What is true, on the other hand, is that policy interventions must be consistent with the behaviour of individual agents. The notion of a monetary regime (Heymann and Leijonhufvud 1994), which postulates a certain type of coherence between the behaviour of monetary authorities and the expectations of individual agents, stresses this point (see Section 2.8 above). This has led these authors to talk of 'Rules *and* Discretion' instead of 'Rules versus Discretion' (ibid. p. 45).

We would rather talk of 'Discretion with Rules', but what exactly do we mean by this?

Problems of complementarity and co-ordination are the necessary result of the attempts to undertake qualitative changes which set the economy out of equilibrium. These problems lead to fluctuations which are likely to render the economy not viable. To check these fluctuations in order to keep the economy within a viability corridor, complementarity over time must be re-established together with coherence of the decision process. This is the task of economic policy. It must not, therefore, consist of interventions which result in the end in further shocks that aggravate the existing complementarity and co-ordination problems. It must rather fill the existing gaps, re-establish the broken links, cover sunk costs. To deal with imbalances which surface along the way not only is an accurate monitoring required, but stocks and reserves of all kinds (real, financial, and human) must also be built in to be available at the right moment in the right amounts.

Discretionary interventions must be conceived in this light. For instance, credit creation is required to sustain an innovation process notwithstanding the increase in prices that it implies. At the same time rules must be conceived, and institutions established, for markets to function in such a way as to contribute to reducing the effects of the oncoming imbalances. The role of intermediaries which allow the smoothing of fluctuations in prices is a good case in point.

The role of economic policy is neither abstention nor punctual intervention. It is to provide the economic agents with the means and the environment for their actions to keep the economy within a viability corridor.

8.6. RE-READING THE RECENT 'STORY' OF WESTERN ECONOMIES

The disequilibria which have affected Western economies in the last decades have been interpreted as the result of the malfunctioning of markets not able to adapt to changes in the environment—whether these are changes in technology, or in the terms on which productive resources can be acquired, or whatever—due mainly to information imperfections and to the absence of institutional and incentive rules able to correct these defects. In particular, the accumulation of capital does not appear as a central element in the explanation of these disequilibria. The policy implications of this analytical set-up are, of course, that we must act upon the institutional constraints which hamper the flexibility of the various markets. At the same time we must have macroeconomic policies which are 'neutral' (in particular, budgetary policies aimed at restoring equilibrium public budgets and monetary policies aimed at the stability of the general price level) in the sense of not being an obstacle to the natural (read 'flexible') working of markets once the institutional constraints have been relaxed.

This perspective has determined how the different crises which Western economies have gone through in the more or less recent past have been interpreted, and, in particular, has determined the main lines along which the process leading to European Monetary Union has been devised. The alternative perspective chosen in this book provides an altogether different line of interpretation of what has happened and what is going on, of the crucial variables involved, and of the policy interventions required (most often just the opposite of those advocated by dominant theory). In this different light the recent evolution of Western economies must be looked at as a process sketched out step by step by sequentially interacting disequilibria rather than as a series of snapshots each one of them reflecting a different long-run equilibrium (whether optimal or sub-optimal) of the economy. This out-of-equilibrium process, as we have stressed in our analysis, is characterized by problems of intertemporal complementarity and co-ordination essentially associated with the process of the accumulation of productive capacity. The sequential order of events, which is completely absent from standard comparative analysis where we can move from one equilibrium to the other by simply shifting curves in one direction or the other, has a crucial role in this analysis.

In this sense 'history matters'. This is why the right way to look at what has happened to Western economies in the recent past is to read it like a story, that is, as stressed by Hicks (1979), 'exhibiting the story, so far as we can, as a logical process' (ibid. p. ix). The starting-point of the story, for all analysts, is the crisis of 1973, but this is actually itself the result of a story which, at least for the countries of Western Europe, had begun much earlier, with the process of reconstruction of these countries after the end of World War II. This reconstruction appears as a process of accumulation of capital not constrained by lack of resources or by the bottleneck of a productive capacity which had only partially been destroyed by the war and was sustained by an economic policy aimed at relaxing the financial constraint rather than at supporting final demand in a standard Keynesian fashion. However, the expansion fed in the late 1950s and in the 1960s by this process of accumulation already contained the seeds of its overthrow. In other words, while at the beginning the only existing barrier to the accumulation was that of full employment, in the early 1970s, as the result of the boom following the collapse of the Bretton Woods system and, in particular, the depreciation of the dollar, a primary resource constraint appears that is usually labelled as the 'oil crisis' but which was always there beneath the surface as the result of all that had been taking place in the previous years. This is where Western Europe and the United States part company.

Our analysis of the effects of credit creation in Section 7.3 above is a faithful recount of the process created in Europe by the collapse of Bretton Woods, which is in the nature of a monetary shock. In presence of a resource constraint the additional money pumped into the economy could no longer go towards increasing construction activity, and hence brought about an increase in wage rates, final demand, and prices (see the chain of effects described in Section 7.3 above and portrayed in Fig. 7.12, which results in the co-existence of inflation and unemployment).

The oil crisis was the first of a series of supply shocks which pushed

252   *Out of Equilibrium*

producers to adopt innovative policies both to react to changes in the relative prices of primary resources and to bring back to full employment of labour a barrier moved nearer by the primary resources constraint, that is, to push back from f to F the barrier shifted to the left by the emergence of this constraint (see Fig. 8.1, derived from Hicks (1977), where the rate of inflation i and the growth rate g are plotted along the vertical axis and the horizontal axis, respectively). For innovative policies to be successful—we have also learned from our analyses in Chapter 7—monetary policy, saving behaviour, and the adjustment mechanism represented by price and wage changes must interact in such a way as to assure co-ordination of economic activity in order to avoid excessive fluctuations of output. We have shown in Section 7.1 above that in this case a stable evolution path would have been represented by an increase in savings associated with a stable money supply and moderately flexible prices and wages. This would have brought about a re-absorption of unemployment and higher real wages (but a constant share of wages) as the result of the successful adoption of more productive technologies (see Fig. 7.2c).

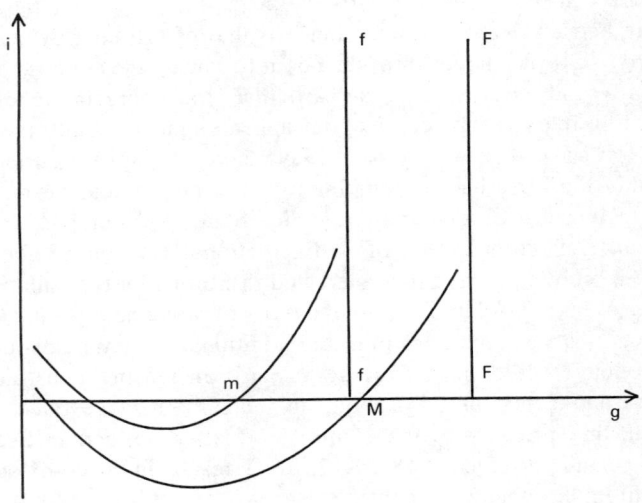

FIG 8.1

What actually happened in Western Europe in the second part of the 1970s, is just the opposite: an increase in public deficits, and hence of the 'take-out', the indexation of wages, with the result of an increase in the share of wages, higher inflation, a fall in the rate of investment, and more unemployment (as shown in Tables 8.1 and 8.2).

The fall in the rate of investment is the main reason for all that and is clearly the result of policies biased towards the utilization of production processes when we would have needed just the opposite, that is, a bias towards construction. This reflects a mistake in inter-

TABLE 8.1 *The share of wages as a percentage of GDP in various OECD countries, 1970–1995*

Year	France	Germany	Italy	UK	USA
1970	49.3	53.4	45.6	59.0	59.7
1971	49.9	54.5	48.0	58.0	58.7
1972	49.9	55.0	48.9	58.6	58.7
1973	50.2	56.1	48.6	59.1	58.8
1974	52.1	57.8	48.0	62.5	59.6
1975	54.6	57.8	51.1	64.7	58.3
1976	54.8	57.2	49.7	62.3	58.4
1977	55.3	57.6	49.6	59.3	58.4
1978	55.1	57.2	48.6	58.7	58.4
1979	54.9	57.2	48.3	58.5	58.8
1980	56.0	58.7	47.5	59.4	59.4
1981	56.6	59.0	48.3	58.7	58.7
1982	56.6	58.8	47.9	56.9	59.5
1983	56.3	57.1	47.4	55.8	58.2
1984	55.5	56.4	46.2	55.7	57.8
1985	54.7	56.3	46.2	55.1	58.0
1986	53.3	56.1	44.9	55.2	58.2
1987	52.8	56.5	44.6	54.4	58.8
1988	51.8	55.8	44.2	54.4	58.9
1989	51.3	54.9	44.3	55.1	58.0
1990	51.8	54.3	45.2	56.8	58.4
1991	52.1	56.5	45.2	57.4	58.4
1992	52.4	56.6	45.2	57.4	58.4
1993	52.8	56.3	44.3	55.8	58.2
1994	51.8	54.7	42.6	54.5	57.8
1995	51.8	54.2	40.6	53.9	58.1

Source: OECD, *Economic Outlook*, 59 (1996).

TABLE 8.2 *The rate of investment as a percentage of GDP in various OECD countries, 1970–1995*

Year	France	Germany	Italy	UK	USA
1970	24.9	26.2	28.4	19.8	16.5
1971	25.4	26.9	27.0	19.8	16.9
1972	25.8	26.5	26.6	19.1	17.6
1973	26.6	25.2	27.0	18.9	17.8
1974	26.1	22.7	26.2	18.8	16.7
1975	24.5	21.8	25.0	18.5	15.3
1976	24.3	21.4	23.4	18.3	15.8
1977	23.1	21.6	23.0	17.6	16.8
1978	22.8	21.8	22.3	17.5	17.7
1979	22.8	22.3	22.2	17.5	18.0
1980	23.0	22.6	23.2	16.9	17.0
1981	22.3	21.4	22.3	15.5	16.6
1982	21.4	20.4	21.2	16.1	15.8
1983	20.5	20.7	20.9	16.3	16.4
1984	19.7	20.2	21.1	17.3	17.7
1985	20.0	19.7	20.7	17.4	18.1
1986	20.4	19.9	20.5	17.1	18.0
1987	20.9	19.9	20.9	18.0	17.5
1988	21.9	20.1	21.3	19.0	17.1
1989	22.7	20.6	21.8	20.3	16.9
1990	22.8	21.1	22.1	19.5	15.5
1991	22.6	23.0	22.0	18.0	15.5
1992	21.7	23.3	21.5	17.9	15.9
1993	20.5	22.2	18.9	17.6	16.3
1994	20.2	22.5	18.4	17.4	17.0
1995	20.3	22.4	18.9	16.9	17.6

Source: OECD, *Economic Outlook*, 59 (1996).

preting the crisis as a problem of lack of demand, along a Keynesian line that considers consumption and investment on a par, rather than as a problem of insufficient accumulation of capital, as would be suggested by a model of a Neo-Austrian type stressing the construction aspect of investment and the utilization aspect of consumption (see Section 8.1 above).

To cut the high inflation caused by this mistake became the main objective of the standard policy interventions carried out in the first half of the 1980s, which consisted mainly in a restrictive monetary policy coupled with the (more or less complete) abandonment of wage indexation. These interventions were actually successful in bringing about lower rates of inflation, paid for in terms of an increase in unemployment, but also had an indirect effect represented by a reduction of the share of wages which, at the end of the 1980s made possible an acceleration of the process of accumulation of capital (as shown in Table 8.3). This was the result of a reversal in the dynamic of the ratio of construction to utilization production processes (now in favour of the former) with respect to the preceding

TABLE 8.3 *The rate of accumulation in the manufacturing sector in various OECD countries, 1970–1995*

Year	France	Germany	Italy	UK	USA
1970	7.6	7.4	6.8	4.4	5.6
1971	7.8	7.4	6.2	4.1	5.5
1972	7.8	6.9	6.1	4.0	5.8
1973	8.0	6.5	6.8	4.3	6.4
1974	7.5	5.6	6.6	4.1	6.2
1975	6.5	5.3	5.6	3.8	5.4
1976	6.6	5.4	5.7	3.8	5.6
1977	6.4	5.6	5.7	4.0	6.0
1978	6.2	5.7	5.7	4.2	6.6
1979	6.2	5.9	5.9	4.2	7.0
1980	6.2	5.9	6.2	3.9	6.7
1981	5.9	5.5	5.6	3.6	6.8
1982	5.7	5.1	5.0	3.8	6.3
1983	5.4	5.2	4.7	3.7	6.1
1984	5.1	5.1	4.9	4.1	6.9
1985	5.3	5.2	4.8	4.6	7.0
1986	5.5	5.3	4.9	4.5	6.6
1987	5.7	5.3	5.2	5.2	6.3
1988	6.1	5.5	5.7	5.9	6.4
1989	6.4	5.7	5.8	6.1	6.5
1990	6.5	6.1	5.9	5.8	6.3
1991	6.3	6.8	5.7	5.2	5.8
1992	5.9	6.6	5.5	4.8	5.8
1993	5.3	5.8	4.4	4.8	6.1
1994	5.3	5.7	4.9	4.8	6.5
1995	5.4	5.7	4.7	4.9	7.0

Source: OECD, *Economic Outlook*, 59 (1996).

years, which was the fortunate side-effect of a policy explicitly pursued with the different objective of bringing about a competitive disinflation. The increase in growth rates and the reduction of unemployment in the latter part of the 1980s confirm the importance of re-establishing the adequate proportion of construction to utilization production processes, which also implies co-ordination over time of investment and consumption.

The new important supply shock represented by the fall of the Berlin Wall at the turn of the decade, which called for a restructuring of productive capacity in the same way as the oil crisis of 1973, together with the changes in rules and institutions required by the prospect of establishing the European Monetary Union, once again put the process of accumulation of capital at the centre of the stage. But once again the prevailing interpretation of what was going on and what was required missed the point. Once again, that is, attention was focused on inflation, the phenomenon that appeared at the surface, and disinflation through restrictive monetary policies was the objective pursued. Unemployment, which quickly reached intolerable levels, was left to the care of institutional measures concerning the labour market and aimed at re-establishing full flexibility of wages. This time, however, we could not rely on the fortunate side-effects of this type of policy as at the end of the 1980s. The situation was not the same: a misinterpretation of the nature of the crisis—a supply shock to be dealt with by making a more intense process of accumulation of capital possible—had crucial negative implications.

The perverse effects on both growth (reduced) and unemployment (increased) of a restrictive monetary policy coupled with flexible prices are clearly shown in the case analysed in Fig. 7.6a. On the other hand slower growth means higher public deficits (an increase in the fraction of output 'taken out', μ in terms of our model) with the result of constraining more and more investment (construction activity). To advocate a cut in spending to cut public deficits so as to make a higher level of investment possible means not to figure out the sequence of disequilibria over time through which adjustments actually take place but just to associate equilibrium values of the magnitudes involved deduced from the comparison of alternative long-run equilibrium positions of the economy. As a matter of fact a cut in expenses would further slow down growth and this would result in reduced investment due this time not to a lack of financial resources but to a fall in final demand (announced by the more or less pronounced reduction of the share of wages in recent years in all major European economies)—in a Harrod-like perspective as depicted in a cavalier but essentially exact way in (Fig. 7.16a).

It is clear that the policy required is rather the opposite of that followed in almost all European countries today. If the problem were to re-establish the equilibrium between utilization and construction activity at a higher level of intensity of the latter, a stronger process of accumulation should have been sustained both by higher savings (through a control of budgetary deficits) and an 'expansive' monetary policy, associated with a 'moderate' price and wage flexibility, as in the case shown in Fig. 7.21a.

The comparison with the experience of the United States over the same period is illuminating. The United States has not suffered and is not suffering levels of unemployment comparable to those in Europe. The standard explanation runs in terms of the flexibility of the labour market. As a matter of fact in the US nominal wages are rigid downwards (see Akerlof, Dickens, and Perry 1996); the flexibility of the labour market depends on labour mobility (geographical and professional) rather than on wage flexibility. On the other hand the share of wages is essentially constant due to the fact that wage increases keep pace with those of productivity. It is interesting to note in this context that the 'separation rate'—that is, the fraction of all people employed who leave their job every year, and likewise find a new job if the rate of unemployment is constant—is 34 per cent in Italy, quite near the 38 per cent of the United States and much higher than the 22 per cent of Germany or even the 30 per cent of France. But notwithstanding this strong labour mobility Italy shares with France the sad priviledge of a rate of unemployment higher than 12 per cent, that is higher than in most European countries with less labour mobility.

The truly important difference between Europe and the United States is that the rate of investment has remained constant in the latter, and that investments have always been augmented in response to supply shocks (in 1975–9 as well as in 1991–5), while in Europe investments and the rate of investment have been reduced in the corresponding periods. This confirms the suspicion that the problem is still the process of accumulation of capital and the conditions for this process to be smoothly carried out, that is, the conditions for re-establishing the equilibrium over time of construction to utilization production processes, disturbed each time by oncoming shocks.

On the other hand if the heart of the matter is the process of accumulation, technology, as well as institutional aspects (and more generally, the 'fundamentals' of dominant theory), have little to do with employment. Whatever the prevailing technology we can carry out a process of accumulation of capital which assures full employment, provided that the growth of complementary resources keeps pace and the adjusting mechanisms make this possible.

Conclusion

The analysis developed in this book puts the emphasis on interdependence as do general equilibrium models. However, in general equilibrium models interdependence is instantaneously obtained as the result of establishing an equilibrium system of prices (whatever the information structure that the prices themselves express) which represents the only interdependence link. In this perspective the temporal order of decisions does not matter by definition. Contemporaneous causality is considered.

The interdependence that we take into account, on the other hand, is interdependence out of equilibrium. This takes the form of feedback mechanisms over time. Different types of disequilibria follow from this and interact with each other sequentially. Different evolution paths of the economy may thus be associated with any kind of original shock. The model proposed is a heuristic tool that makes it possible to explore them. What we are after is not mimicking reality, though. Rather we want to be able to unveil sequential causality relations which represent the backbone of processes of economic change. Unlike in the equilibrium approach these processes are not sketched out by the 'fundamentals' of the economy but are rather the outcome of what happens on the way; this may change according to the decisions taken and the policies followed sequentially.

The ultimate end of economic analysis is the ability to propose policy recommendations. In the equilibrium approach these are derived from models which interpret the world as being systematically in a state of equilibrium, so that it is the world that adjusts to the model, not vice versa.

We believe rather that policy recommendations can only be appropriate if the dynamic mechanisms which determine the genesis of economic phenomena are brought to light. An out-of-equilibrium analysis provides this light, and in this light both the interpretation of the economic phenomena and policy recommendations may be completely different, and in most cases quite the opposite of those advocated by dominant equilibrium theory.

Appendix

Numerical simulations data[1]

Chapter 6

Steady State

$$a^c_{ih} = (8\ 8\ 8\ 8)\ \forall i\ 0, \ldots, n$$
$$a^u_{ih} = (8\ 8\ 8\ 8)\ \forall i\ n+1, \ldots n+N$$
or:
$$a^c_{ih} = (8\ 6\ 4\ 2)\ \forall i$$
$$a^u_{ih} = (8\ 6\ 4\ 2)\ \forall i$$
$$b_i = 100\ \forall i\ n+1, \ldots n+N$$
$$n = 9, N = 10$$
$$\bar{g} = 0.02$$
$$p = 1$$
$$w_h = (0.5\ 1\ 1.5\ 2)$$
$$\mu = 0.3$$
$$\varrho = \sigma = 0$$

Periodic Orbits/Complex Dynamics

Figure	κ	ν	η	c	f	f^D	ϱ
6.1	1	0	1	a	b	Y	0.01
6.2	1	0	1	a	b	Y	0.01
6.3	0.5	0.5	1	a	a	Y	0
6.4	0.5	0.5	1	a	a	Y	0
6.5	0.5	0.5	1	b	b	N	0.001
6.6	0 → 2	0 → 2	1	b	b	N	0.001
6.7	0.5	0.5	1	a	a	N	0.001
6.8	0.5	0.5	1	a	a	N	0.001

The letters a,b (and c and c^* in the following tables) refer to c as determined in equations 42a, 42b, 42c, or 42c^* in the case of $\mu < \bar{\mu}$, respectively.

The letters a,b (and c and c^* in the following tables) refer to f as determined in equations 41a, 41b, 41c, respectively.

Y = Yes; N = No.

---

[1] The program for the simulations was written by Elena Lega and Claude Froeschlé using Fortran 617

Numerical simulations data

Chapter 7

Changes in Technology

From $t = 1$ to $t = 19$
$a_{ih}^c = (8\ 8\ 8\ 8)\ \forall i$
$a_{ih}^u = (8\ 8\ 8\ 8)\ \forall i$

From $t = 20$ onward
$a_{ih}^c = (10\ 10\ 10\ 10)\ \forall i$
$a_{ih}^u = (5\ 5\ 5\ 5)\ \forall i$

Figure	κ	ν	α	η	c	f	hrc	μ(0)	$\lambda_1;\lambda_2$
7.1a	0	0	0	1	a	b	(N/Y)	0.3	0
7.1b	0.5	0.5	0	1	a	b	N	0.3	0
7.1c	0.5	0.5	0	1	a	b	Y	0.3	0
7.2a	0	0	0	1	c	b	Y	0.5	0
7.2b	0	0	0	1	c	b	Y	0.3	0
7.2c	0.1	0.1	0	1	c	b	Y	0.3	0
7.3a	0.5	0	1	1	a	b	Y	0.3	0
7.3b	0.5	0	1	1	c	b	Y	0.5	0

From $t = 20$ onward
a_{ih}^c increases by 5% each 20 periods;
the real productivity of the technology increases by 2% over time

Figure	κ	ν	α	η	c	f	hrc	μ(0)	$\lambda_1;\lambda_2$
7.4a	0	0	0	1	a	b	(N.Y)	0.3	0
7.4b	0.05	0.05	0	1	a	b	N	0.3	0
7.5a	0.5	0.5	0	1	c	b	Y	0.3	0
7.5b	0.1	0.1	0	1	c	b	Y	0.3	0
7.6a	0.1	0.1	0	1	c	c	Y	0.3	0
7.6b	0.05	0	1	1	c	c	Y	0.3	0
7.6c	0.5	0	1	1	c	c	Y	0.3	0

Note: hrc = human resource constraint

Changes in Skill

From $t = 1$ to $t = 19$
$a_{ih}^c = (8\ 6\ 4\ 2)\ \forall i$
$a_{ih}^u = (8\ 6\ 4\ 2)\ \forall i$

From $t = 20$ onward
$a_{ih}^c = (7.6\ 5.8\ 4.1\ 2.1)\ \forall i$
$a_{ih}^u = (7.6\ 5.8\ 4.1\ 2.1)\ \forall i$

Figure	κ	ν	α	η	c	f	$\xi(0)$
7.7	0.05	0.05	0	1	a	b	0.8
7.8	0.05	0.05	0	1	a	b	0.1
7.9a	0.05	0.05	0	1	c	b	0.8
7.9b	0.05	0.05	0	1	c	b	0.02
7.9c	0.05	0.05	0	1	c	b	0.8

From $t = 20$ onward
a_{ih}^c increases by 5% each 20 period $\forall h = 3,4$;
the real productivity of the technology increases by 2% over time

Figure	κ	ν	α	η	c	f	$\xi(0)$
7.10a	0.05	0.05	0	1	a	b	0.1
7.10b	0.01	0.01	0	1	a	b	0.1
7.10c	0.05	0.05	0	1	a	b	0.1
		0.005					
7.11	0.01	0.01	0	1	c	c	0.1

Credit Creation

From $t = 1$ to $t = 19$
$g_f = 0.020$
From $t = 20$ onward
$g_f = 0.025$

Figure	κ	ν	α	η	c	f	hrc	$\lambda_1;\lambda_2$
7.12a	0.5	0.5	0	1	a	b	N	0
7.12b	1.8	1.8	0	1	a	b	N	0
7.13a	0.5	0.5	0	1	a	b	Y	0
7.13b	1.5	1.5	0	1	b	b	Y	0
7.14	0.05	1	0	1	a	b	Y	0
7.15a	0.5	0.5	0	1	a	b	Y	1

Numerical simulations data

From $t = 20$ onward
$g_f = 0.0246$
$a_{ih} = (7.8\ 7.8\ 7.8\ 7.8)\ \forall i$

Figure	κ	ν	α	η	c	f	hrc	$\lambda_1;\lambda_2$
7.15b	1.15	1.15	0	1	a	b	Y	1

Changes in Expectations

From $t = 1$ to $t = 19$
$\varrho = 0$
From $t = 20$ onward
$\varrho = 0.001$

Figure	κ	ν	α	η	c	f^S	f^D	μ_{min}
7.16a	0.05	0.05	0	1	b	b	Y	N
7.16b	0.05	0.05	0	1	b	b	Y	N
7.16c	0.05	0	1	1	b	b	Y	Y
7.17a	0.05	0.05	0	1	a	b	Y	Y
7.17b	0.05 0	0.05	0	1	a	b	Y	Y

Limits to Growth

From $t = 1$ to $t = 19$
$\mu = 0.3;\ g_f = 0.02$
From $t = 20$ onward

Figure	κ	ν	α	η	c	f	μ_{min}	g_f	$\lambda_1\lambda_2$
7.18a	0.5	0.5	0	1	c^*	b	0.28	0.02	1
7.18b	0.5	0.5	0	1	c^*	b	0.05	0.02	1
7.19a	0.5	0.5	0	1	c^*	b	0.28	0.025	1
7.19b	0.01	0.01	0	1	c^*	b	0.28	0.025	1
7.20	0.01	0.01	0	1	c^*	b	0.28	0.02	1

From $t = 1$ to $t = 19$
$a_{ih}^c = (8\ 8\ 8\ 8)\ \forall i$
$a_{ih}^u = (8\ 8\ 8\ 8)\ \forall i$

From $t = 20$ onward
$a_{ih}^c = (10\ 10\ 10\ 10)\ \forall i$
$a_{ih}^u = (5\ 5\ 5\ 5)\ \forall i$

Figure	κ	ν	α	η	c	f	μ_{min}	g_f	$\lambda_1;\lambda_2$
7.21a	0.01	0.01	0	1	c^*	b	0.28	0.0246	1
7.21b	0.5	0.5	0	1	c^*	b	0.28	0.0246	1
7.22	0.01	0.01	0	1	c^*	b	0.28	0.0246	1

Note: $c = c^*$ sudden decrease of the take out

From $t = 1$ to $t = 19$
$a_{ih}^c = (8\ 6\ 4\ 2)\ \forall i$
$a_{ih}^u = (8\ 6\ 4\ 2)\ \forall i$

From $t = 20$ onward
$a_{ih}^c = (7.6\ 5.8\ 4.2\ 2.1)\ \forall i$
$a_{ih}^u = (7.6\ 5.8\ 4.2\ 2.1)\ \forall i$

Figure	κ	ν	α	η	c	f	μ_{min}	g_f	From $t =$
7.23a	0.5	0.5	0	1	c^*	b	0.2	0.03	30
7.23b	0.5	0.5	0	1	c^*	b	0.2	0.025	20
7.23c	0.5	0.5	0	1	c^*	b	0.2	0.025	20
7.23d	0.05	0.05	0	1	c^*	b	0.2	0.025	20
7.24	0.5	0.5	0	1	a	b	0.2	0.025	20

Figure	κ	ν	α	η	c	f	μ_{min}	h_d^h
7.25a	0.005	0.005	0	1	c^*	b	0.28	Y
7.25b	0.005	0.005	0	1	c^*	b	0.28	N
7.25c	0.5	0.5	0	1	c^*	b	0.28	Y

REFERENCES

Abramovitz, M. (1986), 'Catching Up, Forging Ahead and Falling Behind', *Journal of Economic History*, 86: 385–406

Alchian, A., and Demsetz, J. (1972), 'Production, Information Costs and Economic Organization', *American Economic Review*, 62: 777–95.

Aghion, P., and Bolton, S. (1988), 'An Incomplete Contract Approach to Bankruptcy and the Financial Structure of the Firm', MIT Department of Economics *Working Paper* 484.

—— and Howitt, P. (1992), 'A Model of Growth through Creative Destruction', *Econometrica*, 60: 323–51.

—— (1994), 'Growth and Unemployment', *Review of Economic Studies*, 61: 477–94.

Akerlof, G. A., Dickens, W. T, and Perry, G. L. (1996), 'The Macroeconomics of Low Inflation', *Brookings Papers on Economic Activity*, 1: 1–76.

Amendola, M. (1972), 'Modello Neo-Austriaco e transizione fra equilibri dinamici', *Note Economiche*, Jul.—Aug, 4; 53–74.

—— (1991), 'Liquidity, Flexibility and Processes of Economic Change', in L.W. McKenzie and S. Zamagni (eds.), *Value and Capital: Fifty Years Later*, London: Macmillan.

—— and Bruno, S. (1990), 'The Behaviour of the Innovative Firm: Relations to the Environment', *Research Policy*, Oct.: 419–33.

—— and Gaffard, J.L. (1988), *The Innovative Choice*, Oxford: Basil Blackwell.

—— Froeschlé, C. and Gaffard, J.L. (1993), 'Sustaining Structural Change: Malthus's Heritage', *Structural Change and Economic Dynamics*, 4/1: 65–79.

—— —— —— (1996), 'Structure and Cycles', *Journal of Economic Behaviour and Organization*, 29: 409–32.

Aoki, M. (1984), *The Cooperative Game Theory of the Firm*, Oxford: Clarendon Press.

—— (1988), *Information, Incentives and Bargaining in the Japanese Ecomomy*, Cambridge: Cambridge University Press.

—— (1990), 'Towards an Economic Model of the Japanese Firm', *Journal of Economic Literature*, 28/1: 1–27.

Arrow, K. J. (1953), 'Le role des valeurs boursières pour la répartition la meilleure des risques', *Econométrie*, Paris, colloques internationaux du CNRS, 11: 41–8.

—— (1962), 'Economic Welfare and the Allocation of Resources for

Invention', in *The Rate and Direction of Inventive Activity: Economic and Social Factors*, NBER, Princeton: Princeton University Press.
Arrow, K. J. and Debreu, G. (1954), 'Existence of an Equilibrium for a Competitive Economy', *Econometrica*, 22: 265–90
Arthur, B. (1988), 'Self-Reinforcing Mechanisms in Economics', in P. W. Anderson, K. J. Arrow, and D. Pines (eds.), *The Economy as an Evolving Complex System*, Addison Wesley.
—— (1989), 'Competing Technologies, Increasing Returns, and Lock In by Historical Events', *Economic Journal*, 99: 116–31
Baranzini, M., and Scazzieri, R. (1990), *The Economic Theory of Structure and Change*, Cambridge: Cambridge University Press.
Baumol, W. J. (1986), 'Productivity Growth, Convergence and Welfare; What the Long-Run Data Show', *American Economic Review*, 76/5: 1072–85.
—— (1991), 'On Formal Dynamics: From Lundberg to Chaos Analysis', in L. Jonung (ed.), *The Stockholm School of Economics Revisited*, New York: Cambridge University Press.
—— (1993), *Entrepreneurship, Management and the Structure of Pay-offs*, Cambridge, Mass.: MIT Press.
—— Benhabib, J. (1989), 'Chaos: Significance Mechanism and Economic Application', *Journal of Economic Perspectives*, 31: 77–105
Bean, C. R. (1994), 'European Unemployment: A Survey'. *Journal of Economic Literature*, 32/2: 573–620.
—— Layard, R. G., and Nickell, S. J. (1986), 'The Rise in Unemployment: A Multi-Country Study', *Economica*, suppl., 53: S1–S22.
Becker, G. (1964), *Human Capital*, New York: Columbia University Press for the National Bureau of Economic Research.
Benhabib, J., and Nishimura, K.(1979), 'The Hopf's Bifurcation and the Existence and Stability of Closed Orbits in Multisector Models of Optimal Economic Growth', *Journal of Economic Theory*, 21: 421–44.
—— (1985), 'Competitive Equilibrium Cycle', *Journal of Economic Theory*, 35: 288–306.
Blanchard, O. (1989), 'A Traditional Interpretation of Macroeconomic Fluctuations', *American Economic Review*, 79: 1146–64.
—— (1990), 'Unemployment: Getting the Questions Right—and Some of the Answers', in J. H. Dréze and C. R. Bean (eds.), *Europe's Unemployment problem*, Cambridge, Mass.: MIT Press.
—— (1991), 'Wage Bargaining and Unemployment Persistence', *Journal of Money, Credit and Banking*, 23: 277–91.
—— and Fischer, S. (1989), *Lectures on Macroeconomics*, Cambridge, Mass: MIT Press.
Bruno, S., and De Lellis, A. (1993), 'The Economics of Ex-ante Co-ordination', Dipartimento di Scienze Economiche, Università degli Studi di Roma 'La Sapienza'.

References

Cass, D. (1965): 'Optimum Growth in an Aggregate Model of Capital Accumulation', *Review of Economic Studies*, 32; 233–40.

Chandler, A. (1977), *The Visible Hand: The Managerial Revolution in American Business*, Cambridge, Mass.: Belknap/Harvard University Press.

—— (1990), *Scale and Scope: The Dynamics of Industrial Capitalism*, Cambridge, Mass.: Belknap/Harvard University Press.

—— (1992), 'Organizational Capabilities and the Economic History of the Industrial Enterprise', *Journal of Economic Perspectives*, 6: 79–100.

Coase, R. H. (1937), 'The Nature of the Firm', *Economica*, 4: 386–405.

Dasgupta, P., and Stiglitz, J. (1980), 'Uncertainty, Industrial Structure and the Speed of R&D', *Bell Journal*, 90: 266–93.

David, P. A. (1985), 'Clio and the Economics of QWERTY', *American Economic Review*, 75: 332–7.

—— (1988), 'Path-Dependence: Putting the Past into the Future of Economics', *Technical Report* 533, Institute for the Mathematical Studies in the Social Sciences, Stanford University, Stanford, Calif.

—— (1992), 'Path-Dependence in Economic Processes: Implications for Policy Analysis in Dynamical System Contexts', Mimeo, Department of Economics, Stanford University, Sanford, Calif.

Day, R.H. (1975), 'Adaptive Processes and Economic Theory', in R. Day and T. Groves (eds.), *Adaptive Economic Models*, New York: Academic Press.

—— (1986), 'Disequilibrium Economic Dynamics: A Post-Schumpeterian Contribution', in R. Day and G. Eliasson (eds.), *The Dynamics of Market Economics*, Amsterdam: North-Holland, 51–80.

—— (1993), 'Nonlinear Dynamics and Economics: A Historian's Perspective', in R. Day and P. Chen (eds.), *Nonlinear Dynamics and Evolutionary Economics*, Oxford: Oxford University Press.

Debreu, G. (1959), *Theory of Value: An Axiomatic Analysis of Economic Equilibrium*, New York: Wiley

Diamond, D. (1984), 'Financial Intermediation and Delegated Monitoring', *Review of Economic Studies*, 51: 393–414.

Dixit, A. (1980), 'The Role of Investment in Entry Deterrence', *Economic Journal*, 90: 95–106.

Dosi, G. (1982), 'Technological Paradigms and Technological Trajectories: A Suggested Interpretation of the Determinants and Direction of Technical Change', *Research Policy*, 11: 147–62.

Eaton, B. C. (1987), 'Entry and Market Structure', in J. Eatwell, M. Milgate, and P. Newman (eds.), *The New Palgrave: A Dictionary of Economics*, London: Macmillan.

Fischer, F. (1989), 'Games Economists Play: A Non Co-operative View', *Rand Journal of Economics*, 20/1: 113–24.

Froeschlé, C., and Lega, E. (1995), 'From Discrete to Continuous Dynamical Systems and Vice-Versa', *Revue Economique*, 46/5: 1511–26

References

Georgescu-Roegen, N. (1965), 'Process in Farming versus Process in Manufacturing: A Problem of Balanced Development', in id. (ed.), *Energy and Economic Myths* (1976) Oxford: Pergamon Press.
—— (1971), *The Entropy Law and the Economic Process*, Cambridge, Mass.: Harvard University Press.
—— (1976a), *Energy and Economic Myths*, Oxford: Pergamon Press.
—— (1976b), 'Dynamic Models and Economic Growth', in id. (ed.) *Energy and Economic Myths*, Oxford: Pergamon Press.
—— (1990), 'Production Process and Dynamic Economics', in M. Baranzini and R. Scazzieri (eds.), *The Economic Theory of Structure and Change*, Cambridge: Cambridge University Press.
Gilbert, R. J., and Newbery D.M.G. (1982), 'Preemptive Patenting and the Persistence of Monopoly', *American Economic Review*, 72: 514–26.
Gordon, R. J. (1995), 'Is There a Tradeoff Between Unemployment and Productivity Growth?', NBER Working Paper 5081, Apr.
Grandmont, J. M. (1977), 'Temporary General Equilibrium Theory', *Econometrica*, 45: 535–7.
—— (1985), 'On Endogenous Competitive Business Cycles', *Econometrica*, 53: 995–1046.
Greenwald, B. and Stiglitz, J. E. (1990), 'Macroeconomic Models with Equity and Credit Rationing', in R. Glenn Hubbard (ed.), *Information, Capital Markets and Investment*, Chicago: University of Chicago Press.
Grossman, G., and Helpmann, H. (1991). *Innovation and Growth in the Global Economy*, Cambridge, Mass.: MIT Press.
Grossman, S., and Hart, O. (1986), 'The Costs and Benefits of Ownership: A Theory of Vertical and Lateral Integration', *Journal of Political Economy*, 94: 691–719.
Hahn, F. H. (1982), *Money and Inflation*, Oxford: Basil Blackwell.
—— (1990), 'Solow and Growth Models', in P. Diamond (ed.), *Growth, Productivity, Employment*, Cambridge, Mass: MIT Press.
—— (1994), 'On Growth Theory', Universitá degli Sudi di Siena, *Quaderni del Dipartimento di Economia Politica*, 167.
—— and Matthews, R. C. O. (1964), 'The Theory of Economic Growth: A Survey', *Economic Journal*, 74: 779–902
—— and Solow, R. (1995), *A Critical Essay on Modern Macroeconomic Theory*, Cambridge, Mass.: MIT Press.
Harrod, R. (1939), 'An Essay in Dynamic Theory', *Economic Journal*, 49: 14–33.
—— (1948), *Towards a Dynamic Economics*, London: Macmillan.
Hayek, F. A. (1931), *Prices and Production*, London: Routledge.
—— (1933), *Monetary Theory and the Trade Cycle*; rep. in Economic Classics Series (1976), New York: A. M. Kelley.
—— (1937), 'Economics and Knowledge', *Economica*, 4: 33–54.

Heiner, R. (1988), 'The Necessity of Delaying Economic Adjustment', *Journal of Economic Behaviour and Organization*, 10: 255–86.
Heymann, D., and Leijonhufvud, A. (1994), *High Inflation*, Oxford: Oxford University Press.
Hicks, J. R. (1935a), 'A Suggestion for Simplifying the Theory of Money', *Economica*, Feb.
—— (1935b), 'Wages and Interest: The Dynamic Problem'. *Economic Journal*, Sept.; reprinted in *The Theory of Wages* (1963), London: Macmillan, 268–85.
—— (1939), *Value and Capital*, Oxford: Clarendon Press.
—— (1965), *Capital and Growth*, Oxford: Clarendon Press.
—— (1967), 'The Two Triads', in id. (ed.), *Critical Essays in Monetary Theory*, Oxford: Clarendon Press.
—— (1970), 'A Neo-Austrian Growth Theory', *Economic Journal*, 80: 257–79.
—— (1973), *Capital and Time*, Oxford: Clarendon Press.
—— (1974), *The Crisis in Keynesian Economics*, Oxford: Basil Blackwell.
—— (1975), 'The Revival of Political Economy: The Old and the New', *Economic Record*, Sept., 365–7.
—— (1977), 'Capital Controversies: Ancient and Modern', in id. (ed.), *Economic Perspectives*, Oxford: Clarendon Press.
—— (1979), *Causality in Economics*, Oxford: Clarendon Press.
—— (1982), 'Methods of Dynamic Analysis', in id. (ed.), *Collected Essays on Economic Theory*, ii, Oxford: Basil Blackwell.
—— (1985), *Methods of Dynamic Economics*, Oxford: Clarendon Press.
—— (1989), *A Market Theory of Money*, Oxford: Clarendon Press.
—— (1990), 'The Unification of Macroeconomics', *Economic Journal*, 100: 528–38.
—— and Hollander, S. (1977), 'Ricardo and the Moderns', *Quarterly Journal of Economics*, 91: 351–369
Howitt, P. (1994), 'Adjusting to Technical Change', *Canadian Journal of Economics*, 4: 763–5.
Hume, D. (1752), *Essays on Money*, Oxford: Clarendon Press.
Jevons, W. S. (1871), *The Theory of Political Economy*, repr. in Economic Classics Series (1965), New York: A. M. Kelley.
Jones, L., and Manuelli, R.(1990). 'A Complex Model of Equilibrium Growth: Theory and Policy Implication', *Journal of Political Economy*, 98: 1008–38.
Kaldor, N. (1966), 'Causes of the Slow Rate of Economic Growth in the United Kingdom', Cambridge: Cambridge University Press.
—— (1972), 'The Irrelevance of Equilibrium Economics', *Economic Journal*, 82: 1237–55.
—— (1985), *Economics without Equilibrium*, New York: M. E. Sharpe.

Keynes, J. M. (1936), *The General Theory of Employment, Interest and Money*, London: Macmillan.

King, R. G., and Rebelo, S.(1990), 'Public Policy and Economic Growth: Developing Neoclassical Implication', *Journal of Political Economy*, 98: 126–50.

Kohn, M. (1981), 'A Loanable Funds Theory of Unemployment and Monetary Disequilibrium', *American Economic Review*, 71: 859–79.

Koopmans, T. (1964), 'Economic Growth at a Maximal Rate', *Quarterly Journal of Economics*, 78: 355–94.

Krugman, P. (1990), *Rethinking International Trade*, Cambridge, Mass.: MIT Press.

—— (1991), 'History versus Expectations', *Quarterly Journal of Economics*, 106: 651–67.

Kydland, F., and Prescott, E. (1982), 'Time to Build and Aggregate Fluctuations', *Econometrica*, 50: 1345–70.

Laidler, D. W. (1994), 'Hayek on Neutral Money and the Cycle', in M. Colonna and H. Hagemann (eds.), *Money and Business Cycle*, i: 3–26, Aldershot: Edward Elgar.

Layard, R., Nickell, S., and Jackman, R. (1991), *Unemployment*, Oxford: Oxford University Press.

Lazonick, W. (1991), *Business Organization and the Myth of the Market Economy*, Cambridge: Cambridge University Press.

Ledyard, J. O. (1989), 'Market Failure', in J. Eatwell, M. Milgate, and P. Newman (eds.), *The New Palgrave: Allocation, Information and Markets*, London: Macmillan.

Leijonhufvud, A. (1968), *On Keynesian Economics and the Economics of Keynes*, London: Oxford University Press.

—— (1983), 'What was the Matter with the IS.LM?', in J. P. Fitoussi (ed.), *Modern Macroeconomic Theory*, Oxford: Basil Blackwell.

—— (1988), 'Monetary Policy and the Business Cycle under "loose" Convertibility', Mimeo, Department of Economics, University of California, Los Angeles.

—— (1993), 'Towards a Not Too Rational Macroeconomics', *Southern Economic Journal*, 60: 1–13.

Lindahl, E. (1929), 'The Place of Capital in the Theory of Price', in id. (ed.), *Studies in the Theory of Money and Capital*, (1939), London: Allen and Unwin.

—— (1930), 'Penning politikens medel', trans. in id. (ed.), *Studies in the Theory of Money and Capital*, (1939), London: Allen and Unwin.

Loasby, B. J. (1991), *Equilibrium and Evolution*, Manchester: Manchester University Press.

—— (1993a), 'The Organization of Industry', Mimeo, Department of Economics, University of Stirling.

—— (1993b), 'Understanding Markets', Mimeo, Department of Economics, University of Stirling.

Long, J. R., and Plosser, C. (1983), 'Real Business Cycle', *Journal of Political Economy*, 91: 39–69.

Lucas, R. E. (1976), 'Econometric Policy Evaluation: A Critique', *Journal of Monetary Economics*, suppl., Carnegie-Rochester Conference Series on Public Policy, 1: 19–46.

—— (1980), 'Methods and Problems in Business Cycle Theory', *Journal of Money, Credit and Banking*, 12: 696–715.

—— (1987), *Models of Business Cycle*, Oxford: Basil Blackwell.

—— (1988), 'On the Mechanics of Economic Development', *Journal of Monetary Economics*, 22: 2–42.

—— (1993), 'Making a Miracle', *Econometrica*, 61: 251–72.

Lundberg, E. (1937), *Studies in the Theory of Economic Expansion*; repr. in Economic Classics Series (1964), New York: A. M. Kelley.

McNulty, P. J. (1984), 'On the Nature and Theory of Economic Organization: The Role of the Firm Reconsidered', *History of Political Economy*, 16/2: 233–53.

Malthus, T. R. (1820), *Principles of Political Economy*, in P. Sraffa (ed.), *The Works and Correspondence of David Ricardo*, ii (1951), Cambridge: Cambridge University Press.

Marshall, A. (1920), *Principles of Economics*, 8th edn., London: Macmillan.

Meacci, F. (1985), 'On Disjuntive and Conjuntive Principles in the Austrian Theory: A Note and an Extension', *Rivista Internazionale di Scienze Economiche e Commerciali*, 12, 1187–96.

—— (1994), 'On Working and Circulating Capital', in H. Hagemann and H. Kurz (eds.), *Studies in Honour of Adolph Lowe*, Aldershot: Edgar Elgar.

Messori, M. (1995), 'Keynesian, New Keynesians and the Loanable Funds Theory', in A. Cohen, H. Hagemann, and J. Smithin (eds.), *Money, Financial Institutions and Macroeconomics*, Boston: Kluwer.

Milde, H. and Riley, J. G. (1988), 'Signalling in Credit Markets', *Quarterly Journal of Economics*, 103: 101–29.

Milgrom, P. and Roberts, J. (1992), *Economics, Organization and Management*, Englewood Cliffs, NJ: Prentice-Hall.

Morishima, M. (1992), *Capital and Credit*, Cambridge: Cambridge University Press.

Patinkin, D. (1965), *Money, Interest and Prices*, 2nd edn., New York: Harper and Row.

Phelps, E. S. (1972), *Inflation Policy and Unemployment Theory*, London: Macmillan.

Plosser, C. (1989), 'Understanding Real Business Cycles', *Journal of Economic Perspectives*, 3/3: 51–78.

Reinganum, J. F. (1984), 'Practical Implications of Game Theoretic Models of R&D', *AEA Papers and Proceedings*, May, 61–6.
—— (1989), 'The Timing of Innovation: Resesarch, Development and Diffusion', in R. Schmalensee and R. Willig (eds.), *Handbook of Industrial Organization*, i, Amsterdam: North Holland.
Ricardo, D. (1821), 'On the Principles of Political Economy and Taxation', in P. Sraffa (ed.) *The Works and Correspondence of D.Ricardo* (1951), Cambridge University Press.
Richardson, G. B. (1972), 'The Organization of Industry', *Economic Journal*, 82: 883–96.
—— (1975), 'Adam Smith on Competition and Increasing Returns', in A. Skinner and T. Wilson (eds.), *Essays on Adam Smith*, Oxford: Oxford University Press.
—— (1990), *Information and Investment*, Oxford: Clarendon Press; 1st edn. 1960.
Robertson, D. (1926), *Banking Policy and the Price Level*, London: King.
—— (1933), 'Saving and Hoarding', *Economic Journal*, Sept.
—— (1940), *Essays in Monetary Theory*, London: Staples Press.
Robinson, J. (1974), 'History versus Equilibrium', *Thames Papers in Political Economy*, Thames Polytechnic, Autumn.
Romer, P. M. (1986), 'Increasing Returns and Long Run Growth', *Journal of Political Economy*, 94: 1002–37.
—— (1990), 'Endogenous Technical Change', *Journal of Political Economy*, 98: 71–102.
Samuelson, P. (1994), 'The Classical Classical Fallacy', *Journal of Economic Literature*, 32: 620–39.
Schumpeter, J. A. (1934), *The Theory of Economic Development*, Cambridge, Mass.: Harvard University Press.
—— (1954), *History of Economic Analysis*, London: Allen and Unwin.
Shackle, G. L. S. (1972), *Epistemics and Economics*, Cambridge: Cambridge University Press.
Simon, H. A. (1991), 'Organizations and Markets', *Journal of Economic Perspectives*, 5/2: 25–43.
Solow, R. M. (1956), 'A Contribution to the Theory of Economic Growth', *Quarterly Journal of Economics*, 70: 65–94.
—— (1986), 'Unemployment: Getting the Questions Right', *Economica*, suppl., 53: S23–S35.
—— (1990), 'Reaction to Conference Papers', in P. Diamond (ed.), *Growth, Productivity, Employment*, Cambridge, Mass: MIT Press.
—— (1992), 'Siena Lectures on Endogenous Growth Theory', *Collana del Dipartimento di Economia Politica*, Universitá degli studi di Siena.
—— (1994), 'Perspectives on Growth Theory', *Journal of Economic Perspectives*, 8: 45–55.

Stiglitz, J. (1982), 'Alternative Theories of Wage Determination and Unemployment: The Efficiency Wage Model', in M. Boskin (ed.), *Modern Development in Public Finance: Essays in Honor of A. Harberger*, Oxford: Basil Blackwell.

—— and Weiss, A. (1981), 'Credit Rationing in Markets with Imperfect Information', *American Economic Review*, 71/3: 393–410.

—— (1992), 'Asymmetric Information in Credit Markets and its Implications for Macro-Economics', *Oxford Economic Papers*, 44: 694–724.

Tobin, J. (1969), 'A General Equilibrium Approach to Monetary Theory', *Journal of Money, Credit and Banking*, 1: 15–29.

Uzawa, H. (1965), 'Optimal Technical Change in an Aggregative Model of Economic Growth'. *International Economic Review*, 6: 18–31.

Vickers, J. (1986), 'The Evolution of Market Structure when there is a Sequence of Innovations', *Journal of Industrial Economics*, 35: 1–12.

von Neumann, J. (1937), 'A Model of General Economic Equilibrium'. trans. in *Review of Economic Studies* 1945–6, 1–9.

von Tunzelmann, G. N. (1991), 'Malthus's Evolutionary Model, Expectations and Innovation', *Journal of Evolutionary Economics*, 4: 273–91.

Williamson, O. (1985), *The Economics Institutions of Capitalism*, New York: Free Press.

—— (1989), 'Transaction Cost Economics'. in R. Schmalensee and R. Willig (eds.), *Handbook of Industrial Organization*, i, Amsterdam:North Holland.

INDEX

accumulation 112, 234
  of capital 241, 250–1, 258
  of complementary factors 114, 194
  of human capital 113
  rate 118, 255
activity analysis 20
assets
  financial 41, 51
  investment 41, 51
  real 41, 51
  reserve 41, 42, 52, 82, 105, 232, 249
  running 41, 51

banks 47, 57, 59, 98, 144, 197
behaviour
  adaptive 31
  bounded 103
  explosive 118
  optimizing 108, 141; intertemporal 236
  strategic 104
bid 86
business cycles 236, 238
  exogenous or endogenous character 238
  real 108, 120n, 235

capital
  circulating 42, 45, 68, 121n
  ex ante vision 61
  fixed 68, 70, 118
  goods 16, 21, 66–7, 69, 236–7
  human 61, 63, 72, 112
  marginal productivity 111
  as a physical input 62
  shortage 175, 180
catching up 212n
change 106, 107
  qualitative 23, 30, 32, 48, 98, 107, 170, 233
  quantitative 106
  structural 108, 116, 246
choice 13, 14, 238
  between consumption and saving 235
  between real and financial assets 94
  portfolio 38
  real 51, 142
  sequential 123

  set 13, 81; redefinition 31; enlargement 82
  timeless 238
  voluntary 44
commitment 40, 86, 92, 102
complementarity 66
  dynamic 125
  between financial and real assets 42, 45
  intertemporal 90, 94, 107
  between the market and the firm 96
  over time 82
  problems 43, 45, 50, 166
  between productive resources 215, 217, 220
  relation between factors 111, 113, 195
consumption 24, 144, 231
  co-ordination over time (with investment) 198, 228, 256
  decisions 148; intertemporal optimization 171n
  intertemporal complementarity (with investment) 233
  necessary 233
  unproductive 232
constraint(s) 103
  demand 228
  external 140
  financial 39, 43, 45, 74, 251
  human 49, 74, 171, 187, 194
  on production 238
  supply 228
control
  adaptive 100
  rights 89
co-ordination 81, 125
  ex ante 85n
  failures 115, 126, 141, 206, 224, 247
  over time 100, 107, 230
  organizational 84
  problems 77, 79, 83, 166, 237
costs
  dissociation from proceeds 21–4
  investment and disinvestment 94, 95
  sunk 26, 40, 60, 82, 95, 103, 249
  transaction 82, 89, 90, 94
credit 35, 40, 57, 216, 236
  creation 197, 205, 236, 249, 251

rationing 88n
cumulative processes (depressions, hyperinflation) 56, 117, 248

decision(s)
  process (intertemporal complementarity) 50, 108, 127, 228; lack of co-ordination over time 171
  rules (algorithmic representation) 140
disequilibria 103, 128, 130, 250
  forces 141
  interdependence over time 247
  market 157, 238, (labour) 161
  monetary 43
  persistent 157
  real 43
  sequence of 241–2, 250, 259
  short run properties 244
dynamic
  analysis 99, 106, 107
  context 142
  methods 106
  problem 107, 116
dynamics 106, 107
  comparative 213
  complex 72, 139, 160, 246
  disequilibrium 244
  transitional 109, 123

economic policy 111, 242, 245, 247, 250
  budgetary 250
  mix 230
  neutral 246, 249
  optimal 242
efficiency 13, 14, 24, 89
  in the allocation of resources 40, 65
  of different organizational structures 91, 93
  economic 14
  of the human resource 220
  intertemporal 142
  at a point of time 83
  problem 98
  of production 140
  technical 14
employment 15, 31, 68, 69, 77, 131, 150, 161, 170, 232
  full 71, 109, 236, 251, 258; barrier 74
environment 93, 250
  as an exogenous constraint 98
  as a strategic variable 98
  structuring 125
equilibrium

analysis 96, 241
approach 107, 122, 166, 259
convergence 122, 180
intertemporal 16, 86, 108n, 140, 238, 245–6
long-run 240, 243, 247
multiple 124
Nash 86
organizational 92
over time 108
pseudo 159, 204
sub-optimal 250
state 15n, 158, 259
temporary 17, 108n
evolutionary approach 29, 30
expectations 46, 108, 133, 140, 246, 248
  adaptive 118, 124, 132, 159
  changes 206, 239
  long-term 48, 129, 161, 206
  rational 87, 108n, 131, 157
  short-term 118, 157, 207
external demand 227, 234
externalities 65, 113, 124

financial
  intermediaries 38, 39, 56, 59
  products 39
firm 81
  as an aggregate of elements 99
  liquidity preference 156, 161, 206, 210, 248
  modern theory 88, 99
  as a production function 98
  task (role) 98, 100
flexibility 105, 149, 244
  price 183, 187, 243
  wage 173, 187, 239, 244, 256
fluctuations 54, 56, 108, 248–9
  erratic 162, 238
  in expectations 163
  explosive 192, 238
  of output and prices 45
  in prices 250
  regular 156
  in wage rates 77, 239
full performance 71, 120
fundamentals 158, 230, 243, 258–9

game theory 85
growth 231
  acceleration 203, 212, 215, 227
  behaviouristic version 109
  cyclical 59, 154

Index

endogenous 62, 111
  limits 211, 228
  optimizing version 110, 126

hoarding 44, 48, 232
hysteresis 79

incomplete contracts 88, 89, 102
inertia 118, 166, 169, 223, 245, 248
inflation 170, 199, 186, 201, 247, 251–55
information 39, 149, 240, 259
  acquisition 100, 207
  asymmetry 88, 89, 99, 239
  complete (full) 101, 130, 247
  context 240
  incomplete 40, 102, 206, 230, 248, 250
  production 85
  transmission 80, 93
innovation 30, 85, 107, 129, 180
  policies 252
  process 104, 114, 188, 238, 249
inputs
  dissociation from output 21–4
  primary 21, 152
instability 150, 207–8, 210, 245
interdependence 259
interest rate 38, 53–56, 66, 121, 198, 240, 243
interventions 138, 167
  discretionary 245–6, 248, (versus fixed rules) 247
  external 213, 229, 234, 247
  policy 139, 240, 248, (standard) 254
investment 94, 117, 131, 231
  behaviour 157
  competitive 101, 105n
  complementary 52, 101, 105n
  co-ordination over time (with consumption) 198, 228, 256
  decisions 93, 149
  demand determined 245
  goods 53
  rate 253, 257
  residual determination 129

knowledge 40, 57, 81, 100, 246
  acquisition 80, 103
  creation 92
  on-the-spot 91

labour
  demand 74, 147, 187
  input 61, 65

market(s) 56, 77, 79, 153, 196, 240, 242, 256–7
  mismatch 74, 79, 188, 193
  mobility 257
  productive 231–2
  reserves 243
  supply 74, 146, 187
  unproductive 231–2
lacking 44, 47–8, 57
lag(s) 118, 237, 246
  adjustment 240
  construction 82, 101, 103, 166, 238
  one-period 155
  in the transmission of information 82, 101, 103, 127, 129, 166, 238, 248
learning 64, 91, 188, 194, 98, 102–3, 146, 243
  constant rate 189
  as a creative process 31, 78
  increasing rate 188
leisure 113
liquidity 41, 52, 94, 95, 169
  additional 58

machinery effect (Ricardo's) 25, 120–1, 170, 173–7, 183, 187
market(s) 56, 81, 235
  connections 83, 102
  creative functions 96
  failure 84, 87
  functioning 141, 163, 236
  game 86
  intermediaries 141, 151, 223
  non-institutionalized 151
  role 82
  structure 87
mechanism
  adaptive 149
  adjustment 75, 221, 238, 258; price 103, 141, 156, 180, 213; wage 161, 180, 213
  feedback 77, 170, 241, 259
  growth 115, 126, 169, 211, 230
  servo 161
  stock-flow 141
  viability creating 139
microfoundations
  of endogenous growth 93
  of macroeconomics 105
model(s)
  chaotic 106, 139n
  coherence 152
  continuous time 128

Index

discrete time 128
endogenous growth 72, 115, 137, 154
equilibrium 115, 127, 170n
general equilibrium 259
as a heuristic tool 140, 259
Lucas's 113
mathematical 137
neoclassical (Solow's) 109
sequential 127, 128, 142
solution 138, 139, (analytical) 246
stochastic 123
monetary
authority 44, 47, 58–9, 144
control 58
economy 72
policy 37, 45, 56, 59, 247, 250, 252; restrictive 187, 196, 254–6
regime 59, 242, 249
money 35, 144
essential role 36, 37
flow of payments 43
neutral 37
precautionary role 41, 51
speculative role 39, 41
standard theory 38
supply 151, 187, 230; as a control variable 51, 58; endogenization 155
transaction role 40, 42, 51
unneutrality 198
money balances (idle) 44, 48, 72, 129
households' 48
desired 47, 145, 156
non-desired 47, 145
producers' 47
multiplier 232

organization(al)
adaptive 95
design 91
forms 83, 88, 104
innovative 95
quasi-rents 92
role 88
out-of-equilibrium
analysis 142, 166, 233, 259
context 25, 122, 246
modelling 137, 138, 165–66
path 166, 170
process 27, 73, 118; intertemporal complementarity 251
strategy 83, 102
theory 45

parameters 32
preference 112, 113, 154
structural 246
Pareto optimum 85n, 87
path dependence 123
period
elementary 43, 47n, 128
long 115, 117
short 115, 117
periodic orbits 155–6, 246
prey–predator interaction 181
prices
fix(ed) 103, 128, 141, 238
flex– 128
institutionally determined 151
market determined 151
relative 236–7
stability 37, 250
production 11, 12
'circular flow' view 15
decisions 129, 148
ex ante view 28
ex post view 11, 91
as a linear process 85
synchronic representation 16, 22, 121
time dimension 15, 18, 27, 45, 55, 163, 231, 237
from the vantage point of exchange 13
production process(es)
construction phase 22, 55, 63, 143
elementary 143
horizontal structure 69, 70
intertemporal complementarity 19, 22, 25, 47, 108, 141, 171
Neo-Austrian 21, 22, 119, 143
simple profile 153, 167
scrapping 50, 121, 143, 149
utilization phase 22, 55, 143
vertical integration 22, 55, 68, 119
productive capacity 127, 143, 235
age structure 23, 144, 160
bottleneck 251
distortion 27, 33, 36, 48, 132, 156, 235, 238
productive option 11
creation 30, 78, 94, 188
'definition' moment 11, 93
'utilization' moment 11, 93
productive structure 144
horizontal dimension 23, 144
vertical dimension 23, 144
productivity 159, 220
paradox 159, 220, 223–4

Index

rate of starts 55, 71, 119, 143, 150, 155
reaction coefficients 151, 170, 201
  price 163, 186
  wage 163, 245
resources
  allocation 13, 72, 96, 124, 213; optimal 84; intertemporal 87, 92, 237
  creation 30, 73, 75, 91, 98, 107, 125
  financial 37, 60, 127, 130, 144; additional 212; availability 55, 142; external 46, 131, 212
  generic 13, 30, 104
  human 60, 64, 73, 127; homogeneous 147; heterogeneous 147
  specific 30, 73, 104
returns
  constant 113
  diminishing 62, 113, 164
  increasing 65, 97, 112, 137
rigidity
  price (stickiness) 103, 195, 206, 210, 238–9, 245
  wage 195, 239
rules 249
  institutional 250
  simple 245–6

saving(s) 154, 180, 215, 231, 234–5, 257
  behaviour 187, 241, 252
  function 120, 122
  gradual increase 184, 192, 225, 242
  proportional 172, 242
  rate 80, 112, 114,
  shortage 237
  time profile 177
sequence
  'constraints–decisions–constraints' 27, 60, 127, 207, 239
  inter-period 43. 46, 64, 126
  intraperiod 43, 46, 64, 126
  of periods 21, 90
  predetermined 123
sequential
  analysis 46
  context 22, 45, 66, 94
  structure 166
shocks
  demand 194
  expectational 206
  liquidity 169
  monetary 197, 238, 251
  real 108, 238
  supply 194, 196, 251, 256
  technological 170, 180, 205, 235; single 172; repeated 180
simulations (numerical) 77, 139, 163
skills 11n, 19, 63, 74, 127, 143, 151, 190
  acquisition 113–4
  changes 187
  creation 78
  upgrading 78, 147
stability 109, 150, 240
  analysis 119, 243
  corridor 103, 247
stagflation 201
steady state/growth 19, 22, 35, 106, 118, 152, 158, 213, 217, 223–4
stocks 103
  buffer 141
  physical 42
  real 130
strategy 85, 86, 89
  intertemporal optimizing 247
  out-of-equilibrium 99
  optimal 140
  R&D 85, 87, 114
  sequential 103, 141
substitution 19, 66, 87, 233
  between factors 118
  among financial assets 38
  between financial and real assets 41
  intertemporal 41, 91

take-out 71, 120, 145, 152, 230, 253
  constant 171
  gradual reduction 176
  growth 208, 209
technology 13, 29, 31–3, 111, 140, 170, 220, 250, 258
  changes 170, 187
  endogenization 83, 84
  as information 84
  trajectories 29, 33n
time
  continuous 164, 165n
  discrete 164, 165n, 166
  historical 25n
  logical 25n
  periodization 166, 232
traverse 25, 71, 101, 119, 166, 244
turnpike 116, 248

unemployment 121, 139, 163, 199, 225, 241n, 244, 255–8

equilibrium 240
  Keynesian 188
  Ricardian 189
  temporary 180
utility function 92
  intertemporal maximization 105, 113

vacancies (unfilled) 188
variables 32
  control 128n, 131, 18, 164, 248
  endogenous 32; versus exogenous in economic modelling 126
  exogenous 32
  state 127
viability 27, 58, 107, 132, 163, 228, 244
  corridor 249, 250
  of the economy 142, 160, 198, 210
  of out-of-equilibrium processes 33, 51, 76, 100, 102, 125, 167, 233, 239

wage(s)
  differentiation 191
  efficiency 88n
  fund 47, 68–9, 74, 131, 150, 156, 207, 212 ; constrained 147
  indexation 151, 178, 210, 242, 248, 253
  rate(s) 65, 121, 223, 237; market-determined 151; real 71, 193, 203–5, 237, 239
  regimes 75, 196, 213, 229, 242
  share 170, 181, 201, 253, 257
wealth effect 55
welfare
  analysis 116
  economics 108